WHAT HAPPENED TO CHRIS ANN?

Betrayal to Ultimate Freedom

Christine Orsbun

What Happened to Chris Ann? is a memoir. Many names and characteristics have been changed, and certain events compressed. Much of the dialogue is authentic; however, some conversations have been recreated to the best of the authors' memory.

In Memory of Dr. Sally Goforth

PRAISE FOR
WHAT HAPPENED TO CHRIS ANN?

"In my thirty-five-year career as a clinical psychologist, Christine is one client who stood out. As a teenager, she was forced to leave all she had known behind, leaving her alone and afraid. Her courageous spirit to face her abuser is rare. Follow her story of how she found her way through navigating the many pitfalls of enduring a childhood of abuse. *What Happened to Chris Ann?* is written in a transparent, compelling, and inspiring way that speaks to the reader's heart." **Sally Goforth, PhD**

"*What Happened to Chris Ann?* is a riveting true story of a young girl caught in an unimaginable world. A powerful account of abuse, betrayal, redemption, and forgiveness. Be inspired by how an act of kindness from a stranger can change a child's world and give her the will to believe she will find a way out… A captivating read." **Penelope Childers, co-author of stories of Faith, Healing, and Transformation, including** *A Window of Hope: How We Survived COVID-19.*

"*What Happened to Chris Ann?* captures the true epitome of the internal battle of an abused child. As a former child abuse victim, I could literally feel the pain and agony that comes from experiencing such deep destruction from someone you trusted. My body would numb. "Fight or flight," would set in. Christine brings a much-needed awareness of how childhood trauma can affect victims for decades. I cried and rejoiced with her as she navigated through the psychological and emotional wounds, and did the work to find her way to ultimate freedom." **Melissa Stevenson Rogers, Wife, Mom, Survivor**

THANK YOU

Thank you to all who showed kindness to me throughout the years.
You held me up, gave me hope, kept me going, and made
an eternal difference in my life.

1

No Turning Back

MY FEET TOUCHED the ground, and I slammed the car door harder than I intended. I winced but kept my eyes on the ice-covered gravel. The only light in sight came from the living room window. Even the moonlight was obstructed by the trees.

I began to walk up the long driveway. Questions threatened to erode my confidence. *What if I freeze when he looks at me? What if I turn into that little girl again?*

Ice crunched beneath my shoes. *Why not just kill him? He's got no legs; he can't run.* The man never paid for the torture he inflicted on so many, flinging pain nearly everywhere he went. My innocence and childhood shattered. He took pleasure in watching me squirm with fear while he verbally pounded me into the dirt.

Time after time, that man bruised Mama inside and out. Everyone knew he was a bully and a pervert. A coward and a manipulator. One who thrived at using his power to intimidate others.

He scoffed at the pain he caused and somehow managed to escape prison time.

Should I turn back? No! It doesn't matter what he does or says. This is what I have to do, what I want to do. My moment, my chance to take back the power and everything he stole from me. *I will not let this opportunity pass me by.*

This would be the last thing he expected and something I never imagined I was capable of. *Can I do what my heart tells me I must?*

"This is for the tears that fell down Mama's face," I muttered. And for the years none of us would ever get back.

My feet were heavy as I stepped onto the porch and walked to the door. *What am I thinking? No one else would do this!*

I heard the television on the other side, and for a moment, life seemed ordinary.

I knocked and waited.

There was no turning back.

2

When Mama Saw Us

WHEN I CLOSE my eyes, I can still see our little house on 14th Street. It's the first home of my childhood that I remember. Like all the homes on that street, with its tiny front yard, it needed a fresh coat of paint. The thud of my feet echoed through the house as I jumped from the kitchen counter to the wood floor and skipped around. The air was light. I could breathe. A happy time, when being myself was the only thing I knew, and my worst fear involved getting in trouble with Mama after one of my mischievous stunts. A fearless tomboy and yet, a proper tea party hostess. I was free to be both. Never too loud for Mama. Never too ridiculous. My messes were never too big, and I was never too dirty. For the most part, life felt good, and it never dawned on my young mind that it wouldn't always be that way.

Mama stood on her bed, safety-pinning a sprig of mistletoe to the dingy white curtain behind the headboard. With long thick brown hair and a thin frame, many thought her beautiful. Her big brown eyes and the beauty mark above one side of her lip made her look like a movie star, or at least I thought so.

"Mama, what's mistletoe for?"

"It's so the boys will kiss you." Mama stood back in the middle of her bed, admiring her task.

"Eww! If a boy kissed me, I'd cut his head off!" My go-to phrase when I thought something was gross.

"Mm-hmm." Mama never turned around. She didn't seem to mind when I said things like that, so it never dawned on me that I shouldn't.

"Look, I'm bleeding." Mama turned her head and gasped as she jumped off the bed to get a closer look. Her concern turned to anger.

"Chrissy! March yourself to the bathroom and wash that off." I had used her bright red lipstick to make a spectacle of my arms.

"It's lipstick blood." I didn't know *why* Mama didn't like lipstick blood.

The house on 14th street had one bedroom. Mama rented it because it was within walking distance of the hospital and cheap. Fresh out of nursing school and single with two kids, she could not afford a car and didn't have a driver's license.

Most days we played in the front yard with the neighbor kids. On the lucky days, Aunt Jeanie came for a visit and brought our twin cousins, Pam and Theresa.

Pam and Theresa were a year older than me and a year younger than my brother, Lane. They lived at the farm, which was only a little over three acres out in the country, sometimes with farm animals, but often with none. At the farm, we enjoyed the same freedom to be ourselves, but with much more space to roam and explore. Over the years, the farm became a safe haven and a place where we built memories.

Once a month, Aunt Jeanie picked us up to go to town. Lane and I piled into the backseat with our cousins. Most times, I was barefoot and wore the same thing I'd slept in for a couple of days. My face might be dirty, or my hair in need of brushing, but no one seemed to mind. Going to town meant a trip to the used bookstore, stopping at the utility companies where Mama paid the bills, and then to the grocery store. Ah, the grocery store! If I behaved, Mama would open a can of dried shoestring potatoes and let me eat them in the store.

We stopped at yard sales along the way, and I was happy when I climbed back into the car with a new treasure. By the end of the day, the bottoms of my feet were black from running across hot parking lots and walking around inside stores.

Our toys weren't fancy. We made guns and slingshots out of sticks and rubber bands. Our hot wheels cars drove on the dirt roads we formed with our fingers. Tinier sticks and small rocks made nice little fences and garages with no roofs.

"Chrissy!" Mama stood at the front door with a can of raw biscuits and a spoon in her hands. "Where's Bubby?" Lane came running.

"Here. Playdough," she said, handing the can and spoon to us.

We peeled the paper off the can and pressed it with the spoon until it popped open. A rock retaining wall ran in front of our house along the sidewalk. We threw the biscuits against the rock wall to see whose would stick the longest. When our playdough was too full of dirt and leaves to stick, we threw it as far as we could and went back to whatever we were doing.

Our house had a tiny hallway that led to the bathroom and kitchen. What was meant to be the kitchen's dining area was separated by open bookshelves, offering a "bedroom" for Lane and me. Mama was creative like that. We had two twin beds, a window with a blanket tacked over it, cardboard boxes to hold our toys, and a view of the kitchen through the bookshelves. I slept with my face against the mattress with no sheets. Many nights were rudely interrupted by a hard thud on the head from falling out of bed.

Occasionally, my morning involved sitting at the kitchen table in tears while Mama carefully picked a tootsie roll pop out of my stringy blonde hair. I jerked my head away from her hands as if it were her fault.

"Hold still," she'd say and give me that exasperated look.

"It hurts!"

As far as I was concerned, the lollipop could stay there. It wasn't bothering me.

My favorite "toy" was a cardboard refrigerator box Mama had somehow acquired. She cut squares out for windows and a door that opened and closed. As tiny as I was, it felt like the roomiest playhouse I could have imagined. I carried Barbies, crayons, blankets, and pillows into my little house and pretended to live in it. I drew pictures of appliances and furniture on the walls and imagined they were real. Eventually, my playhouse was moved to the backyard and became history with the first rain shower.

Mama had moved back to Arkansas with Lane and me when she and Daddy split up. She enrolled in nursing school and after graduation, began working at the local hospital.

"Mama, where's my daddy?" I often asked.

"He lives in California. But he's gonna send you and Bubby a surprise."

I didn't have any memory of my dad. I only knew he lived far away and sometimes sent toys to Lane and me. I grew excited when Mama said a box was coming. Every day, I sat on my knees, backward on the couch, and looked out the window. I waited for the mailman to bring a box from Daddy. When it didn't come, I asked Mama again.

"Mama, what did my daddy send us?"

"Barbies for you, and a G.I. Joe for Bubby." Mama never seemed bothered about answering the same question over and over. When the box finally came, there were also cap guns and cowboy boots. That began many episodes of "Cowboys and Indians" for Lane, our cousins, and me. I felt loved when Daddy sent us surprises, but I didn't understand why he couldn't come to see us. *What does he look like? I bet he's nice.*

While always distracted by my new prized possessions, that empty space inside me never went away. It would be years before I learned the reasons my daddy wasn't there.

In my childish ways, I sought extra attention from Mama, especially when I felt the void of my absent father. One evening I sat on the bathroom sink, piddling in the medicine cabinet. I found the pink chewable baby aspirin that tasted so good, with a few left in the bottle. I don't know if the container was childproof or if I just knew how to open it, but I got it open and ate all of them like candy. I jumped down and took the empty container to Mama and squealed, "Look, Mama, I ate them *all.*" Mama's eyes grew as she snatched the bottle from my hand. She must have believed me when I told her there were only a few because she calmed down quickly. Then came the scolding.

On payday, we walked to Kress's downtown—a variety store with an ice-cream and lunch counter in the front as soon as you walked in. Near the ice-cream counter were penny and nickel machines. Pennies bought gumballs and nickels bought small trinkets.

Mama once handed Lane and me each a roll of pennies and a paper sack and said we could spend all our pennies right then if we wanted to. So, one at a time, I inserted my penny, turned the knob, and let the gumball drop into my sack. I couldn't believe how much fifty pennies was. Each time my sack caught a gumball, I looked up, and Mama handed me another penny. Then another and another, until I thought I had enough gumballs to last for the rest of my life.

My ornery mind never rested. One hot afternoon, Lane and I played on the sidewalk in front of Grandma Halverson's house, where we often stayed while Mama was in nursing classes, and eventually at work at the hospital. Mama had promised we could walk to the grocery store with her when she picked us up.

I walked down the sidewalk toward Lane, carrying my metal cap gun by the barrel and flinging the hard plastic handle up and down like a hammer. There was something about how that felt in my tiny wrist that I liked. Lane had stopped playing with me earlier that day, saying I was too mean and didn't play nice. So, when I saw his fuzzy brown head sitting on the sidewalk, I had the sudden urge to smack the hard plastic handle right on top of it. It was a glorious snap of the wrist, much more satisfying than hammering air. But my quiet victory was short-lived when Lane started crying, and Mama came running down the sidewalk.

After a few stern words, Mama took Lane's hand and walked toward the store without me. My quivering bottom lip led me back into Grandma's house to sulk.

Within a few days, I skipped alongside Mama again as we went to see a movie downtown. She bought me an orange soda that came in a plastic orange with a straw in it. When the movie was over, I skipped home with my plastic orange and sat on the retaining wall until every last drop of soda was gone.

Those early days whispered sweetness, when Mama *saw* us and took care of us. She enjoyed fun. She smiled. She laughed. She loved us. Mama wasn't perfect, but she was more than enough for us, and we adored her. We had little money but didn't feel poor. Even when there was nothing but bologna in the refrigerator, we weren't hungry. We were dirty but didn't feel neglected. We wore yard sale clothes and hand-me-downs and were as happy as if they had come from a fancy department store.

We had our mama, and I never imagined life would ever be anything but good as long as she was around. But life was about to change. Quickly. And so was Mama.

3

Jack

ALTHOUGH ONLY FIVE years old, the night I was introduced to Jack became forever etched in my memory. Mama had met him at the hospital. As a paramedic, he often went in and out of the emergency room where Mama worked.

A large man with black hair and long sideburns, Jack parted his hair on the side and swooped it over with hair tonic, typical of the early 70s. He had a deep voice, and his behavior seemed odd. Jack talked a lot, and the more he spoke, the less he looked us in the eye. Impressing Mama seemed to be his goal, with his loud laughter and exaggerated facial expressions. I didn't sense any warmth toward Lane and me, but he seemed to be important to Mama. I kept my mouth shut and watched his every move.

At Christmastime Jack brought unwrapped toys for Lane and me.

Mama looked impressed. They made a game out of wrapping the gifts. First, I had to go into the bedroom while Lane stayed in the living room to wrap the toys that were for me. Mama and Jack watched from the couch.

"You can come back in here," Jack called after my gifts were wrapped.

Then it was my turn to help wrap Lane's toys, and he promptly ran to the bedroom. One of Lane's gifts was a metal police car with a red siren on top that flashed when you pressed a button. My excitement grew. *Bubba's gonna love this.* After Lane returned to the living room, I couldn't contain my giddiness.

"Bubba, it's black and white with a cherry on top!" My hands cupped over my mouth as I bounced up and down on the couch.

I don't remember if Mama laughed, but Jack did. There was something about his laugh that grabbed me on the inside. Something odd. Jack's laugh sounded authoritative, and it went on and on, as though he waited for everyone to look at him and agree in laughter over what I had said. And then he snapped.

"I told you not to tell!" For a second, his face became serious and angry. I froze. Then, as quickly as he snapped, his laughter resumed.

I tried to laugh with him but couldn't. Instead, I fought back tears and quickly found a seat next to Mama. I stayed quiet for the rest of the evening and watched him with skeptical eyes. When there were no more gifts to wrap, I waited for Jack to leave. But he never did. In fact, Jack stayed in our life from then on.

Not long after Christmas, we moved into a slightly bigger rental house on 12th Street. Mr. Grimm, Jack's boss and the owner of the ambulance company, had several homes for rent and this was one of them. Once again, Mama converted the tiny dining room into a bedroom for Lane and me. We had bunk beds, and I got to sleep on the top. This house was old, with rats bigger than my feet. I even woke up one night to find one in my bed. There was no air conditioning and it heated with two small space heaters. Mama lit all four burners on the kitchen stove and turned on the oven if it was freezing.

Jack used a sheet of plywood and some two-by-fours for a makeshift table in the living room corner for his model trains. I stood at the doorway many evenings quietly watching as he spent hours making tiny buildings out of balsa wood and strategically gluing fake grass and trees along the train tracks. He set an ashtray on the train table to smoke while he created an intriguing little village.

He's not like Mama.

Life changed quickly. Daily thoughts and conversations revolved around Jack. What Jack liked and didn't like. What made Jack angry. Jack's hobbies and Jack's opinions. He was overly sensitive to things that seemed normal to me, often reacting with anger, sometimes in a split second. I was never sure what triggered him. Mama began to grow distant from Lane and me. For the first time in my life, I became anxious.

Jack changed my name to "Boney-Maroney" when he was teasing me, or "Chris Ann" when he wasn't.

"Come here, Boney-Maroney!" He grabbed my arms and pulled me toward him. My body squirmed to get away. His laughter echoed through my ears as he grasped my ankles with one hand and held my wrists firmly in the other. Unable to escape, the feeling of my bones pressed together sent me into a panic.

"Look at those boney knees!" He howled as though it was the funniest thing ever and looked around to make sure everyone watched.

The more I struggled to get away, the more painful his grip became, and the more dominant his laugh. I screamed, "Let me go!" My mind drowned in a mixture of fury and fear. When he stopped, I scrambled to my feet and ran to my room, pulled a blanket over my legs, and fought off the tears. *Why is he mean to me?*

Every time this happened, I shrunk a little and became painfully self-conscious of my thin body and knobby knees. A voice inside of me said *you're too boney,* the first of many lies that would haunt me for years.

I had always gone by Chrissy or Chris and never used my middle name. Jack called me Chris Ann when he wanted me to do something, or he was angry. I could never move fast enough for him when he summoned me with Chris Ann. I usually heard it two or three times by the time I got to where he was, and each time I yelled, "I'm *coming!*"

Jack frequently used the phrase, "If you would…."

"Chris Ann, if you would, get me a glass of tea." Or "If you would, pull my boots off." It was an order, not a request. If I messed up, he had a way of humiliating me.

"I want you to take your right hand and grab your left ear," he said.

"Now I want you to take your left hand and grab your right ear." I did as I was told.

"Now *pull.*" He waited and watched. "Pull!"

And I had to pull my ears, sending Jack into hysterics.

Day by day, Mama spoke less, and her smiles were less frequent. Her forehead became permanently wrinkled with tension, and she often looked at Jack's face when she spoke. She paid less attention to Lane and me, and more attention to her hair and makeup, among other things. Jack insisted on a spotless house. If Mama cleaned and did laundry while wearing short shorts, a halter top, and heels, he liked that even better.

Mama and Jack spent a lot of time in the bedroom. Jack owned stacks of pornographic magazines that often spilled out of the nightstand or got caught in the vacuum cleaner when we vacuumed under the edge of the bed.

It took me a good thirty minutes to muster up the courage to tap on their bedroom door for permission to ride my bike or go to a friend's house. After the third or fourth knock, Jack yelled, "What do you want?"

"Can I go ride my bike?" I held my breath. Mama never answered me—always Jack.

A very irritated "Yes!" was the norm, sending me straight out the door. I stayed gone all day, roaming the streets on my bike, sometimes many miles from home. If I went to a friend's house, I stayed until the parents politely asked me to leave. Sometimes I went to the grocery store to walk around in the air conditioning or to the donut shop on Towson Avenue, where I sat for hours eating donuts until my money was gone.

On Sundays and Wednesdays, Lane and I walked across the street to an Assembly of God church. For me, it was a way to get out of the house and be around friendly people.

There were two ladies, Mrs. Coots and Miss Winnie, who always greeted me with a smile and invited me to sit with them if I was alone. They made sure the other girls included me in activities, and those ladies didn't tolerate teasing. They didn't ask me about my home life, but I'm sure they knew it wasn't good.

My friend, Laura, attended the same church with her family. Laura and I were in the same grade at Belle Point Elementary. With long brown hair, and a permanent smile, I thought her always happy. During the week, I often wandered over to her house uninvited but was always welcomed in by her parents. Laura and I climbed into her attic and played Barbies for hours, or thumbed through the Sears catalog, pointing out everything we wanted to buy. I watched Laura's parents talk to her. They smiled at her the way Mama used to smile at me. I hid my sadness with phony grins and forged indifference. The difference between her parents and mine baffled me.

On Laura's birthday, her parents ordered a store-bought cake that was too pretty to eat. They gathered the guests around the table and sang "Happy Birthday," followed by clapping and cheers. They hugged her and looked in her eyes when they spoke to her. *I wish I lived here*, I often thought. *Bet my real dad would sing to me.*

Watching Laura's parents showed me that something was very wrong with mine.

THE SUMMER BEFORE kindergarten, my world continued to unravel. On the night of July fourth, Lane and I lit sparklers in the kitchen, from the open flame on the stove. The smell of smoke filled the air, as did our excitement. I squealed when tiny sparks landed on my hands or fell onto my feet.

"It's gonna burn me!"

"No, it's not," Lane insisted. We swirled the sparklers around, drawing lines of smoke in the air until the spark went out. Then we lit another, sometimes two at a time. I felt safe with Lane. If he said something wasn't going to hurt me, I believed him. But I wasn't sure about the floor. Some of the sparks burned tiny brown dots in the linoleum.

"Look!" I pointed to the floor with my mouth open.

"It's okay," Lane assured.

"At least it wasn't my feet!" I squealed and grabbed another sparkler.

Mama and Jack watched from the kitchen table, and for a while, I forgot they were there. From nowhere, Jack stood and grabbed me.

"Come here, Boney Maroney." My squealing abruptly stopped, and my face went blank. With one arm around my waist, Jack hoisted me into the air and grabbed my bare ankles with his other hand. He stepped to the kitchen stove and held my feet over the open flame.

"Hey! Is this gonna burn you?" My insides froze.

"Does this scare you?" His laughter boomed.

"Stop!" My body wrenched back and forth as I felt the heat on my feet. Then Jack jerked me away from the flame, laughed, and did it again.

Over and over, he held my feet above the fire, feeding my panic.

"What's wrong?" "Does this burn you?" "Are you scared?" Each time I felt the heat, the terrifying frenzy started all over again.

After several minutes of torture, he put me down, and I hurried out of the room, glancing at Mama as I left. Mama looked uncomfortable but seemed to be faking a laugh for Jack's sake. Lane looked stunned. I shook for several minutes in my room as I inspected my feet to see if they were burned.

They weren't. But my spirit was.

4

My Brother

AS SUMMER CONTINUED, so did my ways of avoiding Jack.
Even when I was gone all day, Jack and Mama never asked where I'd
been or what I'd been doing. Once kindergarten started, I was thankful
for another place to go.

I always felt special when I spent time with Lane, even if I had
invited myself. I tagged along every chance I could, and he was nice
enough to let me. Lane had plenty of friends, and I wanted to be one
of them. It didn't dawn on me that having his kid sister following him
around, expecting him to play with her, might get annoying. Apart
from the age difference, and the fact that I was a girl, our personalities
were different. He generally stayed quiet. I was only quiet around Jack.

Lane saved every dime he got, while I spent mine. Even before
he was old enough to get a real job, Lane did yardwork and other odd

jobs, saving everything he made. For me, I loved going shopping and bringing home a treasure. Any store would do.

Lane sat still, while I bounced all over the place. He was content to watch television, lay on his bed to do homework, or practice spinning the basketball on his middle finger. I hated being still. There were more exciting things to do than sitting still, unless Jack was in the room.

Lane loved competition. I just wanted to have fun. When we played Monopoly or Chess, he always won, and rarely, if ever, took it easy on me. It wasn't fun to lose, but I still finished because I didn't want to miss a moment with my brother. Then I begged him to play again.

Lane didn't seem to get on Jack's nerves, and I couldn't manage to avoid it. Seemed like every time I turned around, I did some other ridiculous thing that Jack brought to my attention. I didn't understand why I kept messing up. *I'm stupid. If I wasn't, he wouldn't always be mad at me.* I tried to be more like Lane so Jack would like me.

One similarity between Lane and me is that we both worked hard, even at a very young age. We had to. Jack had a lot of demands, and we didn't dare disappoint him.

Whenever Lane and I bickered back and forth, I was usually the one who ran tattling to Mama. I can still see her wrinkled forehead and clenched jaw as she pleaded, "You kids are making my stomach tie up in knots. Stop tattling!"

Mama said that a lot, and I tried to imagine how a person's stomach could get tied up in knots, and worse yet, how I caused that to happen. At the time, I didn't realize she was already stressed to the limit, and what she at one time took in stride had now become intolerable. I hated seeing Mama so tense and upset. It made me sad to see how her life had changed. How *our* lives had changed. I would have loved it if she could have responded with one of her "Umm-hmms" and gone about her housework. I walked away with guilt because I had upset her again, and the voice in my head swooped in with another attack. *You're pathetic. You can't do anything right.*

On Halloween, Lane and I trick-or-treated along with other kids in the neighborhood. In the summer, we walked to Creekmore Park to swim. We cleaned the house. We cooked. We did laundry. We played tricks on each other. I adored him, and I looked up to him.

One sacred memory is of the two of us playing catch in the backyard. Even though I could barely hold the glove in my hand, Lane showed me which hand to use, and which way to turn the glove, depending on how the ball was going to land. Many a ball went right past my glove and smacked me on the chest, or hit the ground rolling, causing me to run after it. But I didn't care because my brother was playing with me. I wanted to be tough for him. I wanted to learn how to catch the ball so he would tell me I was doing a good job.

One time we played catch, and I actually listened to him and caught the ball just the way he said.

"Hey, you caught that as good as Pam. Good job." Cousin Pam was more of a tomboy than me, and she did everything as well as any boy, so she and Lane got along.

As good as Pam. His words were like the Holy Grail.

"Throw it to me like you throw it to Pam," I said. He did. And I thought my jaw was broken after the ball rolled over my glove, up my arm, and into my face. But I had to hear him say it again, so I yelled, "Do it again!"

"You sure?"

"Yes, like you throw it to Pam." Lane kept throwing, and I kept missing. "Throw it again. Hard." Then it happened.

"Okay," Lane said. "Now I'm gonna throw a grounder. And you gotta do what I told you. I'm gonna throw it hard."

"As hard as Pam?" I asked. I nodded my head yes, as if that was going to make him say what I wanted.

"Yes, as hard as Pam. Get ready."

I got ready. Lane threw the ball hard. I saw it coming. I squatted and held the glove like he taught me. It rolled fast, and I clenched my jaw, just in case.

I caught it! I *did*. I thought I might explode from excitement as I jumped up and looked straight at Lane. I waited to hear the words. And he said them.

"You did it as good as Pam. Good job." The universe lifted me up and twirled me around. It filled me with joy to know my brother was proud of me. *I caught it as good as Pam.*

When the sun disappeared, we went inside, straight to the fridge. Lane snatched a frozen popsicle, and I grabbed a pickle. Still reeling from my brother's proclamation of approval, I retreated to our room, flopped onto my bed, and opened a book. Jack didn't exist at that moment. Life had no problems. I had accomplished a great feat, and my brother was proud of me.

That's all that mattered.

5

Fear and Heartache

"CHRIS ANN!" THOSE sharp words forced anxiety through my spine every time.

"Coming," I yelled as I jumped up.

"Chris *Ann!*"

"I'm *coming*." I hurried to the kitchen where Jack sat at the table. I stood straight up in front of him, reporting for duty. *Am I in trouble?*

"If you would, set this table so we can eat." Jack cooked barbeque squirrel that night, and I dreaded it. I had never eaten squirrel before, but Jack's rule was to eat everything on our plate whether we liked it or not.

I set plates, napkins, silverware, and glasses on the table. Then watched as Jack lifted long thin pieces of cooked meat out of the barbeque sauce and piled it onto our plates. My nose wrinkled.

"What's the matter? You don't like squirrel?" he said.

I shook my head.

"Have you ever tried it?"

I shook my head again.

"Well then, you don't know if you like it, do you?"

"No." I noticed he was almost being nice. He spoke flatly, without a smile, but wasn't angry.

As I ate small bites of squirrel, I was glad it was covered in sauce. I didn't like it. Or maybe it was the thought of it. I watched as Jack devoured his food and helped himself to more. Then he stopped and looked at me.

"You like it now?"

I shook my head no as I chewed my last bite. My facial expression must have been comical because Jack actually smiled a little.

"It's gross," I muttered through a mouthful of food. His smile turned into laughter, which made *me* laugh, spitting out my food in the process. The moment was funny but awkward.

"You want me to make it again sometime?"

"Heck no."

Jack laughed again, and a surge of relief ran through me. *He's not mad.* I laughed along, and then it hit me—*I know, I'll throw out my "cut your head off" line. That'll be funny.* For a moment, I imagined impressing him with my wit and the two of us laughing together. *Maybe he'll like me then.*

"If you do, I'll cut your head off," I blurted, expecting more laughter, but there was abrupt silence instead. Jack glared.

"You'll what?" His smile disappeared.

Had he not heard me? "I'll cut your head off."

My smile faded as Jack's eyes narrowed. He leaned inward and put his fork down. I sat motionless, shrinking as I wondered what went wrong.

"You'll cut my head off?" He kept his mouth open.

Silence.

"Mama lets me say it," I whispered and hung my head.

"Your *mama* lets you say it." He snorted and pushed his chair back.

My chest tightened. *Please don't be mad at Mama.*

Jack walked over to a kitchen drawer, pulled out a butcher knife, and returned to the table. He held the knife out for me to take.

"Here. Go ahead. Cut my head off."

I froze. Mama didn't speak.

Jack put the knife in my hand and folded his hand over mine. His face beaded with sweat, and he breathed heavy and slow. He stared wildly at me and pulled the knife up to his neck. "Go ahead. Cut."

When I didn't move, he yelled, "Cut my head off!"

I burst into tears, and Jack watched me cry. Then he let go of my hand with a huff and walked out of the kitchen.

I instinctually got up to clear the table, glancing at Mama as I passed. I ran the dishwater and watched it fill the sink. Mama's chair scooted back, and she walked out of the kitchen. My heart went numb. I didn't understand what had happened. *Mama didn't do anything.* I squirted dish soap into the water and watched it bubble. *Afraid, I guess.* The voice in my head whispered, *It's your fault. Even Mama knows it.*

No one ever said a word about what happened. And I never said, "I'll cut your head off" again.

I COUNTED THE days until school started. First grade sounded so much more important than kindergarten.

"Mama, I'm in *real* school now, because it's a number grade." I watched Mama spray Pledge onto a washcloth and dust the end tables in the living room.

"Here, do that one." She handed me the cloth, then went to get the vacuum cleaner. Her high heels had caused a run in the back of her pantyhose. Her short shorts and halter top barely held her in. Her hair was ratted high above her caked-on makeup.

My teeth gritted as I pushed the rag around. My mind seethed. *She never used to dress like that. He turned her into a clown.*

The Pledge smelled like lemons and made the furniture shine when you rubbed it all around. Jack liked to walk in to the smell of furniture polish and see vacuum tracks on the carpet. That's how he knew we had cleaned.

Mama finished vacuuming and began wrapping the cord.

"Mama," I said quietly. "Number grades mean I'm in *real* school, like Bubba, right?"

Snap! Another rat in the kitchen.

"Go take it out. And take this with you." She handed me the ashtray of cigarette butts. I walked into the kitchen and looked behind the stove. A rat, pinned to the wooden trap, barely moved. I picked the trap up by the corners and held it as far in front of me as I could reach. I carried it outside, dropped it into the trashcan, and dumped the ashes on top of it. It seemed odd to me that we worked so hard, keeping the house clean for Jack, but secondhand smoke and rats weren't a big deal.

My heart filled with joy the day I started first grade. I loved my teacher, I loved my desk, I loved the smell of the crayons, and I loved Thomas, who sat next to me. He didn't speak much, but he smiled at me a lot and was always faithful in picking up my pencil or crayons when they rolled off my desk. Reading came easy, and I was eager when the teacher called on me to read out loud. Never once did she have to help me with the words.

"You're a bright student. Such a good reader." I soaked up her kindness.

One day as I gazed at Thomas, my stomach gave a warning. I stood and threw up all over the floor, in front of everyone.

My teacher called for the janitor, and I was sent to the office, where the secretary took my temperature, then told me to wait in a chair while she went to get my jacket. We didn't have a phone, so she sent me home with a note for Mama. I walked the four blocks to our house and opened the front door. By now I was wobbly and thought I might throw up again.

Mama looked confused as I held out the note. She read it and told me to get in bed. I shivered underneath the blanket until Mama came into my room, propped me up with pillows, and gave me medicine. Several minutes later, she came in with a bowl of chicken noodle soup, and a coffee cup full of grape Kool-Aid. My heart leapt. *Mama made me soup?* She was taking care of me, and it felt wonderful. I wasn't even hungry, but I wasn't going to refuse it. *Mama made it for me.*

My body shivered when I handed back the empty bowl. Mama pulled the pillows from behind me and tucked me in. I would like to say she kissed me on the forehead or brushed my cheek with the back of her hand before I fell asleep, but she didn't. But she *did* make me soup, and for that I melted inside. *I've missed you, Mama.*

I awoke to Lane hurrying into our room and Mama and Jack's voices in the living room. Mama seemed on high alert as she pulled off Jack's boots and told him what she was fixing for dinner, then asked him if that was okay. She didn't tell Jack I had come home sick. Everything returned to normal. Jack, the center of attention again, in charge. The mama who fed me soup had disappeared. My nausea dissipated, and although I still wasn't hungry at dinner time, I ate what Jack put on my plate.

WHILE STILL IN first grade, we moved to another rental house, on North O Street, not far away, but far enough we had to switch schools. Our backyard butted against the schoolyard, and every morning, we walked out the back gate to get there.

Mama said I could invite the kids in my class over for my seventh birthday. I had never had a party with friends, and I was excited. By the time the guests arrived, Mama had already given me one gift. It was a portable record player and a single recording of "Arkansas" by Glen Campbell, the only record I owned. I played it over and over throughout my party. Only two friends showed up, but we nearly finished the cake Mama made.

Every time the record ended, I ran to my record player and started it again. I was sure everyone loved that song as much as I did. I don't know where Jack was that day, but the air felt light and Mama seemed almost normal, even after the party was over.

That evening, Mama took out her ukulele. She'd had it for several years but rarely played. "I'm gonna play Moon River," she said as she began strumming. "It's one of my favorites."

I sat on Mama's bed and watched in awe as her fingers brushed up and down on the strings. She smiled and closed her eyes. I had forgotten what her smile looked like. But the moment was slightly squashed when Mama started singing. *Her singing doesn't sound right.* I felt sorry for her and was glad when the song was over, but happy to still be sitting there. She then decided to dump her purse on the bed and sort its contents.

"Gum," I said as I grabbed a stick of fruity gum.

"Don't swallow it. And spit it out before you go to bed." Mama gathered the rest of the gum and put it in a pile. She separated the trash from the change and put her makeup back in its bag.

"Lipstick," I said.

"No." Mama snatched the lipstick from my hand, but I didn't care. I had my mama.

It was a peaceful moment when I laid my head on my pillow that night. It had been so long since Mama and I connected. But my smile faded as I lay there wondering why it had to be that way.

The sound of Jack yelling startled me out of my sleep. They were fighting again. I blinked over and over, trying to wake up. Jack burst through my bedroom door, then turned around and marched back out. There was more yelling, and the front door slammed. Mama came into my room and turned on the light.

"Get up."

"What?" I held my hand over my eyes to block the glare.

"Get some clothes on." Her eyes were big, her voice shaky. Not the person I sat on the bed with a few hours earlier.

Mama fled with Lane and me that night. I don't remember who she called, but someone picked us up and took us to their house. A few days later Jack showed up to take us back home. Mama never told us why we had to leave, or why we were going back. It was several days of quiet confusion.

Little did I know, this was the beginning of many separations and moves, all with little or no explanation. Lane and I rarely asked questions, and never in front of Jack. We knew Jack was in control, and all three of us were better off keeping our mouths shut.

Darkness filled the night when Jack pulled the car into the driveway in front of our house. Silent, we walked to the front door. Jack opened it, exposing the house in total disarray. Furniture turned over. Lamps thrown against the wall. Drawers emptied onto the floor. Mama stood with her mouth open.

"Oh yeah," Jack muttered. "I forgot about this." Mama didn't speak.

From the living room to the dining room to the kitchen—every room was a disaster. In my bedroom, books were strewn across the floor. My jewelry box with the ballerina lay upside down, with its contents scattered. I carefully wound it up to see if the ballerina still turned. Kneeling next to my bookshelf, tears welled in my eyes as I picked up my books and put them back where they were. I examined each for damage. *These are mine.* They were my friends. I hated him for touching them.

The next day a quietness filled the air as we finished putting the house back together. We swept broken glass, hung clothes onto hangers, put cushions on furniture, and buried our feelings.

"Why did he do that?" I quietly asked, barely able to look at Mama. I had a vision in my head of Jack returning a few nights before to find us gone. I imagined his face red with anger, going from room to room, destroying everything in his path. *We should've stayed gone.*

"Mama, why did he do that?" I asked again. I knew the answer, I just wanted to hear her say it.

"Oh." Mama didn't look at me. "He was just looking for something." I wrinkled my nose and lowered my eyebrows. *Does she think I'm stupid?* I let out a huff and turned away. *Yeah right.*

It was years before I learned from Grandma and Aunt Jeanie that Mama had called them the night we fled. She told them, "If anything happens to me, it was Jack." He threatened to kill her, cut her body into pieces, and mail the pieces to Grandma. It scared Mama enough to call them, but she didn't want to go to the farm where Jack could find her.

I was glad Mama left with us that night, but heartsick she brought us back.

6

Hard Work, Neglect, and Shame

FIRST GRADE ENDED, and summer began. After being gone on my bike for most of the day, I walked through the front door to find boxes everywhere. Jack had demanded Mama quit her job again, and there was no money to pay the rent, so we were moving into another one of Mr. Grimm's rental houses. Mr. Grimm never asked Mama and Jack for a deposit or first month's rent. I suppose that's why we lived in several of his houses throughout the years.

"You can work at that new Arby's over on Rogers Avenue," Jack told Mama. Mama nodded but said nothing. *Why isn't Mama gonna be a nurse anymore?* I couldn't picture Mama at a fast-food place, and I couldn't imagine it paid as much as the hospital. But Jack said to do it.

The new house was right across the street from the ambulance company and catty-corner to the Assembly of God church Lane and I used to walk to. We were back in the Belle Point Elementary school district.

With two stories, the house seemed a bit larger than the other houses we lived in but just as old. One bedroom, a small, floored attic space, and a screened-in porch covered with heavy canvas shades completed the upstairs. My favorite space was the attic where I spent many hours alone. I spread blankets on the floor and made it my playhouse. The front and backyards were tiny, the detached garage had a dirt floor, and the walls smelled like mildew.

Lane turned the upstairs screened porch into his bedroom. He opened the shades to allow a breeze.

"I'll close the shades in the winter," he said. "Should block the cold air."

As we settled in, the chores multiplied, and so did the rules. We weren't allowed to go anywhere unless the house was spotless. Lane and I were charged with making some of the suppers for the family and continued to clean up the dining room and kitchen after dinner, no matter who cooked. We swept, mopped, and hand-dried the dishes before putting them away.

There was no central heat and air. A giant water cooler in the downstairs bedroom kept that part of the house somewhat cool, and we had to regularly add water with a hose. There was a space heater in the living room and a gas stove in the kitchen. When we turned those on, we used small fans to circulate the heat.

We had a washing machine but no dryer at this house, so we used a clothesline in the backyard. Many trips were made back and forth. Hanging up wet clothes. Taking them down. Carrying the clothes in. Carrying more clothes out. I hated laundry.

When the weather turned cold, Lane and I took the clean wet laundry to the laundromat to use the dryers. Our red wagon perfectly fit two round laundry baskets, with two loads in each basket. The wagon was heavy, so Lane and I took turns pulling it. When I couldn't go any farther, Lane pulled it the rest of the way.

"We're big enough, aren't we?" I looked to Lane for assurance. "I'm seven and you're nine. We're big enough to do all the laundry, right?" I didn't feel big enough, but if Lane said we were, I believed him.

"Yes, we're big enough."

When the washing machine broke, Mama loaded the dirty laundry the same way and handed me the quarters. "Don't lose those or you won't have enough."

"By myself?" *Where's Lane?*

"They aren't wet so they won't be as heavy." Mama pulled the wagon through the front door, to the sidewalk. "Now go."

Hours later, as I pulled the wagon home from the laundromat, I noticed a lady in a slow-moving car following me.

"Hey! Do you live far?" She stuck her head out the window but kept glancing at the road in front of her.

I shook my head and kept walking.

"Do you want a ride?"

I shook my head again and pulled faster. Her car crept alongside of me all the way to our house. She was already knocking before I got there with the wagon. Mama opened the door, and before she could say a word, the woman began scolding her.

"That tiny thing shouldn't have to pull that heavy wagon." The lady pointed her finger at Mama. "That laundromat is too far!" She didn't stop for a breath. "You ought to be ashamed!"

Mama stood speechless.

After that day, Lane and I continued to pull the laundry to the laundromat, but I was secretly glad a complete stranger had the guts to stick up for me. *I like her!*

Jack continued to work at the ambulance company but began building furniture on the side. He learned how to build furniture from his father, who built child-size rocking chairs for a living.

One day, he carried power tools into the house. I watched as he turned our dining room into his workshop. The finished furniture was usually sold, but this time it was for *our* house. Jack built bookshelves and end tables for the living room. He made chests of drawers and nightstands for his and Mama's bedroom. Then he designed cornice boards for the tops of the windows. I watched him use a dinner plate to trace a large scallop pattern across the bottoms of each board, then cut it out with a jigsaw. He upholstered them with orange fabric and decorative thumb tacks, then mounted them above the curtains.

Jack even built a cabinet with doors that locked for the dining room. His talent was remarkable, and I secretly wished I could help build. Instead, I stood out of the way, handed him tools when he told me to, and cleaned up the sawdust each evening when he was done.

I liked all the decorating, but I didn't understand what had gotten into him. He seemed to be on a mission of some sort.

Jack bought various bottles of liquor and small glasses to put inside the dining room cabinet, later referred to as the liquor cabinet. This was the first time I had ever seen alcohol in our house. I had never witnessed anyone drink.

Not long after the new furniture was built, Mama and Jack started getting visitors. We heard knocks at the door, always at night, and as soon as someone let the visitors in, Mama and Jack escorted them to their bedroom. They never introduced their guests, usually a lady and a man, but sometimes just a man, and we never saw the same visitors twice.

On one particular night, Lane and I watched television in the living room while Mama and Jack entertained friends in their bedroom. Absorbed in the television program, and content to be left alone, I heard the jingle of keys in the dining room. Mama had unlocked the new liquor cabinet. The light was off, but I saw her silhouette take a bottle from the cabinet and pour drinks. She was naked. I watched from the living room with confusion. *What? Where are her clothes?* She closed the cabinet and carried the drinks to their bedroom. The thought of people looking at Mama naked sickened me. I slid my eyes toward Lane. Had he seen her? I couldn't tell.

While only seven years old, everything became clear. I knew exactly what was going on and my mind swirled with shame and anger. *Must've got some ideas from those magazines.* In that moment, I felt protective of Mama, and I hated Jack.

I don't know if it's called *swinging, wife swapping*, or what, but Mama and Jack did it throughout their marriage from then on, and no one ever talked about it. Just like the bruises that began appearing on Mama's arms and legs. She tried to cover them with makeup, but they were too big and dark. By the time the bruises changed shades and began fading, new bruises appeared.

Mama always had a "silly story" about how the bruises happened. "I was walking to the bathroom and clumsy me tripped over a shoe and fell right into the door." I saw through the phony laughter. "Didn't even see that door—silly me."

Mama changed considerably, leaving me insecure and confused. Her growing obsession with pleasing Jack left little time for Lane and me. She needed Jack's approval, afraid to be without it. Was her appearance okay? Was the house clean enough? Was dinner okay? Was she acting okay? Was it okay to talk to this person or go to that place? We understood the shame on Mama's face but we didn't talk about it. We kept her secrets, and ours, safely buried.

Mama and I didn't walk to the movie theater or Kress's on payday anymore. We walked to the *Funky Candle*, where they sold suggestive adult gifts, incense, and psychedelic candles. If we had to go to the pharmacy, we didn't leave until Mama looked in the gift section for something for Jack.

If we had a car, Jack drove us to the grocery store. When we didn't have a car, we went in a taxi or in the ambulance. We used it like our personal vehicle, and Mr. Grimm didn't seem to mind. As Jack drove, I sat on the stretcher and studied the small compartments that held supplies. Plexiglass doors kept everything from falling out. We piled paper bags of groceries onto the floor and used our feet to keep them from tipping over when Jack rounded a corner. If a bag fell over, groceries went flying and we scrambled to get it all back into the sack before Jack opened the back of the ambulance.

Mama never got a driver's license. She walked to work when she could and often solicited rides from coworkers. I saw her drive once on a back road, when Jack insisted. She shook the entire time and hadn't gone far before she had had enough. Jack seemed pleased with her dependency on him.

Aunt Jeanie still came by occasionally and took us to run errands. If Jack wasn't home when we returned, we got to play with Pam and Theresa. While Mama and Aunt Jeanie chatted and laughed like old times, Theresa and I sat in my room listening to music, and Lane and Pam went outside to play catch or ride bikes. I cherished those days.

Jack didn't like Aunt Jeanie and Uncle Jimmy. "White Trash," he called them. "Can't believe they live that way. And the way she treats her husband—humph."

Aunt Jeanie wasn't Mama. She was outspoken and independent. She was rough around the edges, especially when it came to Uncle Jimmy. If he said, "Jeanie, you wanna get me something to drink?" she smiled and proudly responded, "No, but I will." I giggled when she said that. She reminded me of how Mama used to be.

7

Sinking Further

LIFE BECAME LONELIER and more unpredictable as Mama drifted farther away. I listened from the other side of the bedroom wall when Jack yelled at her. Mama rarely spoke back to him. Sometimes he marched out of the bedroom, opened the front door and left. I'd run into Mama's room just to see if she was okay. She gathered herself and pretended nothing had happened, despite her running mascara and disheveled clothes.

If Jack stayed gone for a while, that meant the fight was over. If he returned quickly, there was more to come. He marched back into the bedroom, closed the door, and yelled again. I never knew how long the tension would last, sometimes hours. Sometimes days. And too often, the two of them emerged from the bedroom together, Mama crying and Jack red-faced. That meant Jack was kicking us out again.

Getting kicked out by Jack became routine. It created a tangled web of emotions, and it always began and ended the same way. Jack stood in the living room while Mama got her purse. She turned to us kids with a soft, "Come on." We followed her out the door, and down the sidewalk. We walked in silence four blocks to the phone booth that stood outside the laundromat. Mama's face burst with shame.

"Mama, who you gonna call this time?" The three of us crammed into the phone booth as Mama inserted the coins and dialed. A deep emptiness kept me still as I listened to her cry into the phone. I clung to her clothing and glued my eyes in the direction of our house. *Please don't let him see us. Please don't let him see us.*

"Tell them to hurry, Mama." I wanted to get away before Jack made us go back home. I sighed when either Mr. Grimm or Aunt Jeanie showed up.

If it was Mr. Grimm, he took us to one of his furnished rental houses and handed Mama a few dollars for food. If Aunt Jeanie picked us up, we went to the farm. For a day or two, Mama's face looked like one of those fragile China dolls, pale and threatening to break any second. By the third day, if Jack hadn't shown up, her face relaxed, but she remained quiet and unsure. That's when I grew hopeful. *Maybe she won't go back this time. Maybe we get to be happy again.* I silently begged her not to go back. But each time Jack caught up with us, he cried, Mama crumbled, and hope died again. He was always *so sorry* and assured her he would never do it again.

Going back home was a grueling chore. We never talked about the kick outs. Ever. We simply picked up where we left off, a little more wounded than the last time.

LANE AND I made spaghetti for supper one night. Jack dished up our plates, and we knew we had to eat it all before we could leave the table. I wasn't hungry, so I knew I would be sitting there for hours after everyone finished eating.

"I have never seen such a slow eater," Jack said. He shook his head. I pretended I didn't hear him and kept eating. I *was* naturally a slow eater, but I didn't bother telling him I wasn't hungry. That wasn't allowed.

"It takes you half an hour to chew one bite."

I kept eating and took a drink of tea to wash it down.

"Hey, what's wrong with you?" Jack laid his fork down and stared at me. I shrunk into my shell.

"Nothing." *Please don't talk to me.*

"I don't know how anyone can eat so slow." He huffed and helped himself to more spaghetti.

Mama wore her usual awkward smile, said nothing, and kept eating.

"Hurry up, Slow Poke!"

Jack's voice made me jump. *Please stop talking to me.*

Soon, Mama and Jack watched television in the living room, and Lane cleared the table. I shoved bites of spaghetti into my mouth, vehemently chewed, and forced myself to swallow it, hoping I didn't explode.

I glanced from the corner of my eye to see if Jack was watching me from the living room. When I thought I might throw up, I glanced one more time, then laid my paper napkin over the rest of my spaghetti and got up from the table. I scurried into the kitchen and scraped the spaghetti into the trash, then helped Lane clean up. Normally, if I got to the point of nausea, I flushed the rest of my food down the toilet. But it was trash night, and the trash can was closer. *Won't make a difference*, I thought.

When the kitchen and dining room were clean, Lane and I ran outside to play on the swing set.

"Chris Ann!" I nearly fell from the swing at Jack's voice. My stomach turned as I scrambled to slow the swing and jump out.

"Chris Ann!"

"I'm *coming*." I ran into the house wondering what we had forgotten. My eyes filled with fear when I spotted my spaghetti smeared down the side of the trash can.

Jack had returned to the living room, where he sat on the couch waiting. I stood in front of him, and my body went numb before he even spoke. The smirk on his face, his folded arms, and arched eyebrows told me he knew. Jack spoke slowly and over-enunciated each word.

"Did you throw your spaghetti away?"

I *couldn't* say yes; I was paralyzed. And somehow, I thought if I kept quiet, he'd have to let me go. I stood motionless.

Jack sat up straight and breathed heavily through his nose. His lips pressed together, and his eyes cut a hole through me. "Did you!"

I flinched.

His face turned red. His nostrils flared. The tension continued for what seemed like an hour. Jack never budged from the edge of the couch, I never moved from standing in front of him, and Mama never stopped watching television. I could no longer feel my legs, and my emotions were starting to break. Jack sat motionless and stared at me. After several seconds of silence, he yelled again, "Did you!"

I jumped, and a faint "Yes" slipped out.

A huge smile formed across his face as he leaned back and drew in a deep breath. He blinked with satisfaction. "Go outside and get me a switch."

I couldn't get away from him fast enough. I carried the stick back to Jack. *Just get it over with.*

"Now go upstairs and pull your pants down. Lay on your bed and get ready for a whipping." He seemed to relish the moment. He stood up and filled his chest with air like he was the champion.

I buried my face in my pillow as he began striking me. Each strike burned, but I wasn't going to cry. He struck me repeatedly, and I realized he wasn't going to stop until he broke me, or at least thought he had. So I let out a fake cry, and after a few more strikes, he left. When my door shut, I pulled my blanket to my neck and cried for real. I hated him. Not because he caught me in a lie and punished me, but because he turned it into a sport, and enjoyed it so much.

The next day was a Saturday. I had been awake for hours, staring out the window of my room. The trees gently swayed back and forth, and the cars on the street quietly rolled by. I wanted to go outside, but with Jack in the living room, the thought of walking past him was demoralizing.

Lane walked into my room, straight to my dresser, where I had a single goldfish in a small round bowl I had won at the fair earlier in the year.

I don't know if my brother ever sensed my emotional struggle with Jack, but he often restored my spirit, whether he was trying to or not. He distracted me from the internal aching.

"Hey, wanna see something?" Lane reached his hand into the bowl, pulled out my goldfish, and put it in his mouth. I stared mortified as he began chewing. *Surely he didn't!* After a few seconds, he opened his mouth and stuck out his tongue, exposing a cluster of minced orange stuff. *Why would he do that? Goldie!*

As soon as Lane saw the look on my face, he put his hand over the fishbowl and dropped Goldie back into the water. He laughed and walked out of my room as he announced, "It was a carrot."

I wanted to be mad, but I admired his cleverness. "That was a good one," I yelled back. It was just enough to make me feel like a person again.

8

Sibling Love

THE SUMMER BETWEEN first and second grade proved to be the longest, most grueling summer I can remember. Mama was pregnant, the yard infested with fleas, and Jack sold our bikes.

We couldn't use the clothesline due to the fleas, so Lane and I made many trips with our wagon to and from the laundromat. When we returned home, we stretched both arms out in front of the water cooler, letting the air blow the sweat dry. Occasionally, we secured a sheet over the front opening and lay underneath to enjoy a more concentrated coolness.

Our bike riding abruptly stopped when Jack came home from work hopping mad. He claimed he'd seen us riding our bikes in the street earlier that day *near that dangerous intersection.* He punished us with shame and humiliation, then sold our bikes to a pawn shop. Lane took it particularly hard as Jack always acted so proud of him, and Lane wasn't used to getting in trouble. It's the only time I remember seeing real hurt on Lane's face.

The loss of freedom was brutal. Neither Jack nor Mama knew how many times we had actually ridden in the street, through *that dangerous intersection*, and miles past it. They hadn't paid attention. It was not uncommon for me to ride my bike down the middle of the road while standing on the seat, bent over, holding onto the handlebars.

I didn't believe Jack sold our bikes to protect us. *Just tryin' to be a big shot.* I hid the dirty look on my face. *Must have needed some cash.*

Jack sold *my* bikes many times throughout the years, but only sold Lane's that once. My heart always sank when Jack walked through the door announcing, "Chris Ann's bike got stolen again." Each time, I panicked and ran to look.

"You shouldn't have left it laying in the front yard," he yelled. I never understood how it repeatedly ended up in the front yard, forcing Jack to sell it to a pawn shop to teach me a lesson.

Years later, Aunt Jeanie confirmed my suspicion. Jack sold my bikes to pawn shops because they needed money, then accused me of leaving it out to be stolen. Mama confessed many things to her sister. But unless she was desperate and afraid, Mama never accepted Aunt Jeanie's offers for help. How would our lives have been different if she had?

So that summer, Lane and I walked ten blocks to Creekmore Park to go to Free Swim. Free swim was every Tuesday and Thursday morning from 9-11 a.m. There was a big lap pool, and a separate deeper pool with diving boards. Mama made my bathing suit from yellow polyester fabric covered with tiny pink flowers. It looked more like a pair of stretchy shorts and a halter top, obviously homemade and embarrassing to wear.

"Why can't I have a real bathing suit?"

"Because there's nothing wrong with this one." We didn't have the money for a store-bought bathing suit. Jack made Mama quit her job at Arby's and wouldn't let her go back to work at the hospital.

I didn't know how to swim but loved how light I felt in the water. I was barely brave enough to go under and always scrambled to the side if I accidentally sucked any up my nose.

Lane went to the deep pool with the diving boards. A good swimmer, he wasn't afraid of anything. He climbed up the ladder to the diving board, and without hesitation, ran to the edge and jumped off.

At eleven o'clock, free swim ended with an announcement over the speaker. We visited the dressing rooms, met at the front entrance, then ran to the playground. We were so young, so far from home, unsupervised, and could be gone as long as we wanted.

The playground had a merry-go-round, swings, and two slides. The straight slide stood tall—really tall. Later it was deemed a safety hazard due to its height and nothing to prevent kids from falling or jumping from the top. My favorite slide was the curly slide, which offered more excitement than going down in a straight line. More than the merry-go-round and curly slide though, I loved to swing. Swinging felt like freedom. I loved flying through the air, as high as I could go, in and out of the branches. I imagined being a bird, hiding in the trees, away from everyone, safe from everyone. *If I was a bird, I would never come down. Nobody could hurt me up here.*

After we played, Lane and I ran across the parking lot to the miniature golf course. We balanced on the concrete curbs that surrounded the parking lot. We jumped on and off the park benches and looked for lost golf balls. We raced across the parking lot and Lane always won.

"You cheated," I insisted.

"I didn't cheat. I'm just faster."

"That's cuz I don't have shoes on, and you do."

When we were tired of the golf course, we decided to return to the playground. We were never ready to go home.

"I'll race you again," I yelled as I ran toward the parking lot.

"I'll just beat you again," Lane yelled back and didn't bother running.

I ran as fast as I could. I thought if I beat Lane to the other side of the parking lot, it meant something. When I got to the curb, I leapt to see how far I could land on the blacktop, as I'd done so many times before, and kept running.

But something was wrong this time. My feet were on fire. I panicked but knew I couldn't stop. *Ouch! Ouch! Ouch! It wasn't this hot the first time!* I glued my eyes to the grass at the edge of the parking lot and kept moving. When I reached the other side, I collapsed, crying and looking for Lane.

"My feet are burning!" I cried more when Lane caught up with me.

"Raise them up." We realized hot gooey tar caked the bottoms of my feet. Unbeknownst to us, while Lane and I explored, city workers had moved in their equipment and were re-covering the parking lot. One machine poured hot asphalt while another machine with a giant roller flattened it out. I had run through the freshly poured goo before the big roller got to it.

We grabbed sticks from the ground and scraped the asphalt from my feet. It burned and I cried even harder.

"We got most of it," Lane said. My feet were bright red and began to blister. "We gotta get your feet in that cool water."

"It's not free swim anymore."

"We'll sneak in."

We walked to the big open gate and on cue, still in our bathing suits, walked separate ways—Lane to the boys' dressing room and me to the girls'. Once inside, I watched the lady behind the counter who made sure people paid. The counter was about three feet tall, so when she turned her head, I ducked and made a run for it, close to the counter, the way Lane told me to. Within a few seconds, I was on the other side in the pool area. *I did it!* I saw Lane and hurried to the edge of the pool, where I quickly sat and stuck in my feet.

I don't remember how long we stayed at the pool this time, but I've never forgotten the trip home, and it still brings tears to my eyes.

I attempted to walk home barefoot, but it was too painful. Lane gave me his socks as a buffer, but it didn't help. After several attempts, Lane said, "Get on my back."

The ten blocks between Creekmore Park and home seemed like ten miles. Lane carried me on his back as far as he could before needing a rest. Then he carried me some more, and we stopped to rest again. He carried me all the way home. More than forty years later, I still get emotional at the act of love from my brother. He never grew frustrated with me. He never let on that it was hard. He never came close to quitting. He never made me feel bad in any way. He just kept going until we were finally home. He was nine. I was seven.

December rolled around, and my baby sister arrived five days after I turned eight. I was in second grade and Lane in fourth. Jack took Lane and me to see Mama in the hospital. He snuck us into a stairway, where we climbed several flights of stairs. We saw her standing at the top in her hospital gown with a smile on her face. I wasn't sure why we had to sneak like that; perhaps the rules regarding visiting children were different then. We saw Mama for only a few minutes, then Jack took us home. I've always thought that that was a nice thing for him to do, even though I didn't understand it.

A few days later, Jack went with Mr. Grimm to pick up Mama and our new sister, Becky. Mr. Grimm came through the front door first. "Here comes the newest member of the family." He grinned from ear to ear, and so did Mama.

Lane and I were excited to meet our new baby sister. We couldn't help but smile as we stared at her in awe, wrapped in a pink blanket from the hospital. She quickly became the highlight of our lives. For a while, we were a different family.

Within a few weeks, Mama went back to work, this time at a nursing home. Both she and Jack worked nightshift, which left Lane and me to take care of Becky during the night. We knew the routine. If she cried, we picked her up, changed her diaper, fixed a bottle, and fed her while we sat on the couch, rocking her back and forth, singing *Go to Sleep Tiny One.*

We stopped every few minutes to burp her, then fed her some more. As soon as she fell asleep, we put Becky back to bed and prayed she didn't wake up as we tip-toed out of the room. Many nights, her bottle was full of tea because that's what Mama and Jack taught us to give her, and we didn't know any better. There were so many nights it took *forever* to get her back to sleep—we were feeding her caffeine. I still feel the nights I sat on the couch in tears, holding Becky's bottle as I rocked her back and forth, arms aching, and singing through my gritted teeth because she would, not, go, to, sleep. By morning, Mama and Jack arrived home, and Lane and I got ourselves ready for school.

Those hard days still bring tears to my eyes. I wanted so much to take care of my baby sister, but I felt like a failure when I couldn't make her happy. I loved her. It never dawned on me that an eight-year-old is not equipped, mentally and physically, to take care of a baby that young.

9

Darker Days

I HAD JUST crossed over Dodson Avenue on my way to school and spotted a wallet in the grass. I fumbled through the wad of cards and coupons and found cash. Thirteen dollars. To my eight-year-old self, thirteen dollars was a lot, especially since we never had much money. I kept the wallet all day and when I got home that afternoon, I handed it to Mama.

"Look, I found this on the ground."

Mama stopped polishing the legs of the coffee table, took the wallet, then sat on the couch and pilfered through it. Her eyes fixated on the money, and she seemed to be in thought. At that moment, Jack walked through the front door.

"What's that?"

Mama looked up and I saw an unfamiliar look cross her face. *Is she hoping for something?* She had her usual wrinkled forehead and timid eyes, but now she bit her lip and seemed to hold her breath. Mama held the cash out for Jack to see.

"Do you think I could go to the doctor now?"

I had never heard her ask Jack for anything; she usually waited to be told and accepted whatever he said. Mama pleaded with her expression and waited for his response. *The doctor? Was Mama sick?* It hurt my heart to think Mama was sick and couldn't go to the doctor. I understood Jack controlled the money, but it hadn't dawned on me before that day, he also decided who went to the doctor and who didn't.

I don't remember what happened to the thirteen dollars, and I don't remember Mama going to the doctor—ever. Years later, Grandma explained Jack never allowed her to go to her gynecologist for annual checkups. This was one of the many things that caused them to loathe Jack, and why Grandma called him *Jack the Ripper.*

The next day at school, after the last bell rang, I lingered on the playground. I didn't want to go home. It was too hard there. The weight of all the secrets was heavy. In addition to Mama and Jack's bedroom visitors, and Mama's bruises, we didn't talk about my real dad.

I often wondered why he didn't send packages anymore, and I was too afraid to ask. We didn't talk about Jack either. His demands. His temper. His control. We kept our mouths shut so we could survive with as little scathing as possible. And we put smiles on our faces, so the outside world didn't see our shame.

I felt confused when something I thought was good happened in our home. *If we have good days, are we a happy family?* At Christmas, there was always a tree and gifts. And on my birthday, there was always a homemade cake and a gift. Becky made us laugh, and occasionally we went out to eat as a family. Why did I feel heavy and alone? So afraid and sad? *Must be something wrong with me.*

The good times never lasted long, and the good feelings never had time to run deep before something else happened, and the world turned upside down again. Anxiety never left my body and the longing to have Mama back, like I used to, never ceased. I grew weary of finding ways to cope. Life had become too hard, too painful.

I looked up and realized the playground was empty, so I began the dreaded walk home. That evening Mama and Jack fought again. Jack's voice rang through the walls, and I tried to ignore it. I sat on the living room floor with Becky, trying to get her to sit, but she hadn't mastered it yet. I put a pillow behind her to catch her head when she flopped backward. Many times, we had all taken turns sitting her up and praising what a *big girl* she was, only to watch her suddenly flop backward and hit her head on the floor. The floor was carpeted, and she didn't seem to mind it, but I decided a pillow would be a good idea.

When it was time to put Becky to bed, she didn't cooperate, crying every time I left her side. She had been fed, burped, and changed. I became exasperated. When she finally calmed down, I tip-toed out of her room, back into the living room, only to hear Jack open their bedroom door and yell at Mama. Becky started crying again, and when Jack reached the living room, he scowled at me.

"Take her to her mother." He marched toward the front door. "If you want to call *her* a mother." Then he walked out and slammed the door behind him.

I took Becky to Mama, then walked to the bathroom, the only room in the house that locked. The only place I could escape when I couldn't leave home. I caught a glimpse of myself in the mirror. *Eww.* My stringy hair stuck to my head and my eyes were dark. My chapped lips bled in the cracks. I ran my fingers over the roughness.

Something about bleeding resonated with a feeling deep inside of me, a feeling I could never escape no matter how much I ran. *There's blood when there's pain.* I used both my hands to slowly pull my lip apart and a dark droplet of blood grew. For a second my emotional pain fled as I stared at the blood. I pulled again, releasing more.

The urge to release all my inner pain took over. Grasping both sides of my lip, I steadily pulled. The blood streaked down my chin. I controlled the pain. I pulled until I couldn't pull anymore, then stood at the mirror watching as the dark liquid dripped from my neck and soaked into my shirt. Soon the darkness within reminded me the pain was still there, and I soaked a washcloth and scolded myself as I quickly wiped the shame off my skin. The voice inside of me swooped in. *No one cares about your pain. It will never go away.*

Second grade ended and summer began. I wandered the streets and when no one answered the door at Laura's home, I decided to walk to my friend Michelle's house. I met Michelle at school a few months earlier, when she moved into the Belle Pointe school district. She was thin with light brown hair. She didn't speak much, but when she did, her voice sounded soft and kind. We had an instant connection from the day we met. There was something about her that told me we were a lot alike.

Michelle was the oldest child in her family, with two sisters and a brother. Like a mother hen to her younger siblings, she walked them to and from school every day, zipping up their coats, and making sure they ate their free lunch in the cafeteria. She once told me where she lived, near the hospital, not far from our old house on 14th Street.

It was a tiny white house with a chain-link fence around the front. I opened the gate, walked up the broken sidewalk, and knocked on the door. Michelle opened it and immediately stepped outside, closing the door behind her. She seemed uncomfortable, but her kind smile told me she was glad I came. Within a minute, her mother came outside and stood next to us. Her arms were tightly folded, and her facial expression seemed to say, *What the hell do you want, and why are you here?*

"Mama, this is my friend, Chris," Michelle spoke gently. "She came to see me." Michelle's mother didn't say a word. Her eyes bore through me.

"Mama, can she come in?"

"Nope," was all her mother said, arms still folded.

Michelle offered me an apologetic look. Her younger siblings watched through the front window. They weren't smiling either. I looked at Michelle, and she stared at the sidewalk as her bare toes curled from the heat.

"It's okay. I gotta go anyway," I finally said. Michelle looked up with a flushed face. I understood.

I let myself out through the gate and walked away as Michelle and her mom watched from their yard.

My chest grew heavy, and my face went numb as I hurried to get out of their sight. I was sorry I had done that to my friend. I felt her hurt, and a new realization entered my mind. *There are others who feel like I do. I'm not alone.*

They were secret-keepers too.

THE FIGHTING BETWEEN Mama and Jack came to a head.

"You kids get in here," Jack called Lane and me into the living room.

"Sit down." Mama was already in a chair by the front door, staring into space, crying. Becky squirmed on Jack's lap, wanting down, but Jack held onto her. The tension in the air was thick. I focused on the shag carpet. The couch made my legs itch. *What is he doing now?*

"Your mother and I are splitting up." *Your mother and I?* This formal gathering in the living room was something new. *Why is he announcing it this time?* "And I will be keeping the baby."

Mama cried harder.

"You kids need to choose who you want to live with." Jack wrestled with Becky to sit still, but his eyes were on Lane and me. *Is he delusional? Is this even a question?*

"Well?" His voice grew louder. "Who's it gonna be?"

Staring.

"Chris Ann," Jack snapped. "Stop wringing your hands." I didn't look at him. Instead, I glanced at Lane. Lane stared at his lap.

"Who!"

"Mama," I whispered. Jack wasn't surprised at my answer.

"Lane? Who's it gonna be?"

Lane didn't hesitate. "I'll go with Mama." He kept his eyes down.

Jack looked at Mama. "As you know, I'll be keeping the baby." Mama hadn't stopped crying. *As you know? The baby?* Couldn't he say her name?

"Please, Jack." Mama's plea was more desperate than when she wanted to go to the doctor. "Please." Her voice cracked and her face twisted in agony.

"You don't need a *baby*. You *killed* a baby!" Jack yelled. Mama slumped forward and buried her face in her hands. Her body shook as tears ran between her fingers.

"Sit still." Jack's frustration grew as Becky whined and tried to pry his fingers from her waist.

My mind lingered on Jack's words—*you killed a baby*. I looked at him with a cringe. *What a stupid thing to say.* Whatever his words meant, they stabbed Mama in the heart, and I wanted to stab *him* for hurting her.

"Go." Jack stood and held Becky tighter. Mama's tears burst again as she stood and took her purse from the coffee table. Lane and I followed her out the front door. We had no bags, no money, no plan—we just walked. Mama crossed Dodson Avenue instead of walking down the sidewalk toward the payphone.

"Mama, are you gonna call Aunt Jeanie?" I grabbed her hand and made sure I kept up.

"Mama?"

"No, she's got the baby." A week before, Aunt Jeanie had given birth to her third child, Julie. I hadn't met my new cousin yet.

"Who you gonna call, Mama?"

"I don't know." Face pale, Mama fixed her eyes straight ahead.

"Where are we going?" I didn't know this street.

"Chrissy, please…" Mama whispered. She blinked back tears and kept walking.

We walked to the old part of town where the courthouse stood. It was late afternoon, and many of the offices were already closed. Mama went from office to office saying, "Can you please help me? My husband kicked us out and kept the baby." Each office directed her to another office. She must have said it five or six times, "Can you please help me? My husband kicked us out and kept the baby," until she was finally told there was nothing they could do.

Mama used the payphone in the hallway of the courthouse to call Mr. Grimm, who once again took us to one of his furnished rental houses in Van Buren, twenty minutes away, and handed Mama some money. We walked to a nearby convenience store for something to eat, and Mama let me pick out one of those cheap toys from an endcap. At the rental house, Mama laid across the bed, crying while Lane and I ate, and I played with my toy.

"Kids, I guess I need to tell you something." *Mama's talking to us.* We stopped to look at her. "When I was working at the hospital, I got pregnant, and I had an abortion." When she said the word abortion, she cried again. "I already had two kids, and I was by myself. I didn't think I could take care of another one."

My eyes didn't know which way to look. *This feels like an adult talk.* I wasn't used to Mama talking to us much anymore, especially about something serious. Pain covered her face. I knew she longed for Becky. *Wish I could hug her.* But I didn't feel brave enough.

"It's okay, Mama." *Please feel better.* "It's okay."

My heart ached for her. I wanted to say more, but I didn't know the words. Mama buried her face in the pillow. I patted her brown hair. "It's okay…it's okay."

By the next afternoon, we were getting into Jack's car and staring at our feet. After a silent drive home, I ran to my room and lay numb under my blanket for hours. A quietness filled the house for a couple of days, then we continued life as though nothing had happened. A little more broken. A little more lost. And as usual, we never talked about it.

10

What Love Looks Like

IT WAS A quiet summer evening at the house on Dodson Avenue. Jack hadn't been home all day, Lane played at a friend's house, and Becky slept in her crib. From the couch in the living room, I saw Mama walking in and out of the dining room. *Is she humming?* I studied her movements. It was rare to see Mama's face so relaxed. She moved around leisurely and unafraid. *Her stomach must not be tied up in knots.*

Mama placed silverware into the drawer of the buffet, walked to the window, and pulled the curtains shut. She picked up the half-eaten birthday cake from the table, carried it to the kitchen, and came back to rake up the crumbs. I had just turned nine, and five days later, Becky turned one, so we shared a cake that Mama and Jack made. I walked to the dining room doorway and watched Mama wipe the table. She saw me staring.

"What's wrong?"

"Nothing." I wished she hadn't seen me.

"Why are you crying?" I became aware of my wet face and wiped it on my sleeve.

"I don't know."

"You don't know? Tell me what's wrong." Mama's face looked a little like it used to, years earlier. Her forehead wasn't wrinkled with stress. Her voice wasn't tense. *She's really looking at me. Is she happy?*

Heaviness burst out of my chest, and I sobbed uncontrollably. I didn't understand what was happening, only that it hurt, and I longed for something. How could I say I felt anxious and desperate? Mama grew impatient.

"Chrissy, what's *wrong?*" *She called me Chrissy.* I couldn't remember the last time she said my name.

The tears flowed and my throat ached, keeping me from speaking. Mama stood in front of me, yet I could only think one thing—*I want my Mama.*

"Are you gonna tell me why you're crying?" I knew Mama really wanted to know, and I desperately did too. *I'm just crazy, I guess.*

"I don't know."

I didn't know I was starving for a lost connection to my mama. I desperately missed the mama who had gradually disappeared over the last few years. I wanted to feel her love. I wanted her to hold me and tell me I still mattered. I wish one of us would have reached out to hug the other, but neither of us did.

When my emotions drained and tears dried, Mama stopped asking me what was wrong. I went to my room and laid my face on my pillow, wishing I knew the words to tell her how I felt. It was too deep for my mind to understand.

I lay on my bed, too numb to cry anymore.

By age nine, I learned there were people like me and my friend Michelle in this world—secret keepers, shame hiders, the unfortunate.

And there were the ladies at church, and people like Melissa and Steve, a nice couple who lived across the street. And there was Laura and her parents. They were like angels sent from somewhere. *God must love them more.*

Melissa and Steve lived in a two-story duplex that faced 12th Street. The small duplexes weren't the nicest, but the rent was cheap. Most of the tenants were a bit shady and never stayed long. But for a few months, in the upstairs duplex lived a sweet young couple who unknowingly made me feel loved. They didn't have children of their own. I don't know how long they had known each other, but they seemed to be very much in love. Melissa and Steve were kind, easy going, and happy. Somehow, I got into the habit of going over to their apartment, and I went as often as I thought I could get away with.

Steve traveled weekly with his job, and Melissa seemed happy to have my company. She always greeted me with a smile and invited me in when I showed up at her door. We spent hours just hanging out and talking. She showed me the macramé plant hanger she had made. She showed me pictures of her younger twin sisters and told me how close the three of them were, even though she was several years older. She showed me how she made iced tea. Seems like she made tea every time I went over there. I listened to her every word, pretending she was my mama, teaching me about the simple things in life.

"Would you like to play Monopoly?" Music to my ears. Melissa set up the Monopoly game on the coffee table, and we sat on the floor to play. I stunk at that game but I loved playing because it took a long time and someone was paying attention to me. Sometimes Lane went with me, and if Steve was home, the four of us played. *Like a family.* Lane usually won, but I didn't care. Often, because I played so badly, Steve felt sorry for me and sold me some of his property for a dollar. Or, if I didn't have the rent money, he made a deal with me and only made me pay a dollar or two. Steve was kind and gentle. He was understanding. *I bet my real dad is just like Steve.*

One Friday, Melissa invited me to spend the night. Her twin sisters were in town, and she thought I might enjoy meeting them. We made pallets on the tiny living room floor and talked and giggled until we fell asleep.

A tap on the front door woke me up. Melissa hurried through the dark living room, quietly unlocked the door, and removed the chain. Steve was home. She touched her finger to her lips, then pointed toward where we were laying. Steve quickly set his bag on the floor and put both arms around her waist. I watched in the dark as Melissa threw her arms around his neck. They hugged tightly for a long time. I studied his arms as he held her close, like he was keeping her safe. *He's strong.* I could almost feel the love they shared. They smiled at each other as if they understood what the other was feeling. I felt my insides relax as I watched how Steve looked at her, like it was the first time he had ever seen someone so beautiful. *That's what I want someday. Somebody to hold me like that. To look at me like that.*

I felt guilty for how often I knocked on Melissa and Steve's door, and I worried they would get tired of me. But they never seemed annoyed, always welcoming me and happy to give me attention. I wish I could tell them today how they changed my world. They made me forget about everything else for a while. To them I was important. I knew I was safe there. They met needs I hadn't known how to express.

I was an unkept little kid from across the street, but somehow those two people happened to be living there at a time when I needed someone like them. Their time, their kindness, their patience—even their own relationship—were all priceless.

They showed me what love looked like, and somehow that gave me hope.

11

Bitterness Grows in the Winter

WE LIVED IN the house at the corner of 12th & Dodson for most of
my elementary years, with many moves to other places and other
schools. We lived in that house when I started 4th grade, but in the
middle of the year, Mama and Jack decided to move us to a run-down
house in Liberty, Oklahoma. Mama was out of a job again. Jack had
gotten angry at her boss and made her quit.

A country community, Liberty was thirty minutes from the
state line. We lived in three different places in Liberty, but the house on
Happy Corner I remember the most. Happy Corner was a sharp
unexpected turn on a small two-lane road. If you drove straight, instead
of turning, you found yourself on a dirt road, and likely in the ditch. I
heard there used to be a small bar down the dirt road, and many of its
patrons ended up in a wreck when they left, having been a little tipsy,

and not quite making the turn. Nevertheless, Happy Corner had no indication of what life was like in that house.

We only lived there for one winter, but it had been a bad one—bitter, with plenty of snow and ice, making it the longest winter I can remember. The water pipes kept freezing, leaving us without running water for weeks at a time.

Once again, Lane and I put the red wagon to use. We could fit eight gallon-size milk jugs in the wagon. We pulled it through the snow to the neighbor's house, where two little old ladies lived. They were kind enough to let us fill our jugs from their kitchen sink. Then we pulled them back to our house.

I carried the big wash pan from the woodstove, and a steak knife, out to the paved road and chopped ice off the top of it. I filled the pan, carried it back to the stove, and let it melt. We used the melted ice to hand-wash the dishes, then poured the water into the toilet so we could flush it. I tried to take a bath once that winter. I heated water on the stove and poured it into the tub. After three wash pans full of water, I stepped into the tub, but the water that came only to my ankles had lost its warmth. It was a quick bath, and the only one I took for weeks.

Nights were cold. Other than the gas range in the kitchen, we only had the wood-burning stove in the living room for heat. Many nights were too cold to sleep, so I climbed out of bed and spread my quilt on the floor, folded it in half, then in half again. I carefully laid it back on my bed and curled up underneath. It got me through the night.

I became friends with Sherry next door. We were the same age, and we both sang in the school choir. Every day, as soon as the school bus dropped us off, we couldn't wait to be together. We spent many hours at her house just being kids, and it didn't take long for me to cherish what we had.

To me, she was my best friend. Our home lives were vastly different, but her friendship made me feel normal. Sherry reminded me of Laura. If she ever noticed that I was dirty, smelly, or unhappy, she never said. Instead, we sat on her bed chattering and laughing like we had known each other all our lives. We played music from cassette tapes and sang into a microphone as we danced around like we were on a stage. Sherry's room was neat and tidy, with everything in its place. She had a perfectly organized closet full of clothes, and shoes that sat in a straight line along the wall. I loved that my friend seemed so perfect, yet still liked *me*.

The field between our houses had a beaten path through the middle, allowing us to run back and forth. Sherry's dad was a woodcutter and used the field to stack rows of chopped wood so it could dry out and season until time to be sold. Lane often helped her dad with the wood and earned money. Even Becky toddled across the field and was welcomed in with the rest of us.

One of my sweetest memories at Sherry's house happened when her mom came home from work. Seeing us as she walked through the door, she immediately prepared fresh popcorn and cold cokes while we sat on the couch and watched television. Sometimes all we had to do is whisper "Popcorn and Coke" and she smiled as she got up to make it for us. It warmed and excited me when she did that, not only because it was a rare and wonderful treat, but because she was being a Mama—a Mama fixing something for her kids.

I doubt Sherry's family ever knew the power of their kindness, how much it helped a few kids get through a rough time of their lives. They provided a happy place with warm smiles and kind gestures, things we desperately needed at that time.

It was in the house on Happy Corner that I felt the gut punch of abandonment and the burn of anger, hotter than ever before. No one noticed I shivered at night. No one noticed I tried to take a bath but couldn't. No one noticed how my skinny ten-year-old arms struggled to pull a wagon with eight gallons of water across the snow. No one blinked when I sat next to the paved road, chopping ice.

And then, there was the snowstorm.

Lane and I were at school as the temperature outside steadily dropped. Snow began falling and the wind blew hard. Finally, the principal announced school would let out early so everyone could get home before the storm got worse. Students loaded onto the busses, but when Lane and I arrived home, no one was there. The house was freezing. By now, the wind picked up and snow blew so hard, it came through the cracks around the living room windows, where they should have been caulked. I stood in front of the woodstove pulling my coat tightly closed as I watched Lane trying to build a fire. *Where are they?*

Lane focused as he piled kindling and small pieces of wood into the stove and tried to light it. He lit match after match, held it to the pile, and gently blew as soon as it started burning. Each time the fire went out he did it again, over and over until it finally began burning.

"We need more wood," he said. So, we went out to the field and stole wood off one of the stacks. *I'm sure they won't mind.*

I stood by the woodstove, shivering inside my coat, waiting for the room to warm. I stared at Lane as he watched the fire. *I love him. Now we're gonna get warm.* I was relieved when the fire began roaring. Lane was twelve at that time and my hero.

As we stood by the woodstove, the brewing anger inside of me spun into utter bitterness. I was angry that no one was home. Angry that there was snow coming in around the window. Angry it took so long to get warm, and we had to steal wood to build a fire. Mostly, I was angry that no one took care of us that day. Were we not valuable?

That same winter I experienced raw hunger. Another cold day home alone. I don't know where my parents were, but I hadn't eaten since the day before, and it hadn't been much. The pipes were still frozen, and the gas had been turned off due to non-payment. I searched the cabinets for something to eat and I found a can of condensed tomato soup. I opened the can, scooped it into a bowl, and stirred it with a spoon. The water jugs were empty, and I didn't think I could wait to melt ice or to get the soup hot on the woodstove. So, I ate it cold. Thoughts of Mama ran through my mind as I ate, remembering the chicken noodle soup she made me that day I was sent home from school sick.

As I scraped every last bite from the bowl, my mind became a mixture of hurt, anger, and relief. Mama wasn't there that day to fix that bowl of tomato soup, but despite being cold, it was the best-tasting soup I had ever had. It filled my belly. To this day, I love tomato soup, and every time I eat it, I am thankful for it as I remember that cold day in the house on Happy Corner.

Mama and Jack continued to meet up with their swinging friends, despite the continual deterioration of our home life. My bitterness boiled every time I saw Mama pack an overnight bag and disappear with Jack until the next day, leaving the three of us at home. They never told us where they were going, when they were leaving or when they were coming back, but I saw the pornographic magazines, the red rubber douche bag, and change of clothes in Mama's overnight bag. Her bag usually sat on the bedroom floor for a day or so, until she decided to unpack it.

Once, I asked Mama, "Where were you?" after they had been gone all night and into the next afternoon. I knew good and well where they had been, but I was angry, and I wanted to hear her say it. I wanted Mama to explain to me why we were left to fend for ourselves, and Becky, in a house that needed a constant fire going, and had no gas and no running water.

"Well…you know," Mama said, trying to sound casual, "We were all just *visiting* and *talking*, and everybody got *tired* and fell asleep…and the next thing we knew, it was morning!"

Mama laughed as if it was funny. It wasn't.

12

The Funeral Home

AFTER FIFTH GRADE began, we moved to Webbers Falls, forty miles west of Liberty. Mama and Jack intended to manage a funeral home for a guy named Franklin. For the first couple of months, they rented a double-wide trailer a few blocks from the elementary school. Fairly new, with central heat and air, the kitchen boasted a dishwasher, something we weren't used to. Lane and I had our own rooms, with soft beige carpet and big closets. There were no roaches or rats, and the bathroom had a clean, shiny tub and shower. The nicest place we had ever lived.

Mama walked us to school on the first day to get us enrolled. The three of us sat in front of the school secretary as Mama gave her information.

"Names of the children?" the secretary said as she typed.

"Chris and Lane Payton," Mama answered. Payton was Jack's last name, and it's what we began going by once he was in the picture, even though he never adopted us.

"Grades?" the secretary asked.

"Chris is in 5th and Lane is in 7th," Mama answered.

"Address?" Mama couldn't remember the address of our new home, so she explained where it was, and the secretary typed as she listened.

"Where do you work?" she asked Mama.

"My husband and I are the new directors of the funeral home on Main." She didn't know that address either. The secretary stopped typing and looked at Mama.

"The funeral home?" she said, lowering her glasses.

"Yes."

I watched as the secretary smiled and seemed to be more interested in Mama now. She asked questions about their new positions, and she wasn't typing any of it down. She and Mama chatted for several minutes. Something about, "…Webbers Falls is a small town" and "…. the only funeral home around" and "…so glad you're here." Then they both stood, and Mama left as the secretary told me and Lane to follow her to our classes. After that day, Lane and I walked ourselves to school.

I never made many friends at this school. I was lonely, and I missed Belle Point. Lane, however, quickly made friends and joined the baseball team. I loved hanging out around the dugout, watching Lane go up to bat. Sometimes, I had Becky with me, and after the game we played on the bleachers, running up and down, stomping, and being as loud as we wanted.

The river was only a few blocks from our home. Lane and I walked there often, and many times I walked there by myself. Next to the river was a small playground offering shade trees, swings, and a merry-go-round. So close to the water, it was easy to find tiny frogs in the grass. I picked up as many as my small dirty hands could hold and stuffed them in my pockets. I wanted to keep them for my pets but forgot about them by the time I got home. I don't know if my frogs somehow made their way out of my pockets, or if they ended up in the washing machine. Mama never said anything about it, and I didn't think to look.

After two months of living in the double-wide, we were moving out.

"The rent's too high," Jack said.

We moved into an older trailer that sat in the parking lot behind the funeral home.

Much smaller than the double-wide, and not as exciting to look at. The front yard was blacktop that stretched to the back door of the funeral home.

Mama and Jack each had their duties at the funeral home. Jack drove the ambulance and hearse and did the embalming. Mama did hair and makeup and helped in the office. Lane and I ran back and forth from our trailer to the funeral home, like an extended part of where we lived.

The back door opened the embalming room. The ambulance driver used this door if there was no need to go to the hospital, and the hearse driver used it to make a pick-up for a funeral. Next to the embalming room was a tiny bedroom that held a small twin bed. The walls were covered with old newspaper clippings, all articles about car wrecks, with photos of smashed-up cars. I didn't bother reading the articles as the photos told enough of the story.

Next was a long windowless room full of empty caskets. This room was especially creepy at night when Jack asked me to run over to his office and fetch something. I held my hands on either side of my face to block my peripheral vision, kept my eyes straight forward, and ran as fast as I could.

I retrieved whatever I was told to get and repeated the process to get back out as quickly as possible. When I reached the parking lot, I let out my breath and wiped the fear from my eyes.

13

Sinking Further

WE LEFT WEBBERS Falls and moved back to Liberty, into a tiny two-room house owned by Aunt Jeanie and Uncle Jimmy. It was an old Shamrock Motel unit they bought years earlier right after they got married. They moved the motel house to the farm and made it their first home together. It sat empty, in between their new trailer and Grandma and Grandpa's little house.

The farm was a sacred place. Even Lane seemed happy out there. If I wasn't down the hill at Pam and Theresa's, I was up the hill at Grandma's. Our conversations were a comfort to my fragile spirit, and I loved being around her. Grandma made comments about Mama and Jack that showed me she understood but didn't know what to do. "Wish your mama would leave that man. She's scared of him. Scared of what he will do to her. He needs someone to teach him a lesson."

Another brutal winter came that year with a lot of snow. I couldn't get warm for months. The only heat in our little house was the electric stovetop that we cooked on and a space heater. Lane and I slept on the bunkbeds in the tiny bedroom. Mama, Jack, and Becky slept in the bed in the main room. Each morning we met Pam and Theresa at the bottom of the dirt driveway to catch the school bus. Now our third time attending Liberty Elementary.

On weekends, Lane, Pam, Theresa, and I played outside for as long as we could stand the cold. We found bent-up hubcaps and filled them full of snowballs, then hid behind the abandoned cars until someone yelled "GO!" We ran from behind the cars, threw snowballs as fast and as hard as we could. When we were out of snowballs, we used the hubcaps as shields and ran back behind the rusty car for safety.

Other days, we found trashcan lids and used them for sleds on the hill next to the farm. There were only trees at the top, which left a wide-open space for our makeshift sleds to slide all the way down to the dirt road at the bottom. We ran inside briefly to warm up and switch out our wet socks on our hands and feet for dry ones. Those days of playing with my cousins at the farm were not only fun, but also daily escapes from our struggles. We could be kids there. Still, my depression remained, and I always felt it as soon as the distractions were gone.

On a typical evening, we walked down the driveway to Aunt Jeanie and Uncle Jimmy's trailer to absorb the warmth. Lane and I retreated into another room to hang out with Pam and Theresa, while Mama and Jack stayed in the living room. Jack's voice was always the loudest, and like anywhere else, if he called our name, we scrambled. He seemed to take pleasure in showing others how well-trained we were.

"Chris Ann." There were only two reasons he would call me into the room with Aunt Jeanie and Uncle Jimmy. Either we were leaving or wanted to demonstrate his ownership. "Chris Ann!"

"I'm *coming.*"

"She's about the slowest thing there ever was," Jack said with a laugh. "Are your legs broke?" He wasn't really seeking an answer. "I think your legs are broke."

"Have you ever seen such a boney kid?" The room grew silent as everyone sat with awkward expressions. Most of the time, no one knew what to say.

I stood in front of my family with my head down, waiting for him to finish and tell me I could go.

Only Jack laughed. Mama and her wrinkled forehead displayed a fake smile just to please him.

Just tell him to shut up, I wanted to say to Mama. But she would have paid for it if she had.

The cold temperatures remained relentless. I wore my coat all day at school, not only to stay warm, but I hoped to disappear. My cracked lips bled and the dark red circle around my mouth burned from excessive licking. I grimaced when the cold air touched my face, pushing needles through the rawness. I often tried to hide my mouth with my hands.

I was self-conscious about my boney knees and sharp elbows. I believed I was scrawny and weak because Jack had said so. At school, some of the kids took jabs at me, further damaging my self-image.

"Ewww... Your hair is dirty."

"Your fingernails are gross!"

"Where'd you get those *pants*?"

"Why do you keep your hand on your face?"

But the real struggle happened at home. Jack never stopped finding things I had done wrong or stupid things I had said. Little by little, he shamed and verbally battered me into a slighter and more wretched existence. Mama was consumed with managing life in a three-room house with no running water, little heat, and a toddler. On top of her own abused existence.

The days got dimmer and my sadness deeper. I was trapped inside a dark heavy cloud that followed me everywhere I went. *I just want something to be easy. I want to be like the other kids.* I wanted to be warm and clean. I wanted Mama to talk to me, and for Jack to stop punishing me. I wanted someone to see my pain.

I began splitting my lip again. It was a pain I could control, that made the other pain disappear for a few minutes at a time. But the results were always the same. Shame. Despair. Nothing changed.

I daydreamed about running away. *I'll go live in the woods. They won't notice for days.* I created a plan to stockpile supplies. I told myself I would carry an item or two to school with me each day, then hide it in the woods at the edge of the playground before getting on the bus in the afternoon. Blankets, clothes, a tarp, canned food. *When I have enough, I'll disappear.*

I still planned on going to school after I ran away. That way, I'd get one hot meal a day. I wasn't worried about water. *I'll melt the snow and drink it. I don't need baths—don't take them anyway.* I had used the bathroom in the woods plenty of times, so that wasn't an issue. I had my battery-operated transistor radio for entertainment. In my mind, it would all work out, and it sounded like heaven. I never did attempt this futile plan, but in my desperation, I came close.

The snow melted, spring came and went, and hot weather settled in. Jack was done with Aunt Jeanie and Uncle Jimmy and with living in the motel house at the farm and couldn't wait to get away from them. Or was it the other way around?

We packed our stuff and loaded it on the back of Uncle Jimmy's truck. Each time the truck was full, Jack drove off, and returned an hour or so later for another load. We packed and loaded all day until the motel house was empty.

Darkness settled in by the time the last of our belongings were loaded. Jack mentioned an apartment in Ft. Smith, so I assumed that's where we were going. My heart dropped as Jack drove away from the farm. I leaned against the truck window and watched silhouettes of trees pass by. The weight of that winter had not completely worn off as I tried to be hopeful about our new home. *Probably have running water. And maybe air conditioning.*

I pressed my face against the glass so I could see the stars. The night sky mesmerized my mind. *So big and far away.* The stars were bright and never moved. Someone once told me God created the stars—just spoke them into place. They were far away where no one could ever touch them. "Wish I could be a star," I whispered, as I drifted off to sleep.

14

The Unthinkable

WE WERE TIRED and dirty when we arrived at the new apartment. A sidewalk ran between two cinder block buildings, giving access to doors on both sides.

"This way. Start grabbing boxes."

Lane and I got out of the truck and began pulling stuff off the back. We followed Jack down the sidewalk to the second door on the left. The cinder blocks were painted burnt orange and the doors were brown. The smell of cat urine lingered in the air, and someone's music blared. Jack opened the door, flipped on the light, and we followed him in.

The inside of the apartment was painted white, and the floors were the kind you see in schools or hospitals, heavy-duty and ready for traffic. The kitchen and living room were just one room and barely held the sofa, television, and small table and chairs. There were two small bedrooms and one bathroom. As usual, Lane and I would share a bedroom with bunk beds. Becky would sleep with Mama and Jack.

The Arkansas summer heat was brutal as the end of sixth grade approached. I returned to Belle Point Elementary and to my friend, Laura. Every time I returned to Belle Point from a kick-out or other move, our friendship resumed as if I had never left. I loved Laura, and her friendship meant more to me than I understood at that time. She was part of my survival.

Mama got a job at another nursing home, working the second shift, and remained internally lost. And Jack continued to be Jack. He no longer drove an ambulance, but built furniture to sell, and remodeled rent houses for Mr. Grimm.

"Chris Ann."

"Coming." I stood in front of him at attention.

"Go down there to that convenience store and buy you some makeup." Jack held out a twenty-dollar bill. *I'm not in trouble?* Had I heard him right?

"They sell makeup down there, don't they?" I stared at the twenty-dollar bill. *That's a lot of money.*

"Well, do they?" *Why is he being weird? I don't even wear makeup.*

"I don't know." *Why would a convenience store sell makeup?* Jack shoved the twenty-dollar bill into my hand. My heart raced. *I don't know how to buy makeup.*

"Go."

I left the house and walked five blocks to the 7-Eleven. Inside, I wandered around until I found an aisle with paper products and a small section of makeup. I bought one of each, took it home, and shoved it in my dresser drawer. It didn't dawn on me that Jack wanted me to wear it. I bought it like he said, but I had no intention of putting it on.

We had only been in the apartment for a little over a month when the electricity shut off because the bill didn't get paid. We spent the next several evenings at Creekmore Park, cooking dinner on the public barbeque grills, and eating at the concrete tables. Lane, Becky, and I ran to the playground when we were finished with supper and played into the dark, until it was time to go back to the apartment at bedtime.

When the heat became too much, I opened our bedroom window. I soaked a bath towel in the kitchen sink, then took it to my bed and curled up underneath to keep cool. I had to be careful to stay completely beneath the towel because there weren't screens on the windows, and mosquitoes loved my damp dirty skin.

With summer break approaching, there was going to be a swimming party at Creekmore Park for my whole class, and I desperately wanted to go. It made me happy to have friends again, and the thought of a pool party made me giddy. It took me three days to muster the courage to ask if I could go as a permission slip had to be signed by a parent. We sat in the dark at the concrete table at Shady Creek when I asked.

"A *pool party*?!" Jack had a horrible look on his face

"Yes," I replied, but couldn't look at him. "It's a school thing. My class will be there." By now, my body was conditioned to go numb whenever Jack spoke to me, and I welcomed it. His heartless words and unpredictable behavior had become expected, and going numb felt like protection, for the time being. I learned to brace myself, inside and out, and wait for the blow. Only one emotion pierced the numbness—fear.

"Why do you want to go to a *pool party*?" Jack couldn't seem to say pool party without wrinkling his whole face.

"Because."

"*Because why,*" he mocked in a girly voice. His chest puffed out as he put both arms on the table, leaned forward, and stared at me. He was gearing up.

"You don't even know *how* to swim, do you?" His smirk was hateful.

"No." I stared at a chip in the concrete table. *I'm stupid. I can't swim.*

"That's right, you don't. There's only one reason you want to go to a *pool party* and that's to show off your legs."

My legs? What's he talking about? Humiliation spread over my face. I was eleven. Showing off my legs sounded creepy.

"Isn't that right? You just want to show off your legs." His deranged smile terrified me, and I knew he liked what he had said.

"No," I muttered. I just wanted the conversation to be over.

"The only reason for you to go to a *pool party* is to show off your legs, because you can't swim." He folded his arms and let out a *humph*, proud of his conclusion. "You're a liar. What a stupid idea."

I lay in bed that night, degraded, demoralized. I didn't want his words to hurt so much. I tried to lessen the pain in my mind. *My legs are dirty anyway.* I rolled over and realized how much he hated me.

The electric bill got paid, and we closed the bedroom window. We turned the air conditioning on and cooked in the kitchen again.

For weeks, the May temperature grew, as did the tension between Jack and Mama. Fragments of Jack's agitation filtered through their bedroom wall. "…. you'll be out on your butt with nothing." "You don't do a damn thing around here." "Stop feeding me a bunch of crap!"

Here we go again. The anticipated drudgery of being sent walking with nothing and no place to go threatened to break me. *Will we survive this time?* The pain on Mama's face. The evil in Jack's eyes. Watching Mama call for help again. The rollercoaster was too much.

I walked outside and wandered to the edge of the parking lot. The drainage ditch lined with dirt and rocks seemed like a fitting place to hide, to disappear. I lay in the ditch, with my face against the hot rocks. The sting felt better than getting kicked out again, only to come back a few days later. It took my mind off the nightmare inside the apartment.

I cried until I couldn't. Then I brushed the dirt from my clothes, rubbed my face where the rocks had made an impression, and climbed out.

We didn't get kicked out that day, but the tension came and went on a daily basis.

I played outside as much as possible. When I wasn't outside, I stayed in my room. Mama left for work a few hours before Jack got home, so Lane and I filled in the gap, taking care of Becky, cleaning, and doing laundry. The apartment complex had a small onsite laundromat, making it a much simpler chore. No more pulling a heavy wagon back and forth.

My skin turned pink after playing outside for hours. Cool air gushed over my face when I ran through the door to the kitchen. I twisted the last four cubes of ice into a glass of grape Kool-Aid. *We're so lucky to have a freezer for ice.* The tap refilled the tray when I heard Jack's voice, loud from his bedroom.

"Chris Ann!"

My stomach squeezed. "Coming." I dropped the ice cube tray in the sink and hurried to the bedroom door.

"Bring me my cigarettes." Jack lay on his bed covered with a sheet.

I walked back to the kitchen and grabbed the cigarettes from the table. *Just hand them to him and get out.* But my body froze when Jack spoke again.

"Chris Ann, close the door." Jack's lips were pressed together, resembling a smile. His nostrils flared. My mind panicked, but my body didn't move. This was new, and I knew it wasn't good.

"I said close the door. Now, come over here."

My feet carried me to the side of the bed. Jack pulled the sheet down, exposing his naked body. I gasped and quickly looked away. I had never seen a naked man before. I couldn't feel my legs. A lump in my throat threatened to choke me. I desperately wanted to run but was too afraid.

"Why don't you rub me down?" *Rub him down?* I didn't know what that meant. An eternity of silence darkened my vision as I began to shake. *What's going on? I want out of here.*

"What's wrong with you? I need you to rub me down." Jack grew impatient and took my hand and put it where he wanted it. Queasiness turned to nausea. I wanted to cry. My mind spun. I couldn't look at him. I caught a glimpse of the fading daylight through the bedroom curtains. Jack forced my hand to do the motions until he was done.

I don't remember leaving the bedroom. I didn't understand what had just happened, but I knew I hated it. I had fallen into a hole of shame and now I was trapped.

The fighting between Jack and Mama persisted, the summer heat was relentless, and Jack's demands continued. While Mama was aware of how Jack treated me verbally, as she silently sat nearby with her awkward smile, the unspeakable secret remained hidden from her. Jack always chose the early evening, before Mama was home from work, to call me into the bedroom.

The last few days of sixth grade were dark. Something inside of me broke. My heart barely limped along, and my emotions were detached. I became paranoid about people looking at me. *Everyone knows what he's making me do.*

When the last bell of the last day of school rang, I lingered on the playground for as long as I thought I could without getting in trouble. I was already afraid of Jack. Now there were new words that brought terror to my heart.

"Chris Ann, bring me my cigarettes!"

15

Making Up

THREE WEEKS INTO the summer break we moved again. This time to another of Mr. Grimm's rental houses on Drennen Street in Van Buren. The same house Mr. Grimm took us to a few years earlier, when Jack kicked us out, but kept Becky. By now I was twelve and Lane fourteen.

Lane saved up enough money to buy a small motorcycle. He was proud, and I couldn't blame him. Mama even showed interest in it and asked Lane to show her how to ride it one day. So, in the vacant field next to our house, Lane gave her a quick lesson that ended with Mama running into the bushes and laying the motorcycle over. She wasn't hurt, but she never got on it again.

My own zeal to ride the motorcycle exploded, and Lane kindly taught me how. It wasn't long before I was riding figure eights in the field next to the house, since I couldn't legally ride on the street. I felt free on the motorcycle, and I never wanted to get off of it. My first thought each morning was to run to the motorcycle and ride all my problems away.

I laugh as I remember how Lane pleaded, "*Please* don't run it out of gas." I always promised I wouldn't, but I didn't know how to check the gas gauge, and once I got on the motorcycle, all I cared about was getting lost in my figure eights. Every single time, I ran it dry, and Lane walked with the empty gas can to the nearest service station. He never scolded me or got angry. He never refused to let me ride the next day. At the time, I couldn't explain the need inside of me that was being met. I only knew I was thankful for his patience and mercy.

Doing *anything* with Lane was exciting. One night, Mama's three to eleven evening shift at the nursing home was about to end. Jack was too tired to go pick her up, so he handed the car keys to Lane and told him to take the back roads since he was only fourteen and didn't have a driver's license. *Lane's driving? I have to go with him!* I was a giddy twelve-year-old, sitting next to my big brother, no seatbelts, riding on the back roads at eleven o'clock at night. I'm sure I talked his ear off and didn't sit still, but Lane focused on driving, and I marveled at the freedom. Any time away from Jack became a relief.

The fighting between Mama and Jack picked up again. When they fought, it wasn't a screaming back-and-forth type of fight. It wasn't a throwing-things across-the-room kind of fight. It took place behind their bedroom door, with Jack shouting at Mama mixed with moments of muffled noises. I never heard Mama cry behind her bedroom door, and rarely when the fight was over did she come out until the next morning.

For days afterward, the air was thicker than usual, the wrinkles on Mama's forehead deeper, her eyes bigger, and her face sterner. As new bruises emerged on her arms and legs, she spoke less and glanced at Jack's face more often to gauge his expressions. She put makeup on the bruises and only spoke of them if someone asked. But she didn't tell the truth.

Jack kicked us out again.

"Pack your crap," Jack snapped at Mama as he slammed the front door and drove away. I emptied my dresser drawers into a pillowcase and followed Mama to the apartment manager's door where she asked to use the phone.

Aunt Jeanie picked us up. Lane, Becky, and me piled into the backseat. No one spoke all the way to the farm.

There was plenty to do for the first two days as we ran around the farm with Pam and Theresa, back and forth between Aunt Jeanie's and Grandma's houses. I pushed Jack out of my thoughts and enjoyed my freedom. *I'm safe right now.*

By the third day, Jack hadn't called or shown up. Sternness edged Grandma's voice as she handed Mama the money to secure a furnished trailer in a trailer park in Van Buren. "I hope you don't go back to that monster this time."

The furniture was old, but we didn't mind—it felt like ours, and we were happy to have it. A day later, some church people brought us sacks of groceries. Dozens of brown paper bags sat all over the kitchen floor. I had never seen so much food. Excitement made my eyes big as I rummaged through the sacks.

"Look." I held up two boxes of macaroni and cheese for Mama to see. "And spaghettios." I loved the freedom I felt when Jack wasn't around. "Mama, can we make spaghettios for supper?"

"We'll see."

The church people must have invited us to their church. I remember standing next to Mama with our heads bowed. When the preacher told everyone to close their eyes and raise their hand if they needed prayer, I peeked at Mama. She raised her hand. At the end of the service, Mama scribbled a note and dropped it in the offering basket. Someone must have read the note right away, because the preacher read it aloud. "Please help me. I'm alone with three kids. I have nothing and I'm scared." Then he asked if the writer of the note would be willing to come forward for prayer. Mama rose and started walking. I followed her. We stood in front of the church as the preacher prayed over us, then people lined up and took turns handing Mama money as they left the service.

Mama cried and thanked each person, and I stood in awe of the dollar bills being shoved into her hands. *Why are they giving us money? They don't even know us.* My heart was tempted to burst as I watched Mama cry freely, without looking away or dabbing her makeup. She didn't seem to mind who saw and wasn't holding anything back. Seeing Mama express honest emotions reminded me of who she used to be, before Jack.

Several weeks passed since Grandma gave Mama the money to rent the trailer, and so far, no sign of Jack. *Are we free?* I dared to allow a little happiness in. *Mama usually goes back by now.* Had Jack called, and Mama said no this time?

It was amazing how good the world seemed when I didn't walk in fear. I could breathe. My body moved more freely, and my mind cleared. Mama talked to us again and occasionally smiled. Worry still creased her face, but not the same worry as when Jack was around. This worry looked like sadness. When Jack was present, the worry became fear.

Lane and I had our own rooms, and Mama's hours at the nursing home changed to an earlier shift, allowing her to be home every evening. This split from Jack had already lasted longer than all of the others, and hope dared to grow in my mind. *Is the bad stuff over? No more bruises for Mama? No more of Jack's disgusting orders to the bedroom? Am I getting my Mama back?* Could it be?

No.

One dark evening after the church people dropped off more sacks of groceries, and Mama put things away in the kitchen, another knock came. I got up from the couch, but Mama had already opened the door. Her face changed.

I couldn't see who it was, and for a second, no one spoke. *Please be the church people again.* Then I heard the voice that made my insides panic.

"Karen."

At the sound of his voice, my gut curled, and I nearly threw up from the rush of hope leaving my body. I peeked through the door to see Jack standing in front of the steps. My fists clenched and my jaw grew tight. *Get away from us!*

"I've missed you." Jack looked at the ground, then up at Mama. Her lips pressed together, forming a frown, but her hand stayed frozen to the doorknob. My mind screamed.

Close the door! Mama silently stared.

"Karen, you know I love you." His eyes pleaded.

Close the door, Mama. Just cloooose the door.

"Can I come in?" *Ha!* Jack never asked Mama for permission to do *anything*. But Mama opened the door wider and stepped back. I darted from the room before he got through the door.

I shrunk into my bed as Jack's voice rang through the thin walls. He was indignant about all the groceries we had.

"Where did all this come from?"

It's not for you! It's ours!

"From the church." Mama's voice was faint.

Jack wanted to know why Mama was *doing this to him*. After all, he was *so sorry*.

She's not gonna make him leave. I clenched my teeth tighter to stop my chin from quivering. As they continued to talk, their voices faded from my ears. The world darkened as my newfound freedom slowly faded, taking my Mama with it.

And that was that. He came back. We were broken again.

I remained secretly angry with Mama for months, but I didn't dare tell her. I felt guilty for my anger. *She already knows she caved. Why make her feel worse?* What little backbone Mama may have developed during the weeks of being away from Jack simply wasn't enough to stand up to his clever manipulation. Face-to-face with Jack, Mama had no courage. *She's still afraid.*

I also felt shame. Shame about what Jack had been doing to my body, making me feel filthy. His perverted words haunted my mind, and I didn't know how to get them out. Somehow, I felt responsible for what was happening, and I couldn't bear to utter the words out loud to tell Mama. *She would cry if I told her. She wouldn't know what to do.* Would I see Grandma any time soon? Should I tell her? Could I? Jack typically banned family visits after returning from a kick-out.

I held onto hope that maybe someday things would change, and Mama would make a permanent break from Jack. I believed that was the only way any of us would ever be free.

Jack continued to summon me with "Chris Ann, bring me my cigarettes," when Mama wasn't home. "Turn the light off and close the door." His abuse escalated and became more frequent, but he did everything quietly. His words were barely audible, but his authority was clear. Shame and fear kept me silent. When I was in front of Jack, my body, voice, and mind froze. When I wasn't in front of Jack, I could only imagine his wrath and Mama's pain if I told anyone what was happening. If I thought Mama would help me, I might have taken the risk. *She's too weak. We'll never be free.*

THE NEW VAN Buren Middle School finished just two weeks before school started. I was twelve and going into seventh grade. There was something about a new school year that made me feel life was going to be different and somehow happier.

Before Jack moved into the trailer with us, Mama walked me over to Clover Leaf Plaza, a small strip mall across the highway, because she heard the department store was clearing out girls' shirts. I felt happy to walk with Mama again. And she was going to buy me something. She found a rack of shirts on sale for $1.00 each and told me I could pick out five. I happily flipped through all the shirts, choosing the best ones.

I only remembered getting new school clothes once before. When we lived in the house on Dodson, Jack took Lane and me to a store and I got one new outfit. It was orange polyester pants and a lighter orange stretchy top that had sparkles in the fabric. I felt pretty wearing clothes that fit and had no holes or stains.

I felt confident others would focus on my new outfit and think of me as a normal person. But my all-time favorite piece of clothing was a pair of white and blue bellbottoms that Mama picked up at a yard sale. They fit me perfectly, and I thought everyone would think I looked cool. I would have been content to wear them every day but was afraid of what others would say. I was heartbroken when I fell at school one day, ripping a hole in the knee of the fabric.

"Chrissy, where did you get this makeup?" Mama found the plastic bag I had thrown into a box that I never bothered to unpack. She opened the packages and tested the colors on the top of her hand.

"Daddy told me to buy it. Long time ago. You can have it." I only called him Daddy around Mama. We were not allowed to call him anything else.

Mama seemed pleased with her discovery. She scooped it all up and took it to the bathroom.

Had she heard me? I watched as Mama spread makeup on her face, then drew heavy lines of eyeliner. My thoughts pulled me in different directions. *Why doesn't she care where it came from? Did Jack forget he told me to buy it? He never made me wear it.*

I felt alone.

Once Jack moved in, Mama gravitated back to her old self. She and I didn't walk together again. She only went to work or places with Jack. She spoke carefully again, if at all. The wrinkles in her forehead returned. And her eyes told me she had left us again. I often thought about that night at the church, when Mama was honest about her emotions. I knew she wouldn't cry like that again, at least not on the outside.

16

Reaching Hell

I WALKED TO the front of the trailer park to catch the bus to middle school. Lane took a different bus to the junior high. The ride felt peaceful. Safe. I sat on the cool vinyl seat, took slow deep breaths, and focused on the vibrations of the road. I didn't have to talk to anyone, and Jack couldn't touch me.

The building smelled like fresh paint, and everything was new and clean. Mrs. Walker and Mrs. Fletcher quickly became my favorite teachers. They both spoke gently and looked at me with smiles. Mrs. Walker taught English and Literature, and Mrs. Fletcher taught Art. Those subjects came easy, and I soaked up every "Good job" or "Great work" they offered.

I had ninety minutes of safety each day after school before Jack got home. At three-thirty, Lane and I walked through the door and turned on the television. Little Rascals, Happy Days, and Laverne and Shirley always came on, in that order. Three half-hour programs that allowed me to temporarily escape. But shortly before the last program ended, anxiety swooped in, reminding me Jack would be home from work. Mama wasn't due for at least another hour or so. Becky, four years old, stayed at a neighbor's house during the day until Mama picked her up on her walk home from work.

At that time, Jack worked at a chair company as part of an assembly line in a hot warehouse. Mr. Grimm no longer ran an ambulance company since hospitals now ran their own ambulance service. Each day, he came home in dirty sweaty overalls, with an exhausted ready-to-die look on his face. As soon as Jack walked through the door, he went straight to his and Mama's bedroom at the back of the trailer and stripped off his smelly clothes. Sometimes I was able to see the end of Laverne and Shirley, but often Jack's harrowing voice cut my television time short. Lane usually went outside when the program was over, to wash Jack's car, something he seemed to enjoy.

"Chris Ann, bring me my cigarettes." My heart sank every time. My vision darkened as I picked up the cigarettes from the coffee table and slowly walked down the hallway. By the time I reached the bedroom door, my body went numb, and my mind panicked as it searched for ways to change the course of what was about to happen. *Maybe if I turn the light on, he won't do it this time.*

"Turn off that light. And close the door." Even though I knew what he wanted me to do, I froze until he gave the next order.

"Come over here and sit down." I watched my feet take me to the edge of the bed where he lay naked.

"Sit down."

Always, for the first few moments, Jack stared at me and said nothing. Those moments seemed like an eternity. My stomach turned hard as a rock. My skinny body shook, and I stared at the floor, at the ceiling, at the wall—whatever I could fix my eyes on. Tension ran through my neck to the top of my head.

I never knew from day-to-day what I was going to be forced to do. "Rubbing Jack down," as he called it, evolved into a list of other demoralizing demands that seemed to never end. I was subjected to repulsive, dispiriting acts, mixed with verbal assaults and explicit comments. When I didn't move at his first command, he forced my body to where he wanted it.

"You know," he said, his voice sly, "I work hard all day. I put food on the table. I put a roof over your head. The least you could do is show some appreciation." He then began whatever act he decided upon that day, sending me into a state of terror and speechlessness every time. Afterward, he stared holes through my exposed body, while stabbing my mind with explicit words and taunting questions. "What's wrong with you?" "Why can't you be more appreciative?" "Are you really that selfish?" "Why are you so quiet?"

I tried desperately to seize the moments in between Jack's demands by counting ceiling tiles. Foam squares glued to the ceiling, typical of trailer homes back then. If I meticulously counted tiles and imagined being on the other side of them, it gave me enough mental escape to protect my sanity.

"What are you looking at!" Jack snapped.

"Nothing" I whispered. *One, two, three, four…*

"Are you counting something?"

"No." *Six, seven, eight…*

Then came his next demand. And then the next.

Jack assaulted me.

Jack molested me.

Jack exploited me.

Jack raped me.

The ugly truth is, five days a week, at around five o'clock, Jack used my body to feed his evil sickness, with no regard for the torment he inflicted. He sexually, mentally, and emotionally abused me beyond my own belief, each time ripping a new hole into the deepest part of my soul. And each time, it was conveniently over with a few minutes to spare, before Mama walked through the front door with Becky. I walked away from him more shattered than the day before and spiraling deeper into my dark terrifying world. Sometimes I walked outside to watch Lane finish drying Jack's car. Sometimes he was already in his room doing homework. I knew Lane wouldn't have heard anything as Jack was so cleverly quiet, and fear held my voice in a vice-grip. Had he noticed how long I was in there? Did he wonder?

Shame kept me from telling Lane. The words were too difficult, too ugly, too painful to say. *I don't want my brother to think badly of me. Besides, he's got his own fears.* Jack controlled him too.

Jack's psychological and emotional manipulation added to my silence. In addition to the guilt-inflicting lectures, he dared me to tell Mama.

"What? You want to tell your mama?" He stared at me with raised eyebrows and a smirk. "Go ahead. She won't believe you." Swelling anger made me long to tell Mama, but the temptation was always squashed with the thoughts in my head. *It will hurt her…she won't believe me…she won't know what to do to help me.*

I hung my head and fought back tears until he told me to leave the room.

I walked through my days wounded and emotionally crippled. I hated my body. I hated my life. I hated myself. I didn't trust people much anymore, especially men. I *watched* others more than I spoke to them, like I did with Jack. Simple daily tasks felt nearly impossible. Getting on the bus each morning was easy, but walking in the school hallways, looking at people, and them looking at me was excruciating. My surroundings didn't seem new and bright anymore. I felt buried beneath a mountain I couldn't move. All I saw was darkness. All I felt was shame, pain, and hopelessness. The voice inside continued its torture.

You're dirty. You're worthless. No one cares. There's no way out.

Every day after school, I told myself I was safe for an hour and a half. *It's just me, Lane, and the television.* I didn't allow myself to think about what happened when it was five o'clock. I couldn't. And every day, when Jack came home, I was forced into Hell again, exposing my wounds and burning them even deeper.

"Chris Ann, bring me my cigarettes."

I hate his guts! I hate his voice! I hate his face!

17

The Rescue

ON A COLD Wednesday, I stepped off the school bus and hurried
into the school to get out of the wind. I didn't want to be there
anymore. I didn't want to be anywhere. The darkness inside of me left
no room for any kind of escape. Even the comfort I used to feel from
Mrs. Walker and Mrs. Fletcher seemed lost. But I didn't want to be at
home either.

My first class was English and Literature with Mrs. Walker.
Class had barely begun when a pretty lady with long black hair walked
in and whispered something to our teacher.

"Class, please give your attention to Mrs. Hill," Mrs. Walker
announced, then sat at her desk.

Slender with bright eyes, Mrs. Hill had soft-looking skin, high
cheekbones, and a narrow nose. Her straight shiny hair nearly reached

her waist. She wore a touch of makeup, with lip-gloss instead of lipstick.

"My name is Mrs. Hill. I'm one of the school counselors."

She's beautiful. I studied her moves and listened to her voice.

Mrs. Hill went on about the things she took care of for the school, where to find her office, and how she hoped to get to know *each and every one of us.* Then she said something that grabbed my attention. In fact, it changed my life forever—I just didn't know it at the time.

I don't remember how her last sentence began, but it ended with "....so if you ever have a problem you'd like to discuss, come see me."

A problem I'd like to discuss... Come see me... My mind reeled for the rest of the day. Could it be that simple? Could I really just go to Mrs. Hill's office and tell her about my problem, and she would tell me things that would make me feel better? I thought about it all the way home.

By the next day, I decided to talk to Mrs. Hill, but I had to get my story straight. I couldn't tell her this was *me* I would be talking about—it was too shameful. Terror filled me at the thought of Jack finding out. It had to be my *friend* and I was *very concerned.*

By the last period of the day, I gathered the courage to ask Mrs. Fletcher if I could go to the office. I walked through Mrs. Hill's open door and handed her my hall pass. She invited me to sit as she got up and closed the door. *She's even prettier than yesterday.*

"Well, Chris, how can I help you?" Her words sparked a little hope. I began telling my *friend's* story. It became harder than I had imagined. I fumbled with the zipper on my jacket and tried to remember what I had rehearsed.

"I have a friend that has a problem."

"What kind of problem?"

"Well… Her name is Tina, and her dad keeps asking her to do stuff that she doesn't want to do. But he makes her."

"What kind of things does her dad make her do?"

I stared at my zipper and began telling the story—how my *friend's dad* makes her come to his bedroom and "rub him down." Mrs. Hill asked questions to get more detail. "So, tell me what else your dad is making you do."

"Not *me*, my *friend*!" I furrowed my brows so she would see frustration, not fear. I told her what happened when my friend took the cigarettes to her dad. How she turned on the light and was told to turn it back off and close the door.

Mrs. Hill continued to speak as if this were happening to *me* and not my friend. She saw through my story, but I couldn't admit the truth. The bell was about to ring, and I hadn't told her everything. I hardly told her anything. And worse yet, she hadn't said anything that made me feel better—no solutions.

"Chris." Mrs. Hill leaned over the top of her desk. "I want you to come back to my office tomorrow, around this time."

Okay, maybe she's gonna work on what to tell me. I left her office, went to my locker, then got on the bus. The seat was cold, and the chatter around me grew as kids piled in. I pressed my face against the window and wondered if I had done the right thing. Although I couldn't imagine what Mrs. Hill would say the next day, I had hope, and I hung onto it. *She'll know what to say. Something to make me feel better.*

The next day was Friday. My chest couldn't catch a full breath as I watched the hours in slow motion. Come on, last period. I imagined myself skipping out of Mrs. Hill's office and getting on the bus feeling much better about life. *She's gonna tell me something to make me feel better. She's smart.*

Finally, the last class of the day began. Mrs. Fletcher gave me another hall pass, and I hurried down the hallway. My throat went dry, and my feet moved faster without me telling them to. *What if she's not here? What if she couldn't think of anything to make me feel better?*

"Please—please—please," I whispered all the way down the hall. *She's here!*

I walked into Mrs. Hill's office, closed the door myself, handed her my hall pass, and sat down. *Sit straight up. Wait for her to talk.*

"How are you doing, Chris?"

"Fine." I was ready. Anxious. Desperate. *Bring it on.* But my readiness came to a screeching halt, and my body froze after her first sentence.

"Chris, by law I had to report what you told me yesterday." She paused as if she was waiting for me to say something.

"About my friend?" I knew the answer.

"I called the Department of Human Services and spoke to the Child Welfare authorities. There are social workers with each of your parents, talking to them right now."

My throat closed, and the room turned dark. Horror. *How could she?* Her words swirled in my ears...*had to report what you told me...talking to them right now...* My mind screamed. I wanted to run, but my feet wouldn't move.

"Oh no," I managed to whisper. *Why did I do this? I should've kept my mouth shut.* Now it would all be out in the open. The horrid shame. The disgraceful truth. I would see Jack's wrath like never before. Then I imagined Mama, and a new horror filled my mind. *Mama's gonna be so hurt.* I hated myself.

"Chris, if you are too afraid to go home, you don't have to. You can leave with me."

I was too afraid *not* to go home! *I've done enough already. I can't make it worse.* Why had she betrayed me?

"Chris?"

"I'll go home."

Mrs. Hill slipped a piece of paper with her phone number on it into my hand. "Just in case you need to call me." I shoved the paper into my jacket pocket, gathered my things, and walked outside to catch the bus. My body surged with adrenalin. My mind couldn't think. The first seat on the left was empty, and I nearly collapsed into it. *What's gonna happen when I get home?*

When the bus stopped in front of the trailer park, I was the first one off. I wanted to cry, but fear trapped my tears. Jack's car wasn't in front of the trailer, offering slight relief. But when I opened the door, my heart sank at the sight of Mama sitting in the living room next to a social worker. *She knows.*

Mama was crying into her hands. My face filled with shame. The social worker motioned to an empty chair that had been placed in front of the two of them for me.

"Sit down, Chris," the social worker instructed. I sat without bothering to take off my jacket.

"My name is Gina. I'm with Child Protective Services." I couldn't look at her. Or at Mama. My face was blank.

"Can you tell your mom what you told Mrs. Hill?"

No, I can't! I wanted to, but the words were too shameful, too horrible. I hung my head and felt streaks of heat run down my cheeks and a drip from my nose. I couldn't stop it.

"Chris, can you tell your mom what has happened?" The social worker patiently waited. Mama broke the silence. "Chris, you don't have to say anything you don't want to." Then she turned to the social worker and cried, "My husband would never do that!"

"Chris, can you tell your mom what your dad has done to you?"

I watched the tears fall to my lap. My heart was desperate to say the words to Mama, but I couldn't move, not even to look up.

After a moment, the social worker stood and asked me if I wanted to leave with her. *Of course* I wanted to leave with her, but I was terrified. Was she crazy? *Jack would kill me.* Besides, Mama would have completely broken in half.

I shook my head, and she left.

Mama didn't have a chance to say anything before we heard Jack's car door slam shut. We were still in our chairs when the front door burst open. And there he was, his face in a state of rage that made me wonder if I was going to survive. He slammed the front door, walked into the kitchen, walked back to the living room, and began pacing back and forth. His eyes steamed. His red face dripped sweat. His jaws clenched as tightly as his fists. His nostrils flared as his lips seemed to be searching for something to say. He stopped once and glared at me. His eyes looked cursed. *Is he going to hit me?* Then he resumed his pace.

Mama disappeared from my vision. I don't know if she actually left her chair, or if in my own fear, everything around me vanished. Except for Jack. His heavy breathing and hammering footsteps were the only noise in the room. Then his words began as he walked toward me. I held tightly to the seat of my chair.

"You!" Jack's finger hovered a few inches from my face. "You are a liar! You're despicable!"

I didn't move. *He didn't hit me.*

"You are ungrateful! After everything I do for you! Ungrateful!"

I waited for his voice to stop, but it didn't.

"Nobody wants you! Your own daddy didn't want you. And I don't want you either." We had never been allowed to talk about my biological dad, but that rule didn't apply to Jack. "You are not my kid anymore, you hear me? You are not a *Payton* anymore!"

I never was. And that doesn't hurt. When you've been stomped into the ground, stabbed in the heart, and stripped of worth and dignity enough times, being disowned by your abuser is hardly upsetting.

"Go down to that schoolhouse right now and tell them your name isn't Payton anymore." Mama resurfaced but sat silently. It was after five o'clock in the afternoon. Was he serious?

"Go! Get out of that chair. Go tell them your name's not Payton anymore." He meant it. He walked toward me, so I jumped out of my chair and rushed to the door. I opened the door and looked back. Jack raised his steel-toed boot into the air and my mind went crazy. *Is he literally kicking me through the doorway and down the steps?*

The next few seconds are a blank in my memory, even now. I found myself on the ground, looking at Lane, washing Jack's car. Lane looked at me, but I had to start walking. This time without Mama. Knowing the school doors were locked by now, I walked to the front of the trailer park and knocked on the park manager's door.

"Can I use your phone?" He let me in and pointed to the phone on a little table at the end of the couch. I pulled the paper out of my pocket and dialed the number for Mrs. Hill, and she answered on the first ring.

"Hello?" *Don't cry. Don't cry.*

"He told me to go tell the school my name isn't Payton anymore. He made me leave." I spoke quietly so the park manager couldn't hear me.

Mrs. Hill was very specific with her instructions. "Chris, listen to me. I want you to walk over to Savemart and go inside to the produce section. Wait for me there. If you see Jack, start screaming. Do you understand?"

"Yes." It took less than five minutes to get to Savemart. I had walked there many times. The produce section was to the right of the front entrance. As I stood next to the bags of potatoes, the world got quiet. *Okay, I'm here.* A few feet away a lady pushed a cart with a toddler in it. An older lady picked up a bag of apples and carried it away. A store worker brushed past me with a wide broom. People were all around me, but I was alone.

When anyone walked near me, I pretended to study the potatoes, then the onions. I glanced at the front door every few seconds. *Where is she?* I prayed Jack wouldn't walk through the door. I wasn't sure if I could scream.

It took Mrs. Hill twenty-five minutes to drive from Fort Smith to Van Buren. She dashed through the glass doors, and I ran to her. She held out her hand and I glanced at it as though it were a foreign object. The only person I had ever held hands with was Mama, but I reluctantly held on to Mrs. Hill.

"Let's go." She rushed me through the doors and into the parking lot where her husband waited in a pickup truck. I let out a sigh of relief as we jumped in and Mr. Hill started driving.

We looked straight ahead in silence. I didn't know where we were going, or what was going to happen next. My mind was in turmoil. Had she just helped me escape? *Had* I escaped? Would they send me back?

Jack's gonna be mad—real mad.

18

Emotions and Hope

THE RUMBLE OF Mr. Hill's truck filled the cab as he drove down Main Street.

My mind replayed Mama sitting in that chair, crying. Denying. *She doesn't believe me. She didn't help me.* Jack's words swirled in my ears, but Mama's silence was louder. Mama lost her backbone a long time ago. She had been beaten down—physically, emotionally, and mentally—for so long, she no longer had a voice. She walked around in a scared muted body, convinced she couldn't live without him. *I'm out, but what about Mama? She will die if they take Jack away from her.*

Mr. Hill drove to the Van Buren Police Department, and we spent the next two hours in a tiny lobby, as Mr. and Mrs. Hill spoke to the officer on the other side of the counter.

"Are they going to take Jack away from my mama?"

Mrs. Hill looked at me with pause.

"I don't know. We just have to tell them what happened."

I must have asked about what was going to happen to Jack several times because at one point Mrs. Hill asked the officer if she could talk to him in private. The officer opened a door and motioned for Mrs. Hill to come through. Even in the lobby I heard fragments of the muffled conversation.

"She keeps asking what's going to happen to Jack."

"Her stepdad?"

"Yes…afraid he'll be taken from her mom."

There were some quiet words from the officer, then they returned to the lobby. From the Van Buren Police Department, we went to the Ft. Smith Police Department.

The Ft. Smith courthouse was a huge stone and concrete building with tall ceilings and Art Deco style floors. Our footsteps echoed down the hallway as we walked to the only office with lights on. By then it was eight-thirty.

The Hills began speaking through the opening of a glass window, the same glass window Mama cried through years earlier, when Jack kicked us out and kept Becky. I looked around at the familiar walls and light fixtures. I heard Mama's voice as if she was standing there, "Please help me. My husband kicked us out of the house and kept the baby."

I spent another two hours in a chair, waiting. I didn't know what I was waiting for. Just waiting.

When the Hills finally finished, we left the courthouse and drove to their home across town. A beautiful home in a nice neighborhood with tall trees and yards of thick grass.

"Chris, you must be hungry." Mrs. Hill opened her refrigerator. "I can make you a sandwich." She looked at me and I shook my head. "What about some milk?" I shook my head again.

I stood in the doorway of the kitchen, taking in my surroundings. Red and white checkered wallpaper. Decorative baskets hanging on the wall. Shiny wood floors. Half-cooked food in a frying pan. *I called her before they had their supper.*

"Chris, are you sure you don't want a sandwich?"

I had no words. No feelings. At that moment, my world consisted of the spot I was standing on. I looked at Mrs. Hill's face as she waited. I had a flashback of the first time I saw her, only a few days ago. That pretty lady barely knew me. *But she rescued me.*

"I'm not hungry," I whispered.

Mrs. Hill showed me the room I would sleep in. "No one uses this room."

There was a twin bed in the corner and empty shelves mounted to the wall. A small nightstand sat next to the bed, with a clock radio and lamp on it. I didn't have anything to put away, so I stood in the middle of the room looking around, not knowing what to do. Everything was foreign, even my emotions.

I turned on the radio and slowly moved the dial to find a station. The song "Can't Smile Without You" by Barry Manilow came on—finally something familiar. I walked around the room, learning every detail. Opened and closed the closet door. Ran my hand across the neatly made bed. Watched my shoes sink into the thick green carpet. Through the window, I saw other homes up and down the street. Brick homes with bright porch lights and chimneys. Shiny cars in wide driveways. *Everybody's got a nice house around here.*

I turned off the light and lay on the bed listening to what felt like my only friend singing through the top of the clock radio. *Now what?*

I wondered if Lane was already asleep. Was he worried about me? *What did they tell him?*

"Social Services said you can stay with us for now, since I'm a school counselor."

I spent the next two days looking around and listening. I wondered if I would ever feel my body again, or if my mind would ever know what to think.

Mrs. Hill introduced me to her three and six-year-old sons. She showed me around the house and said I could call her Janey and her husband Mark. All I could do was nod.

The boys' room had matching beds and nice toys. *Becky would like those toys.* Janey and Mark's bedroom had a shiny brass bed with a rug underneath. I couldn't believe a bed could be so beautiful.

The living room had a fireplace that worked. Janey and I sat as she talked about all the updates she and Mark did when they bought the house. The painted walls to brighten it up. The screened-in porch to enjoy when it rained. The nicely arranged family photos in coordinating frames. My eyes followed where she pointed, and my head nodded to everything she said. I didn't know what it all meant. *Am I gonna live here?*

In my room, I lay on the bed and watched flickering shadows of the branches outside the window. I wondered what Mama was doing at that moment. *Is she sad?* What did Lane think? *Wish I could show them this nice house.* I imagined for a moment that Mama, Lane, Becky, and I lived there, without Jack. *Mama would love that kitchen. Bet Lane would want to sleep on the screened porch.*

Janey popped her head through the open door. "I'll have some lunch ready in a few minutes." And with a smile, she turned and walked away.

In one day, all sense of familiarity disappeared. My mom, my brother, my sister, my home, my clothes, my books, my city, my room—none of it was mine anymore. In one day, I entered into a new world. A bewildering world I had never seen before. I waited minute by minute to be told what would happen next, and what I was supposed to do.

I sat on my bed until Janey invited me to join them in the other room. I followed her around, watching everything she did. I don't remember what she talked about, but she was often interrupted by her two boys who were full of words and energy. Mark was quiet and pleasant to be around. His smile seemed natural, and his eyes spoke the truth. I trusted him.

Later that evening, Janey brought a sewing machine into my bedroom. "This is my mom's. Do you like to sew?" *Sew?* I saw Grandma cut quilt squares from old clothes and use her sewing machine to sew them together into a long strip. Grandma then sewed the strips together to make the top of the quilt. She used a thin blanket for the middle and sewed on a sheet for the bottom. Grandma's quilts were never that pretty, but they were heavy and warm.

"I have some small pieces of fabric." Janey stood patiently by the door.

"Yes, I like to sew." Inside, I was elated. Being reminded of Grandma helped me relax.

Janey brought me several remnants of fabric, and I began cutting out quilt squares. It felt good to have something to do and to reminisce about being at Grandma's.

I ran out of fabric, hence the quilt wasn't very big, so I gave it to the six-year-old. Janey seemed pleased and asked if I could stitch the date and *Made by Chris* in the corner of it. I don't remember if I ever did.

On Monday, I rode with Janey to school.

"You can tell them I'm your aunt if you want. Or a friend. Whatever makes you comfortable." *Them?* I hadn't thought about what my friends might say, seeing me arrive with the school counselor. I decided to say that she was my aunt, who simply gave me a ride to school.

I learned the routine at Janey and Mark's house and quickly went into *stay-out-of-trouble* mode. I looked for ways to earn their approval, like I did when I was at home. I wanted them to like me. I wanted them to think I was a good kid and say nice things about me, even though I still believed the voice inside of me, instilled over the years.

You can't do anything right. You're a stupid boney little kid. No one wants you. If Janey and Mark realized the truth, they would surely regret bringing me to their home. *I'm not as good as their kids. I'm a reject.*

Janey said, "Just be yourself." But I didn't know who myself *was.*

When they started leaving me alone on occasion, I secretly called Aunt Jeanie's house. I didn't know if calling my family was allowed, so I didn't ask. Theresa always answered the phone, and we chatted for a few minutes before she needed to go. I didn't know how to explain things to her, only that I lived with the school counselor now, and I didn't think I was going back home. She didn't seem to understand, and I was too ashamed to tell her what Jack had been doing. I didn't know I had entered the foster care system. I didn't know that was a thing.

I found out years later, Aunt Jeanie became suspicious of my calls, and she loaded up my cousins and drove to Mama and Jack's trailer to confront them. Jack told her I had gotten mixed up with a group of kids doing drugs, and they simply couldn't control me anymore, so they had to send me away. Later, when Grandma heard Jack's story, she shook her finger at everyone and said, "Don't you believe it. He's a liar."

By the time my family understood what had happened, I had already been placed with Janey and Mark, and they felt there was nothing they could do about it.

One evening, Janey invited her parents for dinner. I had never been around them, and the pressure was overwhelming. *What if they see I'm not as good as them?* Now I had to earn their approval too.

I only knew the suppertime ritual that had been engrained in me for years. The one Jack taught us. *Eat everything on my plate, clear the table and start cleaning up. Don't forget to dry the dishes before putting them away. And wipe the counters and sweep the kitchen. That's how to get approval.*

The truth was, I wanted to stay at the table and talk and laugh with Janey, Mark, and her parents. I wanted to relax and for that to be okay. I wanted things I didn't know the words for, a connection to someone, acceptance. I wanted to be good enough, without having to earn it. But I knew I wasn't good enough—I just didn't know why.

I didn't know what they expected, so I did what I knew. When everyone had eaten, I immediately cleared the table and started putting things away. I filled one side of the sink with warm dishwater and washed the dishes, then rinsed, dried, and put them away. I wiped the table and swept the floor.

Janey and Mark and her parents talked at the dining room table. Anxiety filled my mind. *Are they talking about me? Do they approve?* I focused on the dishes and the soapy scrubber in my hand. *I've got to get every-speck-of-food-off-this-plate.* Then I overheard a curious voice.

"What's this?" I glanced into the dining room and saw Janey's mom looking at Janey, then at me. Her eyebrows were raised, and I quickly looked away. *Scrub harder.*

"She just *does* this," Janey said.

Just does this? Does that mean she approves?

"Without being asked?"

"Yes"

"I'm impressed."

She's impressed. I blinked a tear from my eye. *Don't start crying now. She's impressed! This makes me worthy.* In a split second, I buried my longing to sit and laugh with the family and told myself I was right. *This is where my worth is.* Doing things without being asked—the table, the dishes, the floors. I wasn't part of the family, but they might let me stay if I earn my worth.

"When do the hearings start?"

"Next week." Janey's words were barely audible. "Her mom won't fight for her."

My heart pounded. *Did she talk to Mama?* Pounding turned to aching. Not for the mama who sat in the living room chair in denial. I missed the mama from years ago. Before the darkness.

19

The Hearings

I CONTINUED TO stay with Janey and Mark during the months of
court hearings. Confusion and anxiety kept me in a state of despair.
How many hearings do they have to have? What happens in the end?

Some of the hearings were only for the judge, Jack, and Mama.
Others required Janey and Mark, and the social worker to be there. I
was present only once, but Janey explained the outcome of each time
she went to court. I always appreciated her straightforwardness. At
some point, a social worker went to my house, collected a small bag of
my clothes, and brought it to me. *Did she see Lane and Becky? Are they
looking for me?*

The hearing I attended was long and formal. There was a judge,
a social worker, Jack, Mama, me, and Janey. I sat next to the social
worker, faced the front of the courtroom, and watched Jack stiffly walk
to the stand and swear to tell the truth. His pressed lips and clenched
teeth exposed his fear. There was something satisfying about thinking

he was the only one in the room who was afraid. *You can't run*, I silently declared.

After the social worker spoke, the judge turned to Jack and asked him questions. On the stand, Jack performed in his familiar way. He switched from crying to red-faced yelling, and in point-two seconds, cried again. He was like a caged animal, angry and desperate to get away, but trapped. I was on the other side of the bars—safe.

I listened to Jack deny everything as Mama quietly cried. I watched as he snapped with anger and ranted until the judge stopped him. I prayed I wouldn't have to get on the stand, and I didn't. When Jack attempted to talk to me from the stand, the judge told the social worker to take me out of the courtroom, into a waiting area. I marveled at the shelter around me.

When the hearing was over, Janey emerged, and we left the courthouse.

"What happened after they took me out?"

Janey told me the truth. "Jack continued to deny everything, but the judge didn't believe him."

"What about Mama?"

"She never spoke a word." *That's Mama.*

"Chris, you must take a polygraph test. It's part of the process."

"A what?"

"A lie detector test. Jack has to take one too."

Three days later, Janey drove to an office across town. She waited in the lobby while a man led me into another room and showed me a chair next to a strange device. The man was tall and had a deep voice, but he spoke gently.

"Try to relax. This is a piece of cake." He attached wires to me and explained each step. "This is all procedure. We're going to read your mind." The smile on his face told me he might be joking.

The test was lengthy and nerve-wracking. After dozens of questions, the man removed the wires and began to talk to me. The long moments of his voice bounced off my brain. I didn't know him. I didn't know what he was talking about. But through the confusion and hidden emotions, I heard the words "….so in conclusion, the test shows you are telling the truth."

Of course I'm telling the truth! My anger wanted to knock the machine onto the floor because it was the only thing within reach. Instead, I hid my feelings and nodded my head. When I entered the waiting area, the man asked to speak to Janey in the other room.

After a moment, Janey returned. "You ready?"

I nodded.

"Chris, Jack has refused to take the test." Janey never beat around the bush.

"Hmm?"

"Jack refuses to take the polygraph. I'm not surprised."

I didn't know it was a choice.

"But you did the right thing. And everyone believes you. There is proof for you."

I nodded again. Except Mama doesn't believe me.

Janey was required to take me to counseling at the Western Arkansas Counseling and Guidance Center in Fort Smith. Once a week after school, she drove me to the counseling center, where I met with Dr. Sally Goforth.

"Hi, Chris. You can call me Sally." Her soft voice exuded safety. Sally was a pretty lady with brown shoulder-length hair and a smile that made me relax. She looked at me with acceptance and warmth. Sally listened until I finished talking before she responded. And if I interrupted her because I had more to say, she patiently listened again.

When it comes to talking about the abuse, I remember very little of the discussions. But I remember *a lot* about how Sally made me feel, and how she began speaking truth and kindness toward me. I didn't know at the time, Sally entered a special place in my heart, a place she has stayed to this day.

"Chris, I believe you." I still hear her gentle voice. "This wasn't your fault. You didn't do anything wrong."

I cried into her eyes because I felt safe in them.

"Whatever you are feeling is okay." Her words were gushes of fresh air. Sally gave me permission to be real. I didn't have to impress her. She understood my tears even though I couldn't always put words with them. She saw my pain, and she knew what the emotion meant. She comforted me both with, and without words.

For one hour a week, Sally soothed my hurting heart and calmed the chaos inside of me. I wasn't used to adults being so kind, so interested in me. *She really wants to help me.* She made me feel special—like I mattered.

"Chris, you are lovable. You have value."

I soaked up Sally's words even though it was hard for me. Feeling lovable and valuable was foreign. I was too wounded. Torn between knowing what Jack did was wrong and somehow feeling like I deserved it.

Sally planted seeds of truth inside of me—seeds that took a long time to grow. Her words only made sense as my healing allowed them to, but they were there when I needed them. The trust I felt for her was the beginning of new ponderings.

Am I really worth something? Sally thinks I am.

The voice inside of me said Sally was mistaken. Could that voice be wrong?

THERE WAS A short season of family counseling that included Jack, Mama, and Lane. Those sessions never went well.

"It's standard procedure to see if a family can somehow fix the issues at hand and become a family again." Janey closed her eyes and shook her head. "As if the sexual abuse is the only issue."

Being in the same room with Jack felt intense. He had his therapist, and I had Sally. Jack admitted nothing, and Mama kept quiet with her lost eyes, and an occasional nod or shake of her head as Jack did all the talking—all the exploding—all the defending—all the denying. He made a lot of noise, put on a show, but didn't fool anyone.

I can still see the painful look frozen on Lane's face during the counseling sessions. If confusion and anxiety could kill a person, he would have died right there. He was fourteen years old, in the midst of puberty, and trying to survive home life himself. He had no idea what was going on and sat in mandated family counseling sessions because his stepfather had sexually abused his little sister. How was Lane supposed to act? Was he supposed to say something? He didn't do anything. He didn't know.

My chest ached as the adults in the room talked and I snuck peeks at my brother. He hadn't done anything wrong, and there wasn't anything he could do to fix it, yet he had to be there, just like me. Standard procedure.

Lane and I hadn't spoken since the day Jack made me leave the trailer, the day Janey picked me up at Savemart. I only saw him at the family counseling sessions, but never alone.

Questions swarmed my mind. *Did anyone tell Lane what Jack did to me? Is he mad at me? Have I lost my brother?* Flashbacks of the day Lane carried me home from Creekmore Park provided seconds of comfort. I heard his voice in my mind, the days I rode his motorcycle in the field, "Please don't run it out of gas."

My eyes swelled with pain, but I didn't dare let it show—it was too personal. I simply longed for my brother. *I'm sorry, Bubby. I never meant to hurt you too.*

I STARTED RUNNING in P.E. class at school. Our teacher required four laps around the football field. "That's one mile. Now go," he said to the class.

I couldn't run the entire distance, so running turned into jogging, then into a pace barely faster than walking. But I finished my four laps, exhausted and relieved as I ran to the teacher to be dismissed. The sense of accomplishment felt good, and I always secretly hoped Lane would see me at the football field, finishing my mile. *Maybe he'll think I'm something.*

I discovered something about running. When I began the first lap, my mind focused on getting to the second, then the third, then finishing. After being dismissed, I gulped water from the fountain and savored a feeling I hadn't had enough of—an explosive sense of freedom. I could breathe. I was as light as a feather. I could smile and I wanted to. I didn't know anything about endorphins then. All I knew was running gave me a feeling I desperately wanted to hold onto. I was temporarily convinced that the dirt had fallen off of me and all my problems had disappeared.

This must be what happiness feels like.

Others noticed the effect running had on me. "I see you really enjoy running." Janey's smile said *I approve.*

"I hear you've been running. What a great thing. Keep it up." Sally's words made me want to run for the rest of my life. *I'm doing something right!*

I knew Janey and Sally understood the emotional release I received from running, and I melted in their positive attention. But I never spoke of the identity crisis I still dealt with. *Am I a runner?* I desperately wanted to know who I was, where I belonged, and what I could be good at.

Or was I just an insignificant little girl, full of bruises and covered in shame? Could there really be something to like about me? My wounded mind thought if I made running what I was all about, it would bring further approval and acceptance. It would mean I might become *somebody*, and maybe I'd feel worthy of love. I didn't realize then it was myself who hated me the most.

I had been with Janey and Mark for six months when Mark took up jogging, and one evening invited me to go along. Mark had become my only father figure, incredibly different from Jack. I wanted to tell him I loved him, but thought surely he would laugh. He was kind and gentle but reserved. He rarely initiated an activity with me, so I was elated over his invitation.

"Yes," I told Mark. Of course, I wanted to go jogging with him. *This means he likes me.*

I jogged proudly down the street next to Mark, slowing when slowed, turning when he turned. I wanted him to think I was a great jogger and look at me like a daughter. I imagined Mark would be glad he had invited me and would want me to jog with him from then on. I grew exhausted and began lagging behind. Mark jogged a few feet ahead of me, then a few yards.

Gotta catch up. I wanted to impress him. *Go faster, or he won't invite you again.* I got a little closer to Mark but it didn't last. I was breathing so fast my throat was on fire. My legs were getting tangled, and I worried I might fall any second. The gap between us grew. Mark glanced back but kept jogging.

"Are you okay?"

I assured him I was. He couldn't know I was battling the voice inside of me. *You can't do it. He will never like you.*

I saw the house in the distance. *Yes I can!* My jogging turned to running, and for a minute, I thought I might actually catch up with Mark. My legs became rubber with a mind of their own. *How will I stop? Never mind, keep going.* Despite my effort, the gap grew, and I watched from half a block away as Mark jogged across the yard and up the front steps. By the time I got to the porch, he was inside, changing. I gasped repeatedly as I opened the front door, dragged myself to my bedroom, and fell onto the bed. I stared at the ceiling while my lungs worked hard to slow down. *I failed. He will never like me.*

Tap. Tap. Tap. Janey was at my door. "Chris? Are you okay?"

I cleared my voice and forced an answer. "Yes, I'm okay." I held back the tears as Janey walked away and closed her bedroom door. I hid my hurt because I didn't know how to express it. *I'm a failure. He's not impressed.* My needs were so deeply intertwined among a clutter of emotions, it seemed no one knew they were there, except me.

I'm not good enough to be his daughter. I'm not good enough for anyone.

I didn't run after that night, even though I'm sure Mark asked again.

Writing and photography provided other outlets, and possible identity candidates. I worked on the yearbook staff and in a journalism class at the junior high school. I took pictures at many school events, including football and basketball games. Occasionally I wrote a short article to support my photographs.

It made me feel important to carry a big camera around and be allowed onto the field or the court where only the players could go. It felt good to say *I'm a photographer* or *I'm a journalist* when my yearning for identity was intense, or when I was lonely for approval and acceptance. I just wanted to be somebody.

Only one of my photographs made it into the school yearbook. It was one of those *happened to be standing in the right place at the right time* moments when a tackle took place right in front of me, and I snapped the picture.

I imagined because I lived with Janey, other teachers were aware of my situation and took pity on me. My two favorite teachers, Mrs. Walker and Mrs. Fletcher, took a special interest in me, probably because they knew I adored them, and they knew what happened to me. Mrs. Fletcher had a connection to the local newspaper, and made sure my prized photograph got published, along with the accompanying article.

Mrs. Fletcher crouched next to my desk and began speaking in a low voice. "Chris, I just wanted to tell you that the Van Buren Courier is going to print your story."

Oh, she means my article with the picture. "Okay." It sounded like a nice thing for them to do, although I wasn't sure why they would.

"And they are going to give you a byline." Mrs. Fletcher's eyes were big. She tilted her head as if she was waiting for me to say something.

Was a byline a good thing? *I have to say something.* "Okay. Thank you."

Within a few days, there it was—my photograph with a bold headline above it, and the words "by Chris Payton" underneath the headline. *So, that's a byline.* I figured I didn't get this byline because my article was anything special, but because they were trying to make me *feel* special.

And it did.

20

Comparing Lives

JANEY, MARK, AND their boys went on a family trip they had
planned the year before. Janey apologized that I couldn't go and
explained that when they planned it, they didn't know I would be in
their home, and it was too late to change anything. So, Janey arranged
for me to stay with Mark's parents, James and Helen King, in Fort
Smith for the week.

I had been to the King's home a few times with Janey and
Mark, usually on a Saturday, for dinner and to watch football on
television. James always prayed before we ate, and we always sat at the
kitchen table. I secretly tried to sit next to the bay window because I
had never seen such a beautiful thing. After dinner, we piled into the
den to watch the game. I pretended to be interested in football because
I wanted to be part of the family. I watched their faces as they focused

intently on the television, then jumped from their seats with excitement, or slapped their knees after a bad call by the referee.

The King's home was a spacious two-story with a living room *and* a den. I studied the copper basket of wood next to the fireplace and wondered why anyone needed a living room *and* a den.

James and Helen had been especially gracious at Christmas time. They gave me a pearl necklace with a real gold chain. My mouth dropped open when I saw it. They had already given me two presents, and the thought of how much those gifts must have cost made me want to smile and cry at the same time. The voice in my head told me I wasn't worth that kind of money.

WHEN I ARRIVED at The King's for the week, they seemed happy to see me. Helen led me upstairs to the bedroom where I stayed. I had never been upstairs before, and I was drawn to all the family photos hanging on the wall of the staircase.

Each morning, I awoke to an alarm clock and got ready for school. Helen drove me all the way to Van Buren and picked me up every afternoon. She was relaxed and smiled when she spoke. She didn't ask me questions like, "What did you learn in school today?" or "How was your day?" Somehow, she knew that yes and no questions were more comfortable for me—questions I could answer with a nod or a shake of my head.

"By the way, you can call us Helen and James." I knew she was being nice, but her invitation was bittersweet. Helen and James are what you say when they aren't your grandparents.

Even though I didn't speak much, I loved being with Helen in her kitchen while she cooked supper each night. It reminded me of Grandma Halverson, and how she used to let me scour the cupboards and refrigerator for any ingredients I thought I needed for my *special creation*.

I didn't make special creations in Helen's kitchen, but I did enjoy the attention she gave me. She never stopped smiling and turned to look at me when she was telling me something. She whipped up supper as if it was the most joyful thing she could do. I marveled over how someone could be so happy for no apparent reason. *Someday, I'm gonna have my own kitchen. And I'm gonna smile when I cook.*

What was Grandma doing? Did she know how long I'd been gone? Or Aunt Jeanie and Uncle Jimmy for that matter? After Jack moved into the trailer that Grandma had helped Mama get many months ago, the relationships between Mama and the rest of the family were strained. Uncle Jimmy had let it be known that Jack would not be allowed back on their property, and he had no problem shooting him if he trespassed.

James slipped in and out of the kitchen, just to peek inside the oven or lift the lid from the saucepan on the stove. Helen didn't seem to mind. They were easy to be around. No pressure to impress or win their approval. I felt like I already had it.

"You know," Helen said one night, "my first husband passed away." I nodded my head as if I already knew.

"I found myself alone, with four kids to take care of." Helen prepared supper as she spoke. "I was afraid and didn't know what was going to happen."

I nodded again, this time because I could relate.

"But then I met James. He came alongside me and helped me raise my kids like they were his own." She stopped for a second and smiled. *I didn't know they made stepdads like that.*

I wondered if someone was going to come alongside and help me, not realizing at that moment, that Helen was one of those people. After supper, I went to my room but tiptoed back to the staircase to look at the family photos again. I didn't know anyone who took that many pictures, took the time to put them in frames, and hang them on the wall. I stepped up and down the stairs, studying the contents of each frame. Mark and his siblings throughout the years. Birthday parties, Christmas mornings, boys in football uniforms, and high school graduations. *Family must be a big deal.*

One image gripped my attention. It was a photo of James and Helen, sitting on the hearth of the fireplace with all four of their children on the floor in front of them. I studied their faces. They were happy. They belonged. They were a family. The children wore outfits with coordinating colors. Their faces were clean, and their hair was neatly fixed. Mark's sister had a bow in her hair that matched her dress. All three brothers had neatly buttoned shirts tucked into khaki shorts. Their socks matched, and their shoes were shiny. Someone had paid attention to them. They mattered to James and Helen.

I'm gonna have a family like that someday. With pictures in frames on the wall.

On my last night in the kitchen with Helen, James walked in with a brown Bible in his hand. He and Helen both turned to me with warm smiles and James said, "We want to give you this Bible."

"It's the New International Version," Helen said. "A little easier to read."

I remembered the King James Version of the Bible in the library at Belle Point. I picked it up a few times and tried to read it, but none of it made sense to my elementary mind. The voice in my head told me I was too stupid for God anyway.

"We want you to know that God will never allow you to be in a situation that He won't help you through, if you let Him." Their words were sincere, and I felt special, that they would go out of their way to buy me a Bible and speak kindly to me. They didn't preach, they didn't lecture, they didn't push or prod. I soaked up the compassion in their voices and tried to imagine that God would help me.

Why would God do that? I'm too messed up. My throat throbbed, but I managed to mumble the words "Thank you" without taking my eyes off their faces.

They didn't want anything. They weren't waiting for anything. They just wanted to give me that Bible. Although it would be many years before I picked it up, James and Helen's kindness was not wasted. Simply knowing they cared, when they didn't have to, soothed that void inside of me. Their actions softened part of my heart and instilled kernels of hope.

Decades later, I still have the Bible, and it is one of my most prized possessions.

I lived with the Hills for the rest of my seventh-grade year. Even though I remained safe, life continued to be a struggle. Locked in shame and embarrassment, trapped in self-hatred, I felt somehow I deserved what Jack did to me. The voice inside my head controlled most of me, constantly nagging. *You will never be normal. You're too broken.*

And I was angry.

I didn't know where I belonged, and I felt as though I still had to fight for acceptance and find ways to gain approval. I mourned the loss of my family, too ashamed to tell anyone. I had brought it all upon myself by telling on Jack. At least that is what the voice said.

I struggled to fit into a new family, a new lifestyle that I knew nothing about. Janey and Mark were good people, and both came from stable, and what I called *proper* homes. To me they were rich and compared to my upbringing, their lifestyle was formal.

Janey had *real* china, *real* silver and *real* crystal glasses, and it all matched. She and Mark had conversations about vacations and dreams, and when it would be a good time to buy a new car or put in a pool. They talked about goals and college degrees—things I never knew people talked about. Their parents stayed together and bought homes. They had careers and arranged for someone to take care of the kids while they worked. They had calendars and schedules. They taught their kids things, on purpose. Proper etiquette was a must, using certain words, and avoiding certain others. Going to college after high school wasn't optional but expected.

Janey and Mark's home came with a plethora of rules and expectations that were foreign to me.

"Chris, ladies don't chew gum in church."

"Chris, please say *yes*, instead of *yeah*. *Yeah* is not proper."

"Chris, an untucked t-shirt looks tacky."

"Chris, *he's* and *she's* have names. Please use their names."

"Chris, we ask to be excused from the table before getting up."

"Chris, did you eat that bacon in the refrigerator? I had a purpose for that."

I was often hungry but too afraid to ask for food, so I snuck it from the fridge or pantry. I continued to be lonely but didn't know how to ask for attention. The sadness stayed but I couldn't explain why. I was confused but too intimidated to speak up.

And even though I watched, and tried to learn, I didn't understand, and I kept messing up. Every mess-up further confirmed that voice in my head. *You can't do anything right. You're not good enough.*

I told myself I was lucky to be in Janey and Mark's home because it was a good cover-up of my ruined life. Although I didn't feel equal to anyone else, I thought I could fool people if I looked like part of a good family.

"Just be yourself." Janey's words were heart-wrenching. I wanted nothing more than to be myself, but I didn't know how. Everything felt wrong. I felt invisible.

I TURNED THIRTEEN while living with Janey and Mark, and I'm sure they thought independence was something I wanted, like most girls that age. The truth was, I wanted to feel safe more than anything. I knew I was safe from Jack, but I needed to be near someone most of the time. I wasn't ready for more independence. I wanted to be held, gently talked to, and reassured that I would be okay. But I didn't know how to tell someone.

Mark took the family to Hot Springs for the weekend. We stayed in a hotel with a pool. Janey and Mark were tired from the drive, and it was naptime for their boys.

"Chris, we're going to lay down for a quick nap. You can go to the pool if you want to." It didn't feel like it was optional, so I put on my bathing suit and grabbed a hotel towel. I was the only one at the pool that afternoon, and the water was refreshing. I welcomed the sunshine on my face as I leaped and bounced around. I sat on the pool steps, stretched my legs out in front of me, and paddled them up and down. *Wish I could swim.* Lane was such a good swimmer. I scanned the matching lounge chairs surrounding the pool, wishing Lane was there to swim with me.

When the top of my head felt hot, I pinched my nose and dipped underneath the water, coming up quickly to wipe the liquid from my face. Although I felt brave when I went under water, I was certain I couldn't breathe until my face was dry.

The slide on the side of the pool was curved, with a trickle of water running down the middle. I climbed the ladder and imagined a quick dunk at the end. I held my nose and slid, but quickly found myself in a panic when I couldn't feel the bottom. It hadn't dawned on me the water was deeper at the end of the slide—over my head.

I kicked and flailed as I searched for something to touch. I couldn't tell if I was upside down, right side up, or sideways. My mind spun. My arms and legs moved violently. I felt overpowered. Terrified.

I'm drowning! I swallowed water. No!

My mind flashed to Jack's laughter. "What's the matter, Boney-Maroney?" His grip on my ankles crushed the bones together. My wrists broke underneath his clutch.

No! Does anyone see me?

My head briefly bobbed above the surface of the water, then went back under. *That's the top! I'm right-side up!* I doggy paddled to the side of the pool. My hands followed the edge to the ladder. I dripped to the lounge chair and wrapped myself with my towel as my eyes darted around to see if anyone had shown up and noticed me. No one had.

I clung to my towel long after I dried. I was safe, but I wasn't okay. *Why did I see Jack?* I looked at my wrist as I reached down and touched my ankles. *They're not crushed.*

The hurt was there, but the tears wouldn't come out.

It took years to understand what my panic underneath the water had to do with the Boney-Maroney episodes. In both cases, I had been drowning in fear and powerlessness.

"Chris," Janey called from the hotel room door a few yards away. "We're up."

"Be right there."

The tears finally fell. Pain mixed with anger that someone hadn't kept me safe, both in the past and in the pool. I wondered what Janey would have thought if she had walked down to the pool and discovered I had drowned. I wondered what Mama would think—what she would feel.

Would Lane cry in front of Jack?

21

I'm Not That Brave

GOING TO FAYETTEVILLE with Janey usually meant visiting her parents, shopping at the mall, and eating at a nice restaurant. The restaurant was my favorite part of the trip. On one particular trip, we met Janey's parents at The Old Post Office, a restaurant with tasty food and a nostalgic atmosphere.

"This used to be the actual Fayetteville Post Office." I listened to Janey talk as I studied the brick walls, tall ceilings, wood floors, and brass light fixtures. I had never seen such a fancy old building. All the tables wore a white tablecloth with a candle placed in the middle. *Real candles. This must be a special place. Wish Lane could see me here. Bet Mama would feel special here.*

At the mall, Janey told me I could walk around by myself, and arranged to meet me later. I wandered from store to store, looking at mannequins through the glass fronts. Near the entrance of one store was a rack of makeup bags and purse-sized mirrors, so I went in to look. One second I was listening to the overhead music, trying to decide between a solid-colored bag or a flowery one, and the next second I was in a numbing panic as I felt a strange man rub his hand over my crotch from behind.

Oh God!

I wanted to scream, but my voice froze. Just like with Jack. The man kept walking, and I caught a glimpse of him as he disappeared into the mall. He never looked back.

Oh God, what do I do? Did that really happen?

I exited the store and ran to a nearby bench. I couldn't feel my body, and my mind was in a stupor.

I thought I was safe from all of that.

My chin quivered. My eyes stung. My chest threatened to explode.

I'm supposed to be safe from all of that!

I looked in the direction the man had walked. *He just touched me and then walked away. He didn't even hurry. Does the whole world think they can just touch me like that?*

Emotions filled my throat. My surroundings disappeared. My ears went deaf. *I can't breathe.*

It was as if that stranger knew what had happened to me and knew that just one more touch wouldn't be a big deal. *Am I always gonna be a victim?*

I never told Janey about the man in the mall. The voice in my head told me this was somehow my fault. I allowed it to happen. I didn't scream or run. It had to be my fault.

I'll never be safe. Girls like me don't get to be safe.

DURING THE SUMMER break, Janey wanted to send me to a weeklong Christian camp for teenagers. I had never been to a camp, but it sounded like fun.

"Someone from church paid for it. Such a generous gift. Ninety dollars."

Ninety dollars? I couldn't believe it cost so much, and that a perfect stranger actually paid for it—for me.

Lane went camping one time with the Kiwanis Club. Jack bought him all kinds of camping supplies—a canteen, rain poncho, Swiss army knife, even an aluminum plate, and eating utensils. Lane spread it all out on his bed, along with everything he was going to pack for the trip. I wanted to go too, but it was only for boys. Besides, Jack would not have let me. My heart ached from the memory.

I'm going camping now, Lane. But he wasn't there to see me pack.

Janey bought me two sundresses with spaghetti straps that tied over the shoulders to take to camp. I never wore them because I was too self-conscious to bare my shoulders. Showing too much skin made me worry other people would look at me the way Jack did.

Each day at camp featured something different. Horseback riding, swimming, hiking, crafts. Each evening, we gathered in the chapel. The chapel service was *nothing* like the Presbyterian Church that Janey and Mark took us to.

The room was loud and exciting. The speakers talked about God as if He was this wonderful being who loved and adored us no matter what we had done, what had been done to us, or what kind of family we came from. Everyone wore camp clothes to chapel, and no one knew I was a broken kid with a past.

No one knew I lived with a foster family, and someone from the church paid my way to camp. I pretended to be just like all the other campers. I pretended I was normal, and the chapel became my favorite part of camp.

One of the girls in my cabin was painfully shy and afraid to participate in any activities other than swimming. She and I connected at once, and she confided in me that she was living in a foster home and that someone had donated the money for her to come to this camp. I admired her honesty and wished I could be the same. My shame was still too great to share. Part of me wanted to say, "Me too." But a bigger part of me just wanted to be normal for the week. So I let her believe I was a normal kid from a normal family. I regret that decision. She could have used a friend who understood.

WHILE I WAS at camp, Janey and Mark moved into a big Victorian-style home in Fort Smith. They bought the home right before I went to camp. One day Janey came home and announced to Mark, "I found the house I really want." They looked at it, and within a few days, a realtor sat at their formal dining room table with a stack of paperwork.

The new house had been built in 1906. I called it a four-story home because it had a finished basement and an attic in addition to the two main floors of the house. It was by far the biggest house I ever lived in, and the coolest, even though Janey called it a fixer-upper.

I loved exploring the attic, hoping to find forgotten treasures. A door in the finished basement intrigued me, as it only led to dirt. In the front of the house, a foyer boasted a huge staircase. With its tall ceilings, hardwood floors, chandeliers, and giant windows, the house exuded elegance.

From the upstairs windows, I could see the red brick street below; one of the few remaining brick streets in Fort Smith. Beautifully restored homes lined the street, all built in the early 1900s. The porches, the windows, the manicured yards—all so dreamy.

It took days to unpack and settle into the new house. I was used to moving, but this time it wasn't because we had been kicked out of our home or because they couldn't pay the rent. This new kind of move amazed me.

Many evenings, we sat on the front porch after dinner and watched the young boys ride bikes up and down the street. One evening, a neighbor stopped by. "Hey there, do you know who that is?" The neighbor pointed to a white car sitting a half block away, with a man inside of it. "That guy's been there nearly an hour."

We looked down the street, and it only took a second to know. "That's Jack!" I gasped and looked at Janey. *She'll show me what to do.* Anxiety rose inside of me. *I'm not alone. Janey will protect me.*

Janey remained calm. "We'll need to report this." She smiled as she walked into the house to get the phone. I listened as she made the call to the police, then gently hung up the phone. *She's not afraid.* "They'll check it out." She smiled again.

Within a few minutes, Jack drove away, the police arrived and took a report, and that was the end of it.

I lay in bed that night wondering how many times Jack had spied on us. And I replayed Janey's reaction over and over.

She's not scared of him. I wanna be like that someday.

22

They Sent Me Home

I STARTED EIGHTH grade and Janey took me to the junior high each morning before heading to her office at the middle school. Lane now went to the high school, so I still didn't see him. On an unsuspecting Tuesday morning, Janey dropped me off at school, and by that afternoon I was in the car of a social worker.

She came to take me home—to Jack, Mama, Lane, and Becky. I sat stunned as I listened to her words and watched the approach of familiar streets outside the car window.

"The authorities want to see if things can be worked out." *I thought it was already worked out—it wasn't safe for me to live there.* "But we'll check on you to make sure everything's okay." She glanced at the scribbled directions next to her and mumbled them out loud. "Turn left onto Alma Road, then left onto Dixon, then right, after you pass Savemart."

My mind whirled. My chest tightened. *Is she really taking me back? Why?*

"I'll bring your clothes in a day or so, as soon as I talk to Janey." *Does Janey know?*

The car turned passed Savemart, where Janey and Mark picked me up the night Jack kicked me out. *I didn't even say goodbye. Why didn't they let me say goodbye?* Anger. Fear. Confusion.

No one told me I would be taken back.

Is Jack gonna stop abusing me? Is this how things are done?

It had been nearly a year since I sat on my old bed, in my old bedroom, in our shabby trailer at the back of the trailer park. The same trailer Jack kicked me out of and the place the authorities said I could no longer live because of Jack's abuse.

In counseling, Sally had said, "Jack must admit the abuse before any progress can be made."

It's safe now? Did he admit it?

Life in the trailer again *was* different in the beginning, but not in a comforting way. Jack's behavior toward me grew peculiar, as though I was his favorite child, and he missed me *so much*. His tone and facial expressions were carefully controlled as he doted over me, causing my spine to shudder. He took interest in everything I had to say, and everything I said was wonderful to him. And though he smiled, I saw the coldness in his eyes.

My body and mind reverted to protection mode. The tension kept me on my toes. Numbness kept me from being afraid. Blocking my emotions kept me from hurting. I had to survive what I didn't understand.

For weeks, Jack showered me with attention and gifts. I felt guilty for accepting and afraid to reject whatever he brought home. I knew he wanted something.

"A girl needs a nice camera." Jack held out a new camera, still in the box. "Take it." The voice inside of me chided. *You've been so terrible to him. You aren't worthy.* Flooded with shame, I wanted to run. Mama watched with her familiar awkward smile. Getting rescued and removed from Jack had felt like the right thing. Why was I back? *Is this what's best?*

Jack spoke about fixing up my room. "Pink," he said. "All pink. Pink walls. Pink carpet. Pink comforter. Everything pink." I didn't know who he was. All I knew was that so far, he hadn't called me Chris Ann, and hadn't ordered me to bring him his cigarettes. And I hated pink.

Was I supposed to be happy? Did the abuse cease to matter? Was it over with? I wasn't certain about anything. I didn't understand the meaning of Jack's new behavior, except that it provoked anxiety and fear. Nothing made sense. I didn't know who I was. *Nothing feels right.* I wanted Janey to explain things. I wanted Sally to comfort me. Would I see either of them again? Lane smiled but kept his distance. *Does he know?*

Sally once told me anyone can act right for a while, but it's only a matter of time before a person's true colors start showing. I saw a glimpse of the old Jack one afternoon when we were on our way to pick Mama up from work. I didn't want to go with him, but he wouldn't let me out of his sight. The sun beat down on me through the car window. The air conditioner didn't work. My eyes squinted as I watched the passing buildings, then lowered my window a bit to catch some wind.

"You hot?" Jack's voice startled me.

I looked at him but didn't answer.

"I said are you hot?"

"Yes," I whispered. *Just leave me alone.*

"Heat-wise or otherwise?" He laughed.

My insides stiffened. I ignored him and stared out the window.

"Heat-wise or otherwise?" Jack spoke louder. My stomach churned.

"Well, which is it?" Jack's face grinned as his eyes darted between me and the road. I wanted to puke, but I knew I had to answer him.

"Heat-wise," I whispered through my clenched teeth then turned back to the window. The car stopped at a red light, but I refused to look at him again.

Why am I here?

When the supper dishes were put away, I slipped into my bedroom. I could breathe better on the other side of a closed door. I lay on my bed and opened a book but jumped when the door opened, and Jack stood there. *What could he possibly want? Surely not THAT...Mama's in the living room.* He walked over to my bed and dropped two handfuls of condoms next to my pillow.

"Here, I don't want you to be without these if you need them." Then Jack left the room and pulled the door behind him.

I stared at the condoms, mortified. I didn't want to touch them. *Why would I need these?* My body wouldn't move. Anger. Hate. Fear. Shame. It all came back. The little girl inside of me emerged. *Hide those nasty things!*

I pulled an old purse from the back of my closet, stuffed the condoms inside, and zipped it shut. I hid the purse underneath my clothes in the bottom drawer of my dresser, until I could think of a way to get rid of them without Jack knowing.

A few days later, Mama called me into my room. "Chris, come here." She held my purse in one hand, and some of the condoms in the other.

The look on her face made me think she was both surprised and ashamed. But I couldn't tell if she was ashamed of me or of herself.

"Where did you get these?"

Finally! The truth is coming out. I stood straight, ready to be bold, ready to witness my Mama realizing the truth for herself. Surely this was the final straw. She asked me, so she must want to know.

"Daddy gave them to me." *There! Now she's gonna see his true colors like Sally said.* I watched her eyes and waited. Nothing.

Where was the sudden horror? Where were her senses? Where was her run to my rescue? Hadn't I spoken clearly? I wanted to shake her. "Daddy gave them to me!"

Mama put the condoms back in the purse, put the purse back into my drawer, and closed it. She said nothing.

That's it. No rescue here.

As she walked past me, her familiar weary face and fragile eyes told me she was lost in an impermeable denial. I stood with my mind in an empty space where hope used to be. An inkling of hope that Mama would have the courage to see the truth and would help me and help herself. My heart bled at the thought of Mama never escaping her imprisonment.

She's too far gone.

23

Reading Between the Lines

THE FOLLOWING THURSDAY, a social worker made a surprise visit. Mama and Jack were caught off guard as she entered our trailer and explained she was just there to see how things were going.

Jack kicked it into gear as he reassured her *everything was fine—couldn't be better.* He *just loves this kid,* and all was well in the world. Mama nodded in agreement. The social worker then asked me to sit with her in her car.

It was my chance to have a voice, to tell her I was still afraid, things were not normal, and everything wasn't *just fine.* Mama and Jack were silent as I followed the social worker to her car. For a second, I liked thinking they were afraid.

But as soon as I was in the passenger seat, and the car door was shut, so was my mouth. My bravery left me. *What if I tell her the truth, but she doesn't let me leave with her?* I was sure Jack would somehow know if I said anything to the contrary of the picture he had just painted.

I wanted to tell her about the condoms, and about his comment in the car. I wanted to tell her about all the gifts, the expensive camera, and the plans for a pink bedroom. I wanted to tell her that my gut tells me Jack is up to something, and Mama was too afraid to protect me.

No, things were not normal, and I was anxious and confused. Fear paralyzed again.

The social worker asked me simple questions. "How are things going?" "Do you feel safe?" "Is anything on your mind?" "Is there something you want to tell me?" "Has something happened?"

I wanted to unload, but my voice was gone. *Say something!* I didn't know if I would get another chance. So, since my voice wouldn't work, I did the only thing I could think to do. I showed her with body language and facial expressions that something was very wrong. Janey would have known.

With every question, I pressed my lips together, only allowing them to open for a quick "yep" or "nope." I shifted my eyes to show her I was not comfortable with my own answers. I nodded and shook my head nonstop, just like Mama always did when the voice inside of her was screaming.

I didn't know if my juvenile methods were effective with the social worker, but she kept asking questions and taking notes. After twenty minutes, she said we were done and she hoped I would have a good evening. I held my breath all the way through the front door, past Jack, and into my room, where I collapsed onto my bed and closed my eyes. *You're so stupid. Why didn't you tell her?*

I don't remember eating supper that evening, but I do remember it wasn't long before Jack came into my bedroom, sat on my bed, and talked about the beautiful pink bedroom I was going to have soon.

"You know, a beautiful girl needs a beautiful bedroom."

I'd rather live in a pigpen. I didn't want anything from him. I knew it wouldn't be free, and the cost would be unbearable. Mama, Lane, and Becky sat in the living room. *What could he possibly be up to?*

Jack talked about my *really nice* camera, and how he could take pictures of me in my pretty clothes, on my pretty pink bed, in my pretty pink room. My insides squirmed at his words. My instincts stirred, but what were they saying? Was Jack happy I hadn't told the social worker about his unusual behavior? Then he said something that jolted my focus. In the midst of his wordy ramble, Jack's true intentions slipped out of his mouth.

"….and then, when you put your clothes back on, we can…." Jack stopped, then attempted to correct what he said. "Oh, *not* that you'll be taking off your *clothes…* I mean…" His face drained of expression, and his words became a mixture of panic and gibberish.

My mind stood still with the last audible phrase he had spoken. My eyebrows squished together, and I felt my mouth open. *When I put my clothes back on?*

I looked away from Jack as unexpected clarity formed in my mind. A clarity that penetrated the words in the air and dissolved all confusion. Jack's intentions illuminated as if a higher power shined a light on them, saying, "Hold on, Chris. Let me show you what's happening here." And I saw it. A brand-new game. A new angle. Jack's new behavior began making sense.

The gifts, the expensive camera, the lavish attention, the pink room for a *beautiful* girl—he planned to groom me. And even though I didn't know the term at the time, *grooming* is a common tactic used by perpetrators of sexual abuse. Coercion and manipulation to gain their victim's trust and reduce the risk of getting caught. I couldn't put it into words, but I knew inside it was devious and dangerous. And it would lead toward more sexual abuse.

To my relief, Jack stopped talking and left the room. I sat on the edge of my bed and gazed into the air as the voice inside of me crept in. *You're just an object. You're only good for one thing.*

The carpet was matted from years of traffic. The wood around the window was splintered from water damage. The bedroom door stuck at the top, but it still closed, and even though it locked, I knew I was not safe. Images of a pink room with a pink bed—the sound of a snapping camera shutter—the sight of my clothes on the floor—the condoms… I gasped for air. What would Mama think? Would it matter?

"Get out."

I barely heard the words.

"Get out."

I lifted my head. My eyes shifted. No one was there. Had I really heard something?

"Get out, now."

I recognized the source. It was the same authority that made Jack's intentions clear to me only a few minutes earlier. Not audibly, but in my mind and in my gut. *I'm not safe here.*

I pulled clothes off the hangers in my closet, folded each piece, and made neat stacks in my dresser drawers. I pilfered through the pile on my closet floor and pulled out what still fit, then looked around my room for anything I wished to keep. *Gotta make it easy for the social worker.* Surely having to retrieve only the contents of a dresser, and nothing else, would be quick and easy for whoever was sent for my things.

I didn't eat breakfast the next morning. I got dressed, grabbed my school binder, and pulled the purse full of condoms from my dresser. A wave of fear ran through me as I walked down to the corner and waited for the school bus. But I knew what I had to do, although full of fear. *I just gotta do it afraid.*

I rode the bus to the junior high school like normal, but instead of going inside the building, I darted toward the train tracks. I needed to get to Janey's office at the middle school, and the tracks would take me there.

As soon as I was sure no one could see me, I flung the purse full of condoms as hard as I could into the bushes and kept walking. It didn't cross my mind to keep them for proof. When I saw the middle school, I hopped off the track and cut through the ditch. I ran across the parking lot, through the main door, and straight into Janey's office. I sat in a chair in front of her desk and before I could utter a word, began crying.

Janey was remarkably calm. She stopped what she was doing and looked at me. I halfway expected her to scold me, considering I was obviously skipping school. But her voice remained gentle. "Chris, what's going on?"

I told her everything. The creepy behavior, the gifts, the camera, the plans for a pink bedroom, the condoms. I told her about the social worker coming, how I was too afraid to tell her the truth, and about my behavior in her car.

"He's gonna make me take my clothes off and take pictures of me." Janey listened. "And my mama won't protect me." I told her about getting my clothes ready to be picked up, about walking on the railroad tracks, and about throwing the purse of condoms into the bushes.

She sat quietly and let me finish. Then it was her turn. Janey began by saying none of that surprised her. She had been concerned about me being sent home in the first place. She told me the social worker had already turned in her report.

Her report? But I didn't tell her the truth.

"Chris, the report concluded that you need to be removed permanently."

"What?"

"She saw through Jack's façade. She saw your fear."

"But I didn't say the words…"

"She saw your body language. She knew."

It worked.

"In fact, Social Services was going to pick you up at school today, and you would not have gone back."

I sat motionless, then cried again. The social worker had seen me. She validated what I was too afraid to say. *They're gonna protect me. Permanently.*

"Did you hear me? You're not going back."

I rested against the back of the seat and tried to grasp the gravity of the moment. I wouldn't be with my family anymore. For real, this time.

"Yes, I heard you."

I held my breath as I wondered if my heart would leap for joy or if it would break.

24

With the Stroke of a Pen

THE NEXT FEW weeks were somber. The abrupt second removal from my home was nearly as traumatic as the first. I went back to live with Janey and Mark, but with a new array of emotions. Although safe from Jack, losing the rest of my family for good pained me to the deepest part of my soul. Overwhelming.

"Chris, we've agreed to be your permanent foster home." Janey smiled as she waited for a response, but I didn't have one.

"This means, if the judge agrees, we will have custody of you until you turn eighteen."

Eighteen seemed so far away. Did that mean I would move out when I turned eighteen? What if the judge didn't agree?

"Okay?" What else was I going to do? The thought of going to a different foster home added to my fear.

"Chris, you are the daughter I've always wanted. We want to take you in and treat you like our own."

They want me? Like their own child? I tried to imagine what it would be like, to be a permanent part of Janey's family.

"Okay." It's all I could say. The weight of having just lost Mama, Lane, and Becky pushed the air from my lungs.

Weeks, then months, passed. I watched Janey juggle her career, kids, home, and her continuing education. Childcare arrangements changed along with work schedules and daily routines. For a short period, Janey took her now four-year-old to a daycare in Van Buren, close to both the middle school where she worked, and the junior high I attended. One afternoon, I walked with Janey through the gate at the daycare, and I saw Becky in the play yard. My heart sank when she looked at me. *My Becky.*

A few days later, the daycare teacher questioned Janey about me. Becky had been saying, "That's my sister," as she pointed to me. It hurt my heart to hear it. How confused she must have been. She knew I was her sister but didn't know why I wasn't at home with her anymore. I wondered if she told Mama and Jack about seeing me, and what they might have said. I wanted to hug her and tell her I loved her the next time I saw her at the daycare. But I never went back.

It was a Friday and school had just let out. Janey's blue hatchback pulled into the parking lot and I hopped in. She drove a couple of blocks away from the school, then pulled into a parking lot, put the car into park, and turned to me with a solemn face.

"Chris, I have something to tell you."

Her tone was clear. Her eyes were full of thought. I knew it had to be important if she had to stop the car to tell me. *She's never done that before.* I braced myself.

"The hearings are over."

I had forgotten about the hearings. I only went to one, and that seemed so long ago.

"Chris, today your mom signed the paperwork, giving custody of you to the state of Arkansas."

I was confused. What did that mean?

"I'm so sorry." Janey's eyes turned sad. She tilted her head forward as she looked at me.

Giving custody of me to the state of Arkansas. I didn't understand. Hadn't the state of Arkansas already taken me from Mama and Jack?

Janey continued to explain. "The court determined, due to the sexual abuse and Jack's most recent behavior, it was too risky for you to live in the same home as him. The judge offered your mom one last chance to keep you."

I tried to process what she was saying. Was I going back?

"Chris, the judge told your mom that she had to remove herself from Jack or give you up."

Janey's words swirled. Remove herself from Jack. Like, leave him? On purpose? Mama would never do that.

Janey saw my confusion. "Chris, she either had to get rid of Jack or give you up."

"Okay." I didn't get it. Why did she have to give me up? The state already took me away.

"She signed the papers, Chris. She had one more chance, and she gave you up. It's now official. You'll never go back. You'll live with us."

Janey waited for me to respond. My head told me I was supposed to get emotional, but I didn't. Mama had lost her backbone a long time ago. Even my young mind knew she was too wounded, too blind. I knew when she put the condoms back in my dresser drawer and walked out of my room that she needed more help than I did.

I didn't know what *Battered Woman Syndrome* was at that time, but that fits my mama. She somehow believed she deserved Jack's abuse or caused it, and that she couldn't live without him. To think of him as an abuser was much too difficult for her. He had to be her loving husband.

"Okay," I said again, still absorbing what Mama had done. Part of me was relieved because I knew how far she'd drifted away, and that she couldn't—wouldn't—give Jack up. *It's the best thing she could have done for me. It's all she could do.* And part of me sank in disbelief that she picked up a pen and gave me away. Like a car. *Am I worth more than a car?* It was one thing for the state to take me from her. But they gave her another chance and she signed her name instead.

I didn't stop loving Mama for choosing him over me that day. I stopped loving myself.

I struggled to find a new starting point in Janey and Mark's home—a starting point for the rest of my life. I craved belonging, to feel like I was part of their family—the daughter they never had, like Janey said.

"Just be yourself," Janey said, as if it was as easy as flipping a switch.

I don't know who myself is. I felt too stupid to say it out loud. The layers of emotional wounds were deep. I fought anxiety and depression. I wanted to relax and *just be myself*, but I didn't know how.

I wanted desperately for an identity more than ever now. I wasn't the girl I used to be, but I didn't know who I was, or who I was supposed to become. The life I had was now permanently gone. *How do I be myself? Who am I?* I wanted someone to tell me.

AFTER THE CHRISTMAS break, Janey enrolled me in Darby Junior High in Fort Smith. It was the school district in which we lived, and now that my place in their home was officially permanent, Janey thought it best that I transferred. Mark took me to school on his way to work.

Adding another change to my emotionally overwrought mind became daunting. I longed for stability. A new school meant trying to make new friends. I already had friends in Van Buren. I was tired of losing people.

On my first day at Darby, I saw Laura Crouch laughing and chatting with a group of girls. My heart dropped at the sight of my dear old friend from Belle Point Elementary. I wanted to run to her, but my feet refused. It had been over three years since I last saw Laura. Three years of horror that I didn't know how to explain, and I'm not sure she would have understood.

It made sense that Laura was there as her parents were not in the habit of splitting up two or three times a year and moving around. While I was busy surviving, Laura's life moved forward. She had new friends. Normal friends. I didn't want to be a foster kid, an abused kid. I wanted to be normal, like Laura.

There's not room for me in Laura's life anymore. I'm too damaged. She wouldn't want me. So I didn't even try.

I sat in journalism class one day, waiting for the last few minutes of class to pass so the bell would ring. From behind, a soft voice caught my attention.

"Are you Chris?" *Do I know that voice?* The voice seemed familiar, but when I turned around, I wasn't sure whose it was.

"What?" The desk behind me was empty, but a girl my age sat one row over, and two desks back.

"Are you Chris?" *That voice.* My heart knew her, but my eyes didn't.

"Yes"

"It's Michelle, from Belle Point."

It only took a second for me to recognize her kind face and soft brown hair. *My friend!* Even after roughly five years, her voice remained gentle, as I remembered, her smile also as tender, but her eyes—they were different. Darker than I remembered and heavy. The last time I saw Michelle was in front of her tiny white house when we were nine. An image of her mother standing with her arms folded, refusing to let me come inside, flashed in my thoughts.

"Michelle." I spoke softly as if to also say *I've missed you so much.*

"It's me." She looked at me as though she had a story to tell. I sensed the anticipation. I must have asked something like *how have you been?* Because for the next several minutes my heart sank as Michelle summarized the last five years.

She lived in a girls' home only a few blocks from school. Her dad had sexually abused her and her younger siblings for years until they all decided to run away in the middle of the night. Her little brother, Lonnie, grew scared and went back home. But Michelle and her sisters kept running and ended up in foster care.

My eyes welled, and I sat frozen as I listened. The fact that we had both been sexually abused and were both in foster care seemed inconceivable. I had clung to our connection in elementary school even though I didn't understand it, until now.

I wanted to throw my arms around my friend and hold her. I wanted to comfort what I knew she had been through. I wanted to tell her I'm sorry, and that I understood. Part of me didn't want to tell her the truth about myself. As far as she knew, I had led a normal nurtured life and had been the lucky one. But she was my friend. She was safe now. She had been honest, and I knew I needed to do the same.

"Michelle."

She looked at me.

"Me too."

Her lips bent downward, and her eyes brimmed. She listened with intention and nodded when she felt my pain. We talked until the bell rang.

We walked out of the classroom with an unspoken understanding that we might not see each other again. There were no goodbyes in foster care. As we parted, we looked at each other with aching hearts but no words and returned to our personal struggle.

Michelle didn't return to school. I assume her time was up at the girl's home. I've often wondered what happened, where she went, and if she was okay.

25

What Happened?

JANEY AND MARK offered me opportunities I didn't have before, but I didn't understand how to live in their world. I felt guilty because I wasn't like them, and I didn't know how to change. All the etiquette rules felt stifling. I wanted to wear jeans and t-shirts instead of slacks and blazers. I wanted to feel heard instead of worrying about using the correct words. I wanted to know what they wanted from me, so I wasn't constantly guessing.

My mind seemed to slip further each day, into a deep dark hole. I couldn't find the words to talk to Janey about my feelings; I didn't understand them myself. I tried to keep a journal, but I didn't know what to write. At the top of each page, I wrote *sad, lonely,* or *depressed*—whatever my mood was that day. But I didn't know how to recognize the root of my feelings, much less to write about them.

I thought about my family constantly. What were Mama, Lane, and Becky doing? Were Pam and Theresa doing something fun? Did they think about me? Would I ever see them again?

I secretly hoped Janey would read my journal and rescue me from my depression. I missed how she talked to me when I first went to live with them. I wanted her to comfort me. Their home was a safe place, but I felt like my healing was going the opposite direction and it frightened me. I began sinking more.

When Janey and Mark weren't home, I wandered around the house, studying the details of every room. It was my way of learning about this new world I lived in, these new people, this new lifestyle. The tall ceilings and thick molding around the top of the walls were unlike any place I had ever lived. I memorized a path to walk on the wood floors to avoid the boards that creaked when you stepped on them. I counted the big windows. I ran my hands over the carved design around the fireplace. I walked up and down the stairs, counting them as I brushed my fingers along the passing spindles.

I wandered into Janey and Mark's room and admired the shiny brass bed. *Their stuff is so pretty.* On the dresser was a box of trinkets, and I touched each piece carefully as I took in the details. *Why do people get such pretty things and just leave them in a box to get dusty? Someday, I'm gonna have pretty things.*

Janey had been stressed for several days, maybe even weeks, when one evening she called for me to come downstairs to the living room.

"We need to have a talk." Sternness edged Janey's tone.

I must be in trouble again. I felt my body going numb.

"Okay, do you want to tell me about the sewing machine?" Janey didn't waste any time. *The sewing machine?*

It took me a second to realize she was talking about the sewing machine she let me use last year when I stayed with them the first time. I hadn't thought about the sewing machine in months.

"Your Mom's sewing machine? What about it?" I said confused.

"I was wondering why you stopped using it, and now I know. It's broken." She and Mark just looked at me.

It's broken? "I didn't know it was broken."

"I don't believe you. You broke it, and you hid it from me."

Did she really think that? "No, I didn't know it was broken." I really didn't, but Janey wasn't buying it.

"And what about my ring?"

"What ring?" I grew more confused by the minute.

"My *ring*! You know, the antique ring with all the stones in it. Where is it?" Her face turned to anger.

I knew which ring she was talking about. Janey had shown it to me a long time ago, explaining how old and special it was. The different colored stones made it unique, and I could tell she was proud of it. Occasionally, Janey wore it to work, and when we got home in the afternoon, she took it off and lay it on the kitchen counter while she cooked. I *wouldn't* have taken it.

"I don't have your ring." I waffled between hurt and confusion. I spoke the truth, but Janey's agitation grew. She told me I was *sneaky* and a *thief*. I felt stabbed. I wanted nice Janey back.

I supposed for a moment she was talking about how I sometimes wandered around the house, looking at things. And a few months ago, I did steal some old photographs and books from a storage room at school because holding them in my hand somehow made me feel important. But she didn't believe me about the sewing machine, and she wasn't letting go of the ring.

"So, what did you do with it? Did you throw it in a ditch somewhere? Did you get rid of it?"

"I promise, I didn't take your ring." What else could I say? The rest of the conversation was a blur, but Janey's anger rang clear, and so did her belief that I had broken her mothers' sewing machine and stolen her ring.

Once dismissed, I carried my spinning head upstairs and went to bed.

THE MOMENT MY alarm sounded the next morning, the conversation from the night before stirred my memory. *Oh yeah, Janey's mad at me.* I heard Janey and Mark getting ready for work and hurrying the younger boys. Last night's tension still lingered in the air. Janey's tone remained sharp, and her footsteps were heavy on the wood floor.

I don't know which happened first—my door abruptly flinging open with a sharp, "Get Up!"—or hearing Janey call me a *Bitch*. Both scared me and left me speechless. I jumped out of bed and got dressed for school. I was glad Mark took me to school.

Mark and I didn't speak as he drove, and I don't remember walking across the grass or going inside the building that morning. I do remember sitting in my second-period class and hearing my name called over the loudspeaker. When I arrived at the office, the secretary told me to go to my locker for my things because a social worker was on her way to pick me up. She leaned over and whispered, "She's taking you to a new foster home."

Another one? Am I changing schools again?

Within a few minutes, I sat with my belongings on my lap. My journalism teacher walked in and did a double-take when he saw me. With a smile, he asked if everything was okay, and I told him "I'm moving." I just didn't know to where.

He shook his head. "And you were one of the good ones." I knew he was talking about journalism class, but that statement has always rung in my memory. At that time, I didn't feel like I was good. I didn't understand why no matter how good I tried to be, life continued to punish me.

Why is this happening? Hope was slipping. I didn't understand what I had done that was so bad that no one would believe in me. The voice in my head reared its ugly head. *You're worse than you thought. Nobody wants you. You'll never have a home.*

The social worker came into the office and signed me out.

"Chris?" she said and extended her hand. She was tall and thin, with short brown hair and a light complexion. "You ready?"

I nodded, gathered my things, and followed her out. *Ready for what?* I didn't know. I watched the ground as we walked to her car. That familiar fear of the unknown swarmed my mind. I had no idea where she was taking me—or why.

Once we were in the car, the social worker told me her name was Joyce. "I was asked to take you to another foster home. You'll be attending school in Alma for now. I'll see that you get your things."

I said nothing.

Joyce made small talk for most of our twenty-five-minute drive. Her voice eventually faded from my ears, and I turned to stare through the window. *This is really happening.* Tears dropped down my cheeks as Janey's words from many months ago echoed in my thoughts. *You're like the daughter I never had…like our own…we will have custody of you until you are eighteen…we love you…*

I wiped my cheeks with my sleeve and glanced toward Joyce to make sure she hadn't seen me cry. *Don't need her asking me what's wrong.* I had gone to bed the night before at Janey and Mark's. It was the second time I had a home, a family, a room, a school, a city, a sort-of identity. And even though depression challenged my hope and healing, I clung to Janey's words and thought somehow it would all work out. But the shock of this day felt like betrayal, and the hope that dangled in my mind had been severed.

Guess I wasn't good enough after all.

We pulled into the driveway of an old brown house. I sat up straight and swallowed my emotions. It hit me that I didn't have clothes with me. And I didn't know how long I would be staying in the strange brown house in front of me.

I was introduced to the foster parents, Bill and Deborah, but all I could think was, *I don't know this place. I don't know these people.* There were three other kids, but I don't know if they were also foster kids, or biological kids. I didn't ask questions. I didn't make comments. I didn't hear what was said. I stared at the floor and waited to be told what to do.

The foster home was loud and chaotic. Deborah seemed overstressed, with a tense face and disheveled hair. She walked quickly from task to task and spoke little. I had nothing to say anyway.

While staying in the old brown house, Bill and Deborah took us to visit another foster home in Alma. Friends of theirs who lived in a small house in need of outside paint, much like the house Mama rented on 14th Street years before. The foster mom at the small house, Ruth, had several foster kids and bore the same stressed face and hyper movements as Deborah. But Ruth spoke loudly. She had no problem yelling her instructions to the many kids she herded. *Wonder why she wants all them kids. She doesn't seem to like them.*

On the way home, Bill and Deborah took all of us to Wendy's for hamburgers. I wasn't used to eating out much, and I was glad to go. While most restaurants served portions too large for me to eat, the burger and fries in front of me could have fed two children, but I began eating. And as programmed, I was going to eat everything until it was gone.

I was in my zone despite the noise around me. Take a bite, chew and swallow. Take a bite, chew and swallow. The zone wasn't about how the food tasted or even enjoying it. I had to do what was expected—clean up my plate. I didn't know any different. As I ate, I had no feeling, no emotions—only a program to follow.

"Chris, if you want to take that with you, you can." Deborah was ready to go. Her head tilted and her eyebrows raised as if to say *we've been waiting.* I looked around the table and realized I was the only one still eating. No one there knew of the relentless criticism Jack used to heap on me for being a slow eater. I looked at Deborah, but I heard Jack's voice. *You are the slowest eater ever. We're gonna be here all night.* I heard his bellowing laugh as he announced to everyone in the room that no one ate slower than me.

Deborah waited for a response, but I couldn't speak. My gut hardened, my teeth clenched, my eyes became glassy, and my heart became defensive. In my mind, I was sitting in front of Jack. The need to fight surged through me. *I'm not gonna hurry. They can wait.* I had little control over anything else in my life, I resolved I *was not* going to feel bad about how slowly I ate. Not that night. Not ever again.

"Would you like to take the rest with you?" I sensed Deborah's impatience. But I had to win the battle in my mind.

I fixed my eyes on Deborah, chewed the food in my mouth, swallowed, took a sip of coke, then gently smiled. "No, I'm okay." Then took another bite. I was not going to put it in a sack and take it with me. I would finish it here and throw the trash away when I was done.

As I chewed, I imagined one of those puppets with strings. Each part of the puppet had a string attached to a wooden X held by the puppet master. If the master pulled the arm strings, the arms moved. If he pulled the leg strings, the legs moved. The puppet only moved if the master made it. *I'm not a puppet. Not anymore.*

I knew my internal battle was not the doing of the foster mom. People get tired, they get impatient. Deborah had done nothing wrong. My behavior was much more than stubbornness. I needed to control this *one thing*. I needed for this *one thing* about me to be okay, even if I was the only one who thought so. I needed to believe if I fought for this *one thing*, there stood a chance I was not a puppet.

It was also a fight against Jack. I refused to give in or deny who I was because someone made fun of me. I was *not* going to feel bad. I was *not* going to be like Mama. I knew I wouldn't survive if I became like her.

Three days after eating at Wendy's, the social worker showed up to move me to another foster home. No one explained why I was being moved or how long I'd be at the next place. They showed up, told me to gather my things if I had any, and drove me away. That's how it worked.

I was dropped off at a foster home in a rural area. The foster parents were an older-looking couple who had two biological kids, a son, and a daughter. They never told me their names but showed me to the room I would share with their daughter.

Their daughter was close to my age and very chatty, which was okay with me because I had nothing to say, again. She talked about horses, how much she loved them, and how she hoped to have a horse farm one day. She was excited for me to be there because she had never had a sister before. *I'm not your sister!* I didn't even know how long I would be there.

Underneath my shell, I did feel thankful for the kindness around me. While the foster parents didn't say much to me, I watched their behavior. They reminded me of Melissa and Steve in the cinder block duplex across the street from our house on Dodson. They spoke softly, respectfully. They looked at each other and listened. The foster dad didn't criticize, and the foster mom wasn't timid. *Yep, I'm gonna have me somebody like that someday.* But I wasn't sure if I believed it.

I slept in my clothes, and the very next day, the social worker was back to move me again. As she drove, she explained she was taking me to Hope Youth Shelter. I nodded and looked out the window. It was a twenty-minute drive, long enough for my nerves to build and my heart to panic. *What's a youth shelter?*

26

Hope Youth Shelter

IT HAD BEEN over two years of foster homes so far. Uncertainty, fear, loneliness, loss, confusion—all familiar. Somewhere along the way, a deep anger set in. Anger because I wasn't normal, my life wasn't normal. Anger because Jack got to stay in my home, and I had to leave. Anger because Jack got to keep Mama, Lane, and Becky. Anger because Jack told me my daddy didn't want me, just like *he* didn't want me. *He stole everything from me.*

I longed to have a real home. A place no one could take from me, where I was safe and could breathe. A home with a family, *my* family. I wondered if Aunt Jeanie or Grandma knew where I was. Did they know I was now going to a youth shelter?

The social worker pulled into the driveway of Hope Youth Shelter, comprised of two old houses that sat close to each other. The larger of the two was for the girls and the smaller one for the boys. Each house had a pair of "House Parents," a married couple who also lived there. The front yard was mostly dirt, due to years of using it as a parking lot.

"You ready?" the social worker asked.

Would I ever be? "Yes." I opened my car door and followed her to the small, covered porch. The screen door was flimsy and made a screeching noise when she opened it. I followed her inside.

"Wait here while I go find Sandy. She's one of your house parents." I stood just inside the door of the dimly lit living room. The carpet was gold shag, and the walls were lined with mismatched sofas and chairs. In the dining room to my left, there was an old pool table covered with stacks of clothes and a pinball machine in the corner. The ceiling fan spun around in a wobbly fashion as the tarnished chain clanked against the exposed light bulb.

"Chris?" A tall thin lady with a brown ponytail introduced herself. "I'm Sandy. How are you?"

How did she *think* I was? "Good," I lied. *I want a real home. Why is she so cheerful?*

"Let me show you around." The social worker left, and I followed Sandy.

"Here's where we eat." Sandy pointed to a large, carpeted kitchen that smelled like stale food. "And here's where we store donated food and supplies."

I stared at the open shelves holding hundreds of canned goods, twenty-pound bags of beans, five-gallon buckets of rice, and gallons of mayonnaise, mustard, pickles, and ketchup.

Real families don't buy groceries like this. But I pretended they did. I imagined it was Mama's kitchen, stocked full of good food. How wonderful Mama would have felt, knowing there was plenty to eat.

My mind drifted to a day when Mama said, "You know what I dream about?" I was only about seven years old and hadn't thought much about dreams. "I dream about walking into a grocery store and being able to buy whatever I want."

"Like candy and soda?"

"No, like all the things that look delicious, but are too expensive to buy." Mama closed her eyes as if she was imagining what that would be like. *Someday, I'm gonna take Mama to the store and buy her everything she wants.*

"Let me show you your bedroom." Sandy hadn't noticed my despondence or ignored it. Each bedroom contained three twin beds, with a laundry basket at the foot, for the personal belongings of the girl who slept there.

Sandy's words faded as I thought about Mama filling up a grocery cart.

"Chris?" Sandy paused.

"Hm?"

"This is your new home." *My new home?* Her words pulled me back to the moment. Back to my panicking heart and growing anxiety. *No, it's not!* I couldn't look anymore so I stared at the floor. *This isn't a home. There's no Mama here.*

"You'll adjust, you'll see. Now put your things away. Supper will be soon." Sandy left, and I stood in numbness. *Wonder what Mama's doing?* Did she know they picked me up from Darby and told me I wasn't going back to Janey and Mark's? Did she have any idea I was in my fourth foster home? Did she know the authorities were having trouble finding a place that could keep me for more than a few days? Surely, she would scold them if she did. She would tell them to get their act together and find this girl a proper home! *Surely....*

I sat on my new bed and waited for someone to tell me what was next for me in this world. I caught a glimpse of myself in the mirror on the wall. I didn't recognize the dark brown eyes and splotchy forehead. Dirty hair was matted against the top of my head. I didn't know that girl, and I sure didn't like her. But I stared.

Nobody wants you.

I learned the routine. We ate in rotating groups because the table only seated six people at a time. The house parents didn't eat with us. There was a chore chart on the wall explaining our daily responsibilities.

Each morning, we stood in a group next to the highway and waited for the school bus. When the bus door opened, we filed in, taking up several seats. I held my breath and stared straight ahead, pretending I was invisible to the dozens of stares, until the door closed, and the bus began moving again. I watched out the window, so I didn't have to look at anyone. At the end of the school day, I exited the bus as quickly as I could without making eye contact. I hurried across the yard and through the front door so I could disappear again.

The longer I lived at the youth shelter, the more I learned about why each girl was there. Once all the formalities of arriving at the shelter were over with, the girls swarmed around the new girl and asked, "What are you in for?" as if we had committed crimes and were getting locked up.

One girl was twelve years old and pregnant. She stayed in her room as much as the house parents let her. She didn't talk to anyone and grew paranoid if someone was friendly toward her. Another girl had repeatedly run away from home, and her parents didn't know what to do with her. She bragged that no one could control her, and she eventually ran away from the youth shelter. Another girl had been sexually abused by a relative. When the abuse was discovered, it caused a huge upheaval in her family, and she had nowhere to go. *Imagine that. She got abused and she had to leave, not the abuser.*

The girl who stood out the most to me was Lisa. She arrived two days after me, and we had an instant connection deeper than words. Lisa starved for love and attention, a desperation I knew well. But, while I wore baggy clothes to hide my body, Lisa preferred hers to be tight—very tight. She did anything for anyone in her silent cries for fulfillment. Rumors of Lisa and boys on the school bus or behind the gymnasium quickly emerged. My heart broke when I heard one boy told her she was worthless. A couple of weeks later, the house parents took us all to the health department for a routine checkup, and Lisa found out she was two months pregnant.

The routine checkups were awful. Not that anything was intrusive or out of the ordinary, but it was the fact that we were loaded into a van, driven to the free clinic, and paraded into the lobby like a small herd of cattle, all waiting to be checked out to see how healthy we were. We were the *government kids*.

My only outlet at the youth shelter was the donated pinball machine in the dining room. After school each day, we inspected the folded clothes on the pool table to see if any of them belonged to us. Once we put our clothes away, we had one hour of free time. I was able to escape my thoughts for one hour thanks to someone's generous donation.

After a month at Hope Youth Shelter, depression had me firmly trapped in a far corner of a very dark place. I could no longer smile. My head hung everywhere I went. I rarely spoke. I had broken into pieces and gone back into a dark hopeless world. I struggled fiercely with a powerful, yet unmet inherent need to feel connected to someone.

I couldn't pinpoint the moment I lost Mama. I wasn't sure if it was the day she met Jack, the day she failed to protect me, or the day she gave me away. All I knew was over time she slowly drifted away until one day I realized she would never come back.

She didn't know how.

27

A Bowl of Soup

LUNCHTIME AT SCHOOL. I wandered the playground as others hurried past me to get to the cafeteria. The government kids ate free, but I wasn't hungry. The school had an open campus, and many students lived close enough to walk home for lunch. Cars pulled up and kids jumped in to be taken for a quick bite to eat with their parents. I leaned against the brick building and pulled my jacket closed so I could hide from the cold wind and from my life.

Two girls about my age walked past me. They chatted and giggled with excitement, and I watched with envy. *Probably best friends.* I halfway listened, and I heard something that got my attention.

"Come on, my mom made soup today." *Soup?* I looked up, but she wasn't talking to me. They hadn't even noticed me. The girls walked away from the school toward a nearby neighborhood.

Soup? My heart dropped. *Her mom made soup.* My mind raced back to the day I threw up in first grade, and the school sent me home.

Mama made me soup. My body shivered with fever that day, but my emotions danced from the warmth of Mama's attention. Mama did things just for me that day—made me soup, took my temperature, and gave me medicine. It felt so long ago.

The two girls crossed the street.

Depression turned into desperation. More than anything in the world, what I needed at that moment was a bowl of soup made by a mama, even if it wasn't *my* mama. In an instant, I became brave, and blind to rationality. I pulled myself from the wall and followed the two girls. *I'm gonna have soup made by a mama.* My heart needed it to survive.

When the girls realized they were being followed, their open chatter turned into a quiet whisper, with several quick glances behind them. At any moment, I expected one of them to turn around and ask me where I thought I was going, but neither did. Their quick looks and darting eyes told me they were confused, but I wasn't fazed. *They can't stop me. I don't care what they think.*

I didn't care that I didn't know them. I didn't care that I wasn't invited. I wasn't thinking about rejection or shame. None of that compared to the hole in my soul and the darkness surrounding it. A mama made soup and I was going to have some. My heart might stop without it.

I walked several feet behind the girls. They must have turned to look at me fifty times. They finally arrived, and I shamelessly followed as they walked around to the side door of the house. They looked at me one more time before going inside, perhaps thinking I wouldn't dare walk into their house.

But I did. The smell of soup led me to the kitchen. The mom faced the stove and slowly stirred a big pot that released the most wonderful aroma.

"It's almost ready girls, just have a seat. Bowls are on the table."

Then the mom turned around. We all stood speechless, taking turns looking at one another. The mom looked at me, then toward the two girls. The two girls looked at the mom, then at me, then back at the mom. Their eyebrows were raised, and their chins were pulled back into their scrunched shoulders as if to say, "I have no idea."

My feet were glued to the floor, as my eyes fixated on the soup. For a brief second, I was afraid I might be asked to explain myself. I was tempted to feel ashamed, but my desperation wouldn't let me. I felt the mom's eyes on me. *Oh God, what do I do?*

Then, as if someone heard the cry of my heart, and choreographed the next few moments, without a word, the mom opened the cupboard and pulled out another bowl. She took a spoon from a drawer, walked over to the table, and placed it in front of an empty chair, then smiled.

"Now let's eat," she said with a quick nod.

I sat as the mom carried the pot to the table and filled the bowls with soup. No one had much to say. What *could* they say? It was a quiet twenty minutes as I filled my belly with love. I don't remember who finished first, who got up first, or even the walk back to school. I only remember on that cold desperate day, someone else's mama was *my* mama for twenty minutes. She kept my world from crashing in. The bowl of soup was nothing, but that stranger's simple act of kindness changed my life.

28

Survival

PEOPLE DON'T ALWAYS understand when someone is laden with depression, even the simplest task becomes an impossible mountain to move, leaving the depressed person feeling desperately hopeless.

I'd moved six times in the last nine months, each move abrupt and frightening. Emotional exhaustion consumed me. A mental hollowness. The world around me was too painful. I blocked out as much as I could, hoping my mind would go numb. I stopped allowing myself the desire to be normal. I gave up on normal. Life felt unmanageable. I strived to stay in my safety zone, where I didn't have to think or feel. I developed an aversion to new or unfamiliar things. I just had to survive.

Something about the first bell at the beginning of the school day threatened to steal my safety and send me into a panic. The bell meant I had to go to class—around people. *They might look at me. Or talk to me.* Teachers expected me to answer questions and think about things. I just couldn't. It was too much. Everything was just too much. I decided to be sick so I didn't have to face anyone.

Instead of going to class, I went to the nurse's office. I had a *bad stomachache.* Surely she would call the youth shelter and tell them to pick me up. I walked down a small hallway, just past the school's main office. The nurse's door hung open, but the light wasn't on. *Guess she's not here yet.* I sat in a chair right outside her door and waited. The bell rang, the hallways grew quiet, and the first period began. And I waited.

Where is she? I rehearsed my story in my head in case one of my teachers saw me. *I have a terrible stomachache. I've been waiting for the nurse. Can barely walk.* After fifty minutes, the bell rang again, and students spilled into the hallways. Locker doors rattled open and slammed shut, voices chattered, then the clamor slowly died down, and the bell rang once more.

Second period. They're gonna be looking for me.

I was confused and a bit surprised that no one walked into the hallway and noticed me sitting there. Still I waited. The quietness made me sleepy. I convinced myself to lie on the cot inside the nurse's office. I reworded my story and went over it a couple of times before closing my eyes.

Oh hi, I'd say when the nurse arrived. *I had a terrible stomachache, and I came to see you. It got so bad, I needed to lie down and must have fallen asleep.* Sounded reasonable. *That should get me an excused absence.* But the nurse never came. I lay on the cot all day, dozing in and out of sleep, looking up each time I awoke to see if anyone was there. By now I assumed the nurse had the day off.

The final bell of the day rang. I got up and walked out onto the playground, toward the bus that would take me back to the shelter. I stared out the window for the entire ride, coming up with an extension to my story. I could already hear the conversation between me and the house parents. Surely the school called them to report my absence. I was prepared to say it, just like I had rehearsed.

To my surprise, no one questioned me. I walked in and went straight to the pool table for my laundry. I didn't have much clothing, so I never had much to put away. I put my jacket and school binder in the laundry basket underneath my bed, and hurried back to the dining room, to lose myself for one hour, playing pinball.

Chore time, then dinner time rolled around, and still, no one asked me about skipping classes that day. I went to bed not knowing what to think. *Did I get away with it? Would the school call tomorrow?*

The next morning, I opened my eyes to the sound of the alarm, and it hit me. *Oh. Classes.* I let my mind go numb and went through the morning motions, only allowing the necessary thoughts. *Get dressed. Eat cereal. Wash bowl. Grab jacket. Walk to bus stop. Get on bus. Sit. Get off bus.*

When the first bell rang, panic set in again. The thought of going to class terrified me again. *The nurse's office.* It worked the day before, surely it would work again. *Same story—terrible stomachache. Yes!* So off to the nurse's office I went. Again, the door was open, but the light was off. *She'll be here today. I'm ready with my story.*

The next bell rang, the hallways became quiet, and I waited. *Any minute.* The bell rang again, and the hallways filled. *I can't believe she's not here again.* But I had my story engrained in stone by now. I would get yesterday *and* today excused.

The nurse never came. I eventually walked to the cot again and went to sleep. Every time a bell rang, I woke up and looked at the clock. Third period. Fourth period. Fifth. When the last bell of the day rang, I got up, gathered my things, and went to the bus stop.

I went to the nurse's office every day that week and slept on the cot without one person questioning me. I don't know if the nurse had a second office that I was unaware of, or maybe she was off that week. I could only speculate.

For one full week of school, I avoided the painful task of going to class, and the people therein, without being detected. All I can fathom is either I somehow slipped through the school's cracks or God understood and rescued me again.

It was Friday. I had just started my hour of escape into the pinball machine, still reeling with relief I had gotten away with skipping a whole week of school. Sandy walked into the dining room with an armful of laundry.

"Ah, there you are. The social worker needs to speak to you. She's out on the porch."

I'm busted. I met the social worker on the front porch, the same lady who took me to the previous two foster homes and brought me to the youth shelter. I had my story ready. And she didn't waste time telling me why she was there.

"Chris, the maximum time you can stay at the youth shelter is six weeks, and your six weeks are up."

I heard what she said, but my mind hesitated. *Was I in trouble for skipping classes? Wait, my time is up? Is she taking me?*

"Are you taking me again?"

"Not yet. We don't have a place for you." Her words cut. I lost my real home, and now I was out of foster homes. My stomach heaved and my body grew cold. *Don't have a place for me? Where am I supposed to go?*

"Chris, we have a dilemma. You're only fourteen. You're too young for emancipation."

Emancipation?

"There's a shortage of foster homes. Do you have any relatives who might take you in?" My face flushed at her words. Relatives who might *take me in?* I felt like a rescue pet in need of a home, hoping someone would feel sorry for me and *take me in.* The only relatives I could think of were Aunt Jeanie and Uncle Jimmy. *But do they even know where I am? Did Mama ever tell them?*

"I have an aunt."

"What's her name? Do you know her phone number or address?" She began writing down what little information I could give her.

"We'll contact them."

Her energy told me she thought she was onto something, but I secretly doubted. Aunt Jeanie and Uncle Jimmie were *white trash* according to Jack. Over the years, the farm became a catch-all for anything too big to take inside the trailer. Old vehicles were scattered on the property waiting for Uncle Jimmie to *fix up* someday. Broken lawnmowers and random pieces of junk sat in the tall grass, waiting to go to the dump. Yard sale finds sat under the carport until someone remembered to do something with it. The farm's driveway was shale mixed with mud and very rough to drive on. Their trailer was old and reeked of smoke from Uncle Jimmy's cigarettes. Grandma's little house sat near the trailer and was little more than a run-down shack.

Even the neighbors got together and stopped by for a *neighborly chat* as they asked, "Jim, what can we do to get your stuff cleaned up?" But Aunt Jeanie and Uncle Jimmy were offended and saw no need to do anything about their *stuff*. They liked their *stuff*. So their *stuff* stayed and grew with each passing year.

Despite the clutter, the farm was still a happy place for me. Everyone was safe and no one went hungry. Grandma was there. Pam, Theresa, and little Julie were there. It was where Mama and us kids often took refuge from Jack when he kicked us out. I wanted the social worker to say I could go there, but I knew once she saw the place, she wouldn't approve. "I'll get back to you soon."

I didn't get my hopes up. I didn't even know if Aunt Jeanie and Uncle Jimmy would agree to *take me in.*

Three days later, the social worker came back to the youth shelter. "Good news," she said. "Your Aunt and Uncle have agreed to let you live with them."

My heartbeat slowed down as I waited for her to say something like, *but we can't approve them because of all the clutter* or *because they can't afford another kid.* I heard her say "Good news", but I was waiting for the letdown.

"There are a couple of changes they have to make, and the approval will be final. Then they can take you in."

Those words again. She told me my aunt and uncle lived in a house in Van Buren now. *What? Van Buren?* Had it really been so long since I'd seen them, I didn't even know where they lived? Apparently so. Uncle Jimmy agreed to build a wall in the bedroom that I'd be sharing with Theresa, a wall that created a hallway leading to the only bathroom in the house.

"Once that's done, I'll come and get you."

Could I believe what I was hearing? Was I really going to live with family? *My family?* Was the overwhelming weight of the last two years really coming to an end? My throat grew painfully tight, and my chin quivered. Was it really the end of foster homes and youth shelters? Another rescue?

I looked up at the social worker and barely choked out the words, "They got approved?" I had to hear it again.

She nodded and tilted her head to the side. "Yes, they got approved."

I hunched over and sobbed into my hands. I couldn't stop it. Layers of suppressed anguish made their way up through my core and spilled out. My body shook as a grain of hope came to life. I cried for several minutes before looking up at the social worker again. With my chest hitching, I asked one more time.

"I—I'm going to live—to live with my aunt and uncle?"

"They didn't hesitate," she said with a smile. "They didn't know where you were or what to do." *But they knew I was gone?* "I don't think your mom and stepdad told them the truth."

My weeping continued. Behind the anguish came relief. Sweet relief. Just a couple of weeks ago, the darkest most painful state of mind I had ever experienced trapped me. Hope had died, and I didn't want to go on. But as I stood in front of the social worker on that glorious afternoon, I heard words I thought were no longer possible. Words that felt like miracles. A home for me. My family. They got approved.

29

A Home for Me

IT TOOK LESS than a minute to dump my laundry basket of worldly possessions into the trash bag I snatched from the social worker's hand. I ran to the front door and stood waiting.

"I'm ready." Eyebrows raised and chin tilted, I looked at the social worker, who thumbed through the paperwork in her briefcase. I was going to live with my aunt and uncle, and I couldn't get there fast enough.

The farther we drove from the youth shelter, the more my excitement grew. With every passing building, the weight on my chest lightened. As the car merged onto the interstate, the corners of my mouth curled upward. The vibration of the tires on the road reassured me. *This is really happening.*

We arrived at a tiny red house on Lafayette Street. The carport barely covered Aunt Jeanie and Uncle Jimmy's car. *I've never been to this house.* We walked to the front door, and it felt like Christmas.

Moving in with my aunt and uncle was a homecoming, not only because I had been in foster care for over two years, but also because I had been rescued from the years of abuse before that. *And now I'm back.* It wasn't Mama, Lane, and Becky but it was still family—*my* family.

"Come on in!" Aunt Jeanie opened the door with a grin and quickly motioned toward the living room. Uncle Jimmy stood behind her. Pam and Theresa barreled into the living room. My emotions forced a smile across my face as I waited for the social worker to finish the formalities. *Hurry up, I'm home!*

WHEN SHE LEFT, I ran with Theresa to our room where we chattered and picked up our bond where it was left over two years ago. I listened to Theresa's voice and looked at her face. I had missed her. I had missed *this*. Connection. Relationship. Belonging. Breathing.

We were typical fourteen and fifteen-year-old girls. We spent a lot of time in our room, applied makeup, fixed each other's hair, and talked about boys and our perfect future life.

Pam had the bedroom in the back of the house and wanted nothing to do with girly stuff. She was much quieter than Theresa and me, often content to lay in her bed reading or listening to music. To be around my cousins without Lane felt different. If he had been there, I imagined he and Pam would have hung out in Pam's room, seeing who could spin the basketball on their finger the longest.

My aunt and uncle's kitchen barely had counter space. Aunt Jeanie stayed stocked up on groceries and there was never enough room inside the cabinets, so she stacked them on the countertops and table, wherever she found room. The stacks of cereal boxes, pasta bags, and canned vegetables gave me comfort. At mealtime, we dished up our own plates and ate wherever we wanted, usually in the living room or our bedroom. We didn't have to eat everything on our plate or eat at all if we weren't hungry.

Cousin Julie, now five years old and always under Aunt Jeanie's feet, followed her around with a million questions. Julie slept with my aunt and uncle and was a happy little girl. Even so, it was rare for us to allow her in our room.

One evening, we sat in the living room watching television and eating baked chicken and peas. Uncle Jimmy had his work clothes on and would leave after *Dukes of Hazzard* was over.

"Jim, you want chicken in your lunch?" Aunt Jeanie always packed Uncle Jimmy's lunch and filled his thermos with coffee. He needed the caffeine to get through the twelve-hour night shift.

"Chicken's fine." He wasn't picky.

"Mom, I'm skipping school tomorrow," Theresa announced.

"Okay." Aunt Jeanie kept eating.

"Me too." Julie giggled.

"You don't go to school," Aunt Jeanie reminded her, then got up to take her plate into the kitchen. "Girls, ya'll get some more chicken."

"Jeanie," Uncle Jimmy yelled into the kitchen. "Could you put one of those snack cakes in my lunch?"

"Sure."

I watched from the couch as Aunt Jeanie dropped a snack cake into Uncle Jimmy's lunch box. The smell of fresh-brewed coffee made me sigh as she poured it into his thermos and screwed the lid on. Her face was relaxed. Her tone was peaceful. The air was light. She wrapped a piece of chicken in plastic wrap, dropped it into the lunch box, then snapped it shut.

"Jim, your lunch is on the table." She walked back to the living room, sat down, folded her arms, and looked at the television.

"Thanks."

"Welcome."

So that's what it looks like—parents getting along, being themselves. Nobody demanded. Nobody was anxious. They said *thank you* and *welcome*. They were friendly. They were...nice.

It reminded me of Melissa and Steve, our neighbors from years earlier, and of James and Helen King, Mark's parents. They were calm. No one dominated. No one tippy-toed.

"You done?" Theresa passed by me with her empty plate and headed to the kitchen. "Want me to braid your hair?"

I ran my plate to the kitchen sink and followed Theresa to our room.

"You'll look like a model!" Aunt Jeanie hollered.

I smiled on the inside. I watched in the mirror as Theresa brushed my hair, then began braiding. I melted underneath the human touch. How long had it been since someone had touched my hair, hugged me, or patted me on the back? How long had it been since someone noticed me?

I had a place to be myself, to be loved and accepted just as I was. I understood the rules there, the lifestyle. No eggshells. No wondering how long I'd be there. I was there for good. I was one of them. I could be a kid, for what was left of my childhood. Hope grew. It was the beginning of feeling loved again. *They want me here.*

There wasn't much money, certainly no *extra* money, but there was plenty to eat, the rent was always paid, and the utilities never got shut off. There was at least one car, albeit old and embarrassing, to get us where we needed to go. Most days, Pam, Theresa, and I walked to school. On cold or rainy days, Aunt Jeanie drove us, but we begged her to let us out at the corner so no one would see the car we were in. We would rather run through the rain for that last half block than be seen in a car so uncool. Aunt Jeanie smiled and obliged.

We were free to be ourselves, even when we were being difficult. Yes, there was bickering among Pam, Theresa, and me at times. And some teasing and occasional hurt feelings. We argued about who was messier or the most stuck-up.

Aunt Jeanie became the mediator, and when she didn't know how to resolve our squabbling or was just plain sick of it, she threw up her hands and yelled, "You kids get along!" She'd walk out of the room, and little Julie followed, mimicking her words, "Yeah, you kids get along."

I knew my place in Aunt Jeanie's heart was secure, even when she was frustrated with me. I didn't worry about getting kicked out if I said the wrong thing or acted in the wrong way. She never indicated I was any different than her other three girls. Even as I write this, I squeeze my eyes shut to hold back the tears. Aunt Jeanie filled a void bigger than she ever knew. A void left by Jack and Mama.

My bond with my aunt grew. I soaked up every ounce of nurturing she poured over me. At times I couldn't believe she actually seemed to enjoy being there for me. She did plenty for all four of us girls, probably too much. If we got on her nerves, she said so with a smile, and if we *really* got on her nerves she said so *loudly*, but with a smile. She wasn't afraid to say how she felt, and she allowed us the same liberty. A freedom I never had with Jack. She looked at us and listened, showing us our words mattered. Sometimes she agreed with us and sometimes she didn't. And to my amazement, we weren't mocked or humiliated.

Aunt Jeanie empathized and went to bat for us when Uncle Jimmy acted stubborn. She became the messenger when he needed to know about something. This arrangement worked well for them, and us kids. A comfort and support I never had before.

Aunt Jeanie's birth name was Margaret Jean. Sometimes, we called her Margaret just to be funny. Grandma called her Margie. Nearly everyone else called her Jeanie. One day Aunt Jeanie and I were bantering back and forth, and I thought of a new name for her, *Maggie*.

But when I said it, I got tongue-tied with Margaret and Maggie, and it came out "Maggot!"

"Maggot?" Aunt Jeanie laughed.

I couldn't believe that came out of my mouth, and I pleaded through my laughter, "Oops, I didn't mean to say that."

"Chrissy, of all things." Aunt Jeanie pretended to be shocked. "I can't believe you! Maggot? Really?"

I was thrilled she found it funny. Her relentless teasing kept us laughing for several more minutes, but in the end, I decided I liked the idea of having my own special name for her. No, not Maggot, but Maggie.

"From now on, I'm going to call you Maggie. And no one else gets to call you that." I announced.

"Well at least it's not Maggot!" she laughed. And from that day on, she was my Maggie.

While life with my aunt and uncle was exactly what I needed at that time of my life, were they perfect? Absolutely not. They argued but quickly made up. They got on each other's nerves but didn't hold grudges. Together, they did what needed to be done.

Uncle Jimmy worked hard and paid the bills. When he was off work, he worked on their cars, and the cars of friends or other family members. In later years, it was often *my* car that needed a free mechanic, and Uncle Jimmy was always there. He did all the home repairs and yard work, not just for his own family, but for Grandma and Grandpa too. They were my parents when I didn't have any. *I wished they had known where I was sooner, and what to do about it.*

My eighth-grade year came to an end, and summer activities began. Maggie dropped us off at the public pool several days each week. The pool was cheap, and we enjoyed going, even though I still did not know how to swim.

Since moving in with my aunt and uncle, there had been only one visit from the social worker. She showed up one day as we were getting ready to go to the pool. I had on a bright pink bathing suit, with a towel in one hand and my money in the other. Maggie invited the social worker in, and the visit stayed short. She asked the usual questions, and I made sure I looked her straight in the eye and spoke the truth.

"Chris, how are things going?"

"Good." And they were.

"Is there anything you'd like to tell me about?"

"I'm getting ready to go swimming. And tonight, Maggie's gonna make us a pizza." It was the only thing I could think to say. She smiled.

"What kind of pizza?"

"Cheese."

After a few more questions, the social worker must have sensed all was well. She didn't ask to speak to me in her car. I was glad she came by, and I was glad I could give her such a good honest report. Her visit confirmed to me I really did have a home, and as it turns out, she didn't come back—ever.

The case was closed, and my aunt and uncle had permanent custody of me.

Brrrrrrrrring.

"Hello?" I had never heard Grandma's voice over the phone.

"Grandma?"

"Chrissy?"

"I get to stay for good!"

Grandma was silent for a second. "Oh, Chrissy. You're free from that monster. And you're home."

I smiled and nodded as if she could see me. "Well, we're going to the pool now. Talk to you later." My chest swelled as I hung up the phone. *I'm home.*

30

Aftermath

FOR MONTHS, I basked in the comfort of being with family. Knowing I was there to stay was an indescribable relief. I understood that life, and I knew I was loved. My mind began to relax. My days were brighter and the air lighter. But as I settled into my new phase of life, layers of buried emotions stirred deep within.

My inner voice reminded me I was still *less than* because I had so many secrets. *You'll never be normal.* Depression and anxiety flared up again, making daily tasks feel impossible. I didn't understand I was still living in the aftermath of growing up in abuse. My body had healed from the trauma, but my brain wasn't there yet.

Schoolwork in the ninth grade overwhelmed me, and each day, I fell farther behind. I had witnessed other students get their hands smacked with a wooden ruler for missing assignments. Rumor was that if the teacher took a ruler to your hands, he hit harder and harder until you broke down in tears. If it didn't break you, it didn't teach you. Some kids fake cried right away, just to make it quick. Through the classroom walls, we counted how many swats it took to break someone.

My struggle with schoolwork finally caught up with me. I sat at my desk avoiding eye contact as the teacher gathered yesterday's assignments. Two of us didn't have it. He called both of us to the front of the class and told us to hold out our hands. The other girl was first. She immediately cried and even buckled over, but I didn't think she was faking. *He must hit harder than I expected.*

I thought about how Jack took pride in punishing me. Still in my memory loomed his puffed-up chest and eager face as he prepared to whip me with a switch or bully me with his authority. I could not allow myself to be broken by this teacher. *Nobody's ever gonna break me again.* I was sure of it. Did I have my assignment? No. Did I deserve some kind of consequence? Probably. But something welled up inside of me. I would endure this punishment. *BUT I WILL NOT BREAK.* I couldn't—I needed to survive something, to break through something inside of me. Years of brokenness depended on my refusal to break now. I needed to fight.

I offered my hands to the teacher, and he began hitting me with the ruler. I stared. I was used to pain. Each strike was harder than the one before. The teacher paused only to look at my stone face. My hands stayed out, red and throbbing. *I won't give in.*

The teacher grew irritated and gave up. "Sit down!"

I lowered my hands and walked to my desk, meeting the eyes of each classmate as I passed. I didn't smile. No need to speak. I sat down and opened my book. *Damaged but not destroyed.*

Of course, the school called Maggie. I had been *defiant* and *needed to be reprimanded.*

Like so many times in my life, I wavered on the edge of emotional disaster, desperate for an understanding hand to pull me back to safety. Even if I didn't deserve it.

On the outside, I appeared rebellious and disobedient. My stubbornness was an internal fight to survive. When understanding wasn't there, I sometimes slipped over the edge into a deeper place of despair. It was a cycle I didn't know how to break.

The day the school called Maggie, her reaction was perfect for me, as if she knew exactly what I needed. Mine was not a regular parent-child situation. I was a kid from trauma. My brain worked differently, and *regular* parental responses didn't always work with me, sometimes causing more damage. Maggie hadn't been educated about the needs of kids from trauma, but she did follow her instincts even if she didn't understand them.

"Chrissy, the school called."

I froze. *Is she mad at me?*

"They said you need to turn in your assignments." Maggie smiled at me. I nodded. "How about you do that?"

What? No lecture?

"They said you refused to cry."

I nodded again. *I'm not sorry.* At that moment, my entire world teetered on the edge of a cliff, waiting to see what Maggie said next. Would her words push me over the edge or pull me back to safety?

"Don't you ever feel bad for not being perfect." And with that, she walked out of the room.

Did Maggie's response make sense? To me it did. It said a lot of things. She didn't fully understand my behavior. She didn't fully understand my needs. She wasn't sure what to say or do with the situation. But she saw me. And somehow the words came to her, and she said them. And because of that, I knew I was still safe with her, and that she still loved me.

31

Broken Relationships

A BROKEN SPIRIT and broken mind are much harder to see than broken bones and bruises. The damage runs deep, and in many layers. I subconsciously disconnected from people who I thought had their life together. *They are the lucky ones. I am damaged.* I didn't feel good enough for those people. I didn't want the pain of rejection, so I rejected them first. I was afraid to be laughed at. Afraid to be thought of as stupid. Afraid of being humiliated. Afraid of my worthlessness being exposed. All the ways Jack made me feel.

I believed I was the person the voice in my head described. Ashamed of myself and of my life. I hated being the little girl no one wanted and was not enough to fight for.

Maggie and Uncle Jimmy decided we were moving back out to the farm. *Yes!* Grandma and Grandpa were there.

Uncle Jimmy connected two used single-wide trailers to make a double-wide. It was ugly but roomy. I didn't mind the appearance of our home much, since we were out in the country, and Maggie took us to school. *Who's gonna see it?* I was glad to have a home, with my family, at a place that meant so much. Grandma was elated to have us back at the farm. She had been lonely without us. Jack hadn't allowed Mama to see her family in many months.

Life settled down, and I was happy for the most part. I had become an expert at hiding my past from my friends, convinced I wouldn't be accepted if they knew the truth.

I struggled over Janey and Mark making me leave their home. It took a long time for me to know what to do with my feelings. Janey had rescued me. She made me feel special. I had loved her, trusted her. When they changed their minds about wanting me in their home, my devastation ran deep. I felt betrayed. Was trusting someone worth the risk?

I called Janey a few times, thinking we could still be friends. The conversations were light-hearted and awkward. I phased back and forth between wanting and not wanting a relationship with her. It took years to conclude that a relationship with Janey would never be like I wanted. We were too different. And things between us were too broken.

It's sad how a child will accept guilt and carry it around for years, sometimes a lifetime, for something they never did. It hurt to be accused of stealing Janey's ring. For years, I imagined the satisfaction of somehow hearing Janey had found her ring. Would she call me up and apologize?

"Even if you had taken it, weren't you more important than a ring?" Sally said to me one day, and it still rings in my ears.

Maggie initiated visits with Mama, Lane, and Becky. If Maggie picked them up, or if Lane drove, Jack allowed them to go. Seeing their faces stirred my emotions. I felt like we should hug and say how much we missed each other, but awkwardness kept us apart. They seemed full of their own mixed thoughts. We smiled a lot but spoke little. Maggie kept the conversations going as I caught glimpses of my old life in their eyes.

Mama still sported her uncomfortable smile as she attempted to cover her real feelings. She and Maggie chatted as Lane and I sat and half-listened. Mama's usual *everything is just fine* survival act made me sad.

I hurt for Lane. I saw his uneasiness. *Does he even want to be here?* Whatever he felt, I couldn't blame him. We didn't talk about what happened. The thought of discussing what Jack did to me was mortifying.

Becky stayed near Mama. She was six now, oblivious to anything that had happened. I wondered if she had questions in her young mind and if she ever asked anyone for answers. I doubt she got the truth if she had. I wanted to tell Becky I loved her, and I was still her big sister, but I didn't know if it would mean anything. She was only four when I was removed from the home. Did she even remember me?

During my visits with Mama, we didn't mention the past or the sexual abuse. Mama didn't ask me how I was doing, maybe because she could see I was in good hands.

The way life used to be was over. I had clung to the hope that somehow, I wouldn't really lose my Mama, brother, and sister. And even though we sat in the same room, I knew in many ways, I had already lost them.

I barely remember lighthearted hugs and goodbyes as Mama, Lane, and Becky loaded into the car to go home. Mama never called me in between the few visits we had. Probably because Jack hated me and calling me would only add fuel to the fire. She still had to survive. My throat ached when they drove away, and I wondered how long it would be before I saw them again.

I never went with Maggie to pick them up or take them back. Jack did not allow me near where they lived. I was the enemy.

"Vicious lies!" Jack told the family. As he battled his demons, he had a variety of stories about how I was the problem, not him. Guilt? Embarrassment? The sting of exposure? Jack had to explain to anyone who questioned why I was no longer in the home.

Maggie and Grandma filled me in on the stories they were told but knew were untrue. "Well, that Chris," Jack told Maggie. "She was running with the wrong crowd. Drugs. We just couldn't control her anymore. Had to send her away."

Every lie Jack told exposed him more and more. People weren't stupid. Mama obediently kept her mouth shut and supported his disgraceful circus. I hated it for her, but I hated it more for Lane and Becky. I had no idea what they had been told or what they believed, but I knew they hadn't heard the truth.

It was summertime at the farm. Grandma had been busy in her garden for months and was already picking some of her harvests. I walked around with purplish-black fingers from picking blackberries. We sold them by the quart to the locals. This was an all-summer job that provided money for school clothes the following August.

Theresa and I hung out in our rooms a lot and when we had gas money, we jumped in the car and went someplace, any place would do. We were happy to embrace our freedom and the fact that Theresa had her driver's license.

"Chris, I want to ask you about something." Maggie stood in my bedroom doorway. I turned off my radio. "Do you want to meet your biological dad?" She never was one to beat around the bush.

"How?" I asked. I didn't even know where he was, or if he wanted to meet me. All I knew was that his name was Jim, like my uncle.

"I contacted him and told him that you live with us now. He wants to see you." For a moment my mind was blank. *He wants to see me?* I had been conditioned to not talk about him. *Did he actually say he wants to see me?* That was hard for me to fathom. I wondered what Maggie had told him. Surely not the *truth*. But I didn't ask her.

"Okay," I said.

"Okay?"

"Yes, I'll meet him."

Two weeks later my dad, also named Jim, flew in from California. He visited his mom first, in Ft. Smith, then drove out to the farm.

"Four o'clock," Maggie said.

"Hmm?" I had been restless all morning.

"He'll be here at four o'clock."

"Okay." My head spun. What will he look like? What if he doesn't like me?

I was thankful that Maggie and Uncle Jimmy went about their normal day, not making a fuss over my dad's visit. Maggie did laundry, and Uncle Jimmy changed the battery in his truck. The routine gave me comfort.

Four o'clock came slowly. The sound of a car on the dirt road stiffened my chest. *He's here.*

Maggie stood at the door. "Jim get in here!' She wanted Uncle Jimmy to wash the grime off his hands before my dad reached the door.

I heard the car engine stop and a door open and shut.

"Well, hello stranger. It's been a long time. Come in and sit down." Maggie was a good ice breaker. I stood a few feet back and waited until he spoke.

"Hi, Chris. It's good to meet you." He seemed relaxed and spoke as though it had only been a few days since he last saw me. "How are you?"

"Just fine," I answered in my unintended southern accent that accompanied my routine southern smile, regardless of how I felt. I glanced at Maggie. Uncle Jimmy entered the room. *They're my parents now.*

My dad was a short Italian man with black hair. I saw Lane in his handsome face. He had been married to a lady named Dodie for ten years and had another daughter. My half-sister, Carrie Jo, was thirteen. He owned a business called Sea Junk, a place where people bought, sold, or traded anything related to boating. He liked to bowl and go to horse races in Hollywood, and he managed a rock-n-roll band.

I listened and tried to navigate the myriad of thoughts swarming my mind. *He has a store? And another daughter?* He filled us with stories about his growing up, and his life now, but none about Lane and me. Those stories came later.

Every morning for two weeks, my dad picked me up at the farm and took me to a different place. I met some of his old school friends and we drove around Fort Smith as he pointed to places he had hung out as a teenager. We spent time at his mom's house talking and looking at old photos.

I had met my paternal grandmother when I stayed with Janey and Mark. It was a visit I agreed to but left me wondering where I belonged. I hadn't seen her since that visit.

He showed me a box of canceled checks he had sent to Mama for child support. "I kept these so I could show you someday that I cared…in case someone said I didn't."

By the end of the two weeks, my screaming emotions were impossible to sort out. Jim was a stranger, but he was still my dad. He seemed to care, but he wasn't there for me as a child. I felt compelled to love him, but I didn't know him. He called me his daughter, but we had just met. I wanted to celebrate getting my dad back, but I felt angry and threatened, and I didn't know why.

Did he have any idea what I had been through? *I needed him, and he wasn't there.* Those years weren't just hard, they were hell. After years of abuse and foster care, I finally found a good place with Maggie and Uncle Jimmy. *Is he going to take me away from them?* After all, how could I refuse to live with my real dad if he wanted me to?

At the end of the two weeks, my dad left Oklahoma, and that night I lay in bed absorbing the comfort of Maggie and Uncle Jimmy's voices in the other room. He didn't take me away from them. Instead, he invited me to go to California for a visit, and to meet my half-sister and stepmom. He bought me an airplane ticket and two weeks later, Maggie took me to the airport.

I was sure I should feel a certain way, having just met my biological father, but I didn't know what that way was. I only felt a whirlwind of unknowns. Excitement about flying. Curiosity to see his life in California. *Is it happily ever after now? Does this makeup for when he wasn't there?*

32

California

MAGGIE WAITED AT the airport until I boarded the plane. I fidgeted with everything around me as people placed their bags above my head. One by one, the seats filled, and the door closed. Surrounded by strangers, I wondered where everyone was going. No one else looked nearly as excited or as nervous as me. I fixed my eyes outside of the window and took everything in as the plane took off.

The ground became a patchwork quilt that reminded me of Grandma. I watched it get smaller and smaller until all I could see was silky white.

I settled into my seat as the plane grew quiet. *Bet my dad's flown a hundred times.*

"There you are." My dad stood at the baggage claim. My nerves exploded. *Am I supposed to hug him?* I focused on the moving carousel and watched for the suitcase Maggie bought me from a thrift shop. I couldn't look at him. Instead, I prayed. *Please stay nice. Please love me.* He seemed nice enough in Oklahoma, but I wasn't in the habit of trusting anyone.

On the two-hour drive my eyes frenzied at my surroundings. Los Angeles swarmed with people, traffic, and buildings. More than my mind could take in. As we left the city, I felt soothed by the beauty of mountains and palm trees.

"The beach isn't far from where we live." I had never seen a beach. "We'll go there while you're here."

I looked at my dad and nodded, now in a world I wasn't sure was real.

The car stopped in the driveway of a beautiful stucco home in a manicured suburb called Camarillo. Nerves again. I was about to meet my stepmother and half-sister who, only a month ago, didn't even exist.

Carrie Jo was one-and-a-half years younger than me. My dad dated her mom after he and Mama split up, but his relationship with Carrie Jo's mother didn't last. He was now married to Dodie, and Carrie Jo lived with them. My new sister had beautiful long blonde hair and perfectly tanned skin. She stood barefoot in the entryway as we were introduced. My stepmother had not come home from work yet.

"Chris, this is your sister, Carrie Jo. Carrie Jo, this is your sister, Chris."

Carrie Jo hugged me, and two Shih Tzu's ran around us barking frantically. I noticed her connection to her dad—*our* dad. Her eyes lit up as she told him something the dogs had done while he was away. She had held the story in all day and was about to burst. She spoke so fast, I barely kept up with her words. All I remember is she began her story by calling our dad *Pa* and ended with "....and the dogs were barking and jumping around something fierce!" *Something fierce?* I had never heard anyone use that phrase or get so excited about dogs.

I felt instant ease with Carrie Jo, and she seemed to have an honest curiosity about me. Her eagerness made me feel special. She took me upstairs and showed me the room where I would sleep, then showed me her room. Carrie Jo pointed to some scarves hanging on a hook on her wall, the kind girls wore around their necks in the 80s.

"Pa got me these." Carrie Jo brushed her hands across the scarves. "I wear them when I go to the skating rink."

I studied the furnishings and caught a glimpse of an orange tree through the window. Everything was foreign. I became deaf to Carrie Jo's words as emotions and thoughts poured into my mind. It was obvious this was her home. She belonged here.

We went back downstairs as Carrie Jo showed me the kitchen that opened up into a room with a pool table.

"Show her the game room." My dad stood next to the kitchen cabinet and poured bourbon into a small glass of coke.

"And *this* is the game room." Carrie Jo raised both hands toward the coolest room I had ever seen. The red-felted pool table had dark stained wood and leather pockets.

"I had that pool table custom-built," my dad explained as he joined us.

To my left, a vintage jukebox stood in the corner. "And that jukebox is a Wurlitzer from the forties."

He pointed out the long, wet bar with a padded edge and several swiveling stools along the front. "Had this bar added when we built the house."

I nodded and kept walking. There was a pinball machine and an elaborate stereo system.

"Over here is Dodie's music box collection." My dad showed me a built-in cabinet that housed a huge assortment of music boxes. "She's collected for over ten years."

I could have stared at them all day.

He showed me a picture of his mom and brother, the year he flew them to California and took them to Disneyland. *You went to Disneyland?* My mind wondered for a moment as I tried to think of what my life looked like that year. *Oh, that was the year when Jack started... Don't go there—not right now.*

The sliding glass doors led to a pool, hot tub, and a gas fire pit. I was awestruck.

"Over here is where the band sets up when we have Fourth of July parties."

My dad pointed to an open area of the patio. *People have Fourth of July parties?* "Carrie Jo sings in the band." *In front of people? By herself?*

My dad looked like James Dean in some of his old photos. In other pictures, he looked like Elvis Presley. In my mind, I imagined what he had been like in his teenage years, and during the years he dated Mama. He was a cool, smooth, good-looking guy who played pool and stood around the jukebox in a white t-shirt and jeans, with his hair slicked back. I liked my mental scenario, and I decided it must be close to the way it was. I learned about my dad by looking and listening and using a little imagination.

Dodie appeared through the front door and walked straight to the kitchen, where she dropped her purse onto the table and sat down with a sigh, "I'm exhausted. You know, accounting is mentally exhausting." She poured vodka into a glass and started sipping.

"Dodie, this is Chris." My dad looked at her with raised eyebrows and waited for her to respond.

Dodie looked at me with a combination of a smile and a smirk. "Hi. I'm Dodie." She took a pack of cigarettes from her purse and placed one between her lips. "So, you're from Arkansas?" She lit the cigarette, took a puff, blew it out, and looked at me again.

"Oklahoma now. I used to live in Arkansas."

"Oh, Oklahoma." Dodie didn't seem to mind that she didn't know much about me. The tone in her voice was dry. I worried she might not like me.

"Now, Chris." My dad leaned against the kitchen cabinet. "You girls call me Pa, and that's Ma." He pointed to Dodie. *Pa and Ma? Old people names.* My heart dropped as I realized I would not be able to call him *Dad.* Growing up, I had imagined meeting him someday and calling him Dad. Pa was awkward to say, but that's what I called him from that point on. I was never able to utter the name Ma, so I called my stepmother Dodie.

"Why don't you girls take the suitcase upstairs?" Dodie was finished talking.

The smile on my face hurt, and I wondered if I was going to gasp for air. It was almost too much, the reality I had just been shown. California, the house, the life they lived without me. I didn't know how to process any of it. And the contrast to my own life struck anger.

Pa, Dodie, and Carrie Jo were a family. They had bonded. They had a history together. They lived an incredibly different life, millions of miles from Oklahoma. While Pa moved on with his life in California, Jack shacked up with Mama. While Carrie Jo was being raised by our biological father, I was being raised by an abuser.

While Pa built a new stucco home on "…the best lot in the whole subdivision," Mama, Lane, and I were getting kicked out of our home and sent walking again. While Pa watched Carrie Jo jump into the backyard pool, Lane and I walked ourselves twenty blocks to free swim. While Pa took pictures of Carrie Jo in her pigtails, I knocked on the neighbor's door for attention.

While Pa carted Carrie Jo to the skating rink, bought her scarves, and booked her singing gigs, his first daughter was carted around by social workers and foster parents. While he was busy being a father to his second daughter, his first daughter was getting molested and raped.

I stood in the bedroom next to my suitcase, listening to Pa and Dodie talk from downstairs. Dodie vented bout her stressful job, and how she'd like to tell her boss to "Shove it." The dogs barked until someone opened the sliding glass doors. Carrie Jo had gone into her room, and I was left with my emotions. I felt lost again.

How could he just move on? Why did he raise Carrie Jo, but not Lane and me?

The wounds from years with Jack had followed me to California and into my biological father's house. I held back a scream. *It's not fair!* I knew Carrie Jo deserved to have her father in her life, and I never thought otherwise. But I deserved to have him all those years too.

I needed him too.

After a two-week visit, Pa drove me back to the airport, and I returned to Oklahoma.

"We'll do this again next summer," he said as he saw me off.

I was glad there was no talk about me living with him in California. I wasn't ready for that. I just wanted to go home to Maggie and Uncle Jimmy.

33

Grace, Grit, and Unmet Needs

A FEW WEEKS after returning from California, I got my learner's permit, and Maggie began teaching me to drive our only car, a stick shift. Learning how to coordinate the clutch and gear shifter was brutal, but I finally caught on. Maggie patiently rode next to me as I hugged the steering wheel and stretched my scrawny neck to see over the hood.

On my first attempt to turn the car back into our driveway, I slammed into the ditch. I hadn't yet mastered turning while slowing down, pressing the clutch, and shifting all at the same time.

When the car hit the bottom of the ditch, I looked at Maggie. Her lips were pressed together, and her eyes were big. She sported a smile and held back the frustration. Uncle Jimmy came running down the driveway with a curious face. He stood at the ditch and scratched his head. I stared at him, then at Maggie, then back at Uncle Jimmy. *Somebody say something.*

"I'll get a chain."

"He'll get a chain." Maggie's eyes were still big, but the frustration had left. She smiled at me. "He'll get a chain."

The car might be damaged. Is this the end of my driving lessons? Will I be scolded? Criticized? Laughed at?

"Chris, turn the wheel straight when I say now." Uncle Jimmy parked his truck behind the car and hooked a chain to the bumper. He slowly backed the truck up, and when the chain was tight, he yelled, "Now!" I turned the wheel and the car backed onto the road.

"Press the brakes!"

I pressed the brakes. Uncle Jimmy unhooked the chain and shot me a smile. "Turn sooner next time."

Embarrassed. Relieved. Speechless. But not demoralized. *I love him.*

At fifteen and a half, Maggie allowed me to start dating, although by now I had already snuck around and gone on a couple of dates when I was supposed to be at the local skating rink. The thought of a boy liking me, and the independence of going somewhere with him, seemed exciting.

I struggled with telling my date where I lived. The farm was my safe place, my secret refuge. It was sacred to me, and I didn't want someone to judge how we lived. No matter what our place looked like, there was love and safety inside. Not everyone understood. And superficially, I didn't want the appearance of our old trailer to make me look bad. I worried my date would think less of me if he saw how I lived, but I didn't have a choice. Maggie said they had to meet my date before I could go.

I continued to feel safe and happy with my aunt and uncle, but my self-esteem stayed shattered. I battled with the voice in my head that told me *I was less than* and *of little value.*

I still longed to feel normal and as though I had nothing to hide. Although Maggie and Uncle Jimmy loved me, I still felt a void, and I searched for ways to fill it. Sometimes, if I allowed myself to feel it for long enough, I gasped for air. Pain stayed deep beneath the layers, and I desperately wanted it to go away. So I searched for comfort, but in many wrong places.

I began to realize that some guys valued my appearance more than anything else about me. They asked me out on dates, were eager to make out, but never tried to get to know me. The attention didn't feel right to me, but it was still attention. I thought if they dated me, they saw me as valuable and desirable. It took me years to learn they only really wanted one thing. I drifted in and out of seasons of promiscuity as I battled wanting to feel loved but ended up feeling used.

I was afraid to set boundaries or raise my standards because I thought no one would want me if I did. The voice in my head said, *I don't hold real value, so I can't expect to be treated as such.* I believed I had to take whatever I could get.

There were times when a genuinely respectable guy asked me out and I turned him down. I didn't feel worthy of respect. I believed if he liked me, there must be something wrong with him. And once he saw that underneath my pretty face and long blonde hair was a royal mess, he'd dump me.

Girls like me don't get guys like that.

Theresa worked part-time at a local pizza restaurant, and I tagged along to hang out while she worked. I badly wanted a job so I could earn my own money, but I was just shy of the hiring age of sixteen. However, one evening, people poured in after a football game, and there weren't enough servers to keep everyone happy.

I had watched Theresa enough, so I knew what to do. I jumped up and started carrying orders from the kitchen to the customers. I walked from table to table, refilling drinks. And as customers left, I cleared the table and wiped it off. After a couple of hours, the owner showed up to help with the crowd. She saw me working and pointed to tables that might need something. I rushed to the tables, eager to please.

From across the room, the owner mouthed the words, "I will pay you." And I couldn't contain my smile as I kept moving. *She's going to pay me?* I was having the time of my life, and now I was going to get paid! Jack had never let me do odd jobs for money. He smirked and told me *no* before I could finish asking. He told me I wasn't capable of work, and I wondered if he was right.

When the pizza place closed, I helped clean up, and the owner paid me thirty dollars cash. The feeling of that cash in my hand amazed me. *She paid me. I earned money.*

I continued to go to work with Theresa, and helped out for free, until the owner finally offered me a job, even though I still had two weeks to go from turning sixteen. I had a real job!

Theresa eventually took a different job. She thought selling magic show tickets over the phone sounded more fun. But I stayed on at the pizza place. After three months, at the end of my shift, the owner told me about a car she was selling—a 1972 Toyota Corolla. It was eleven years old, and she wanted $1350 for it. She said she knew the people at the local bank and would cosign if I wanted to buy it and make payments to the bank. I eagerly agreed without even asking Maggie and Uncle Jimmy for advice.

I probably paid too much, but I didn't know enough to negotiate. *My own car.* At the bank, we sat in two chairs facing the loan officer and signed papers. For the next several minutes, my boss and the loan officer chatted, and I stared at my keys, rubbing them like precious metal.

I wondered how one becomes the owner of a pizza place or a loan officer at a bank. And how did they become friends? And why were they helping me? In my little world, people like that were only friends with you if you were important or had a lot of money. *Are they just…nice?*

For twelve months, I paid the bank $115 a month until the car was all mine. Proud when my old car was paid off, I was overcome with a strong desire to shove my fist-held keys into Jack's face.

I wish I could say at sixteen I felt like a well-balanced person, and I suppose in some ways I was. While still in high school, I held down a job, bought a car, paid for my own extras, and followed Maggie's rules—for the most part.

Life put distance between Lane and me, but he was constantly in my thoughts. It had been almost two years since I had seen him.

I heard he got married, and lived on his own with his wife, Megan, and their new son. The thought of Lane moving out, away from Jack, felt comforting. And now he had a *wife*? And a *son*? I couldn't wrap my mind around it. In my heart, he was my big brother. I couldn't imagine him any other way. Did he ever think about me? What kind of girl did he marry?

I wanted him to know the truth. But I didn't think I could utter the words. Shame still had its grip.

I could write him a letter. Nothing too detailed, I thought. A quick letter, in which Lane could read between the lines. My heart needed him to know I wasn't a bad kid. Mama and Jack didn't send me away—I was taken away and not because I got in trouble at school, but because of Jack, because of what he did to me. *Maybe he'll read it and understand.*

So I wrote to Lane. I mentioned I had heard he was married and had a son. I told him where I lived now. And I attempted to tell him what happened with Jack, as minimally as possible. I struggled to explain how things started, and I couldn't bring myself to write the words *sexual abuse* or *rape*. Not even *molested*. The shame would have killed me. I hinted at the truth instead. *I can't say those words to my brother.*

I dropped the letter into the mailbox and panicked when it left my fingers.

Lane wrote back.

Interestingly, we lived in towns next to each other and could have driven or called, but letters felt safer. Lane acknowledged receiving my letter but didn't say anything about what I had hinted to him. He invited me to spend the night with him and Megan. And I accepted. They lived in a brick duplex in Van Buren. Their son, Jacob, less than a year old, was the cutest little boy I had ever seen. *I have a nephew.* I instantly loved him.

I slept on the couch, and the next morning, I heard Lane stirring, getting Jacob dressed, then leaving with his son. The evening before, Megan had explained Lane liked to show up at his work on his day off, with his son in tow, to show him off. Lane was a manager at Savemart. The one I had run to the night Jack made me leave, years before.

I was careful to keep quiet as Megan had not yet woken up. I studied the furnishings Lane had built—no doubt he learned from Jack. A framed picture of baby Jacob sat on the table next to the couch. *I have a nephew.*

Sadness swept over me. Loss. I knew what Lane and I had before was now gone. I couldn't get it back and wasn't sure how to start over. All I knew was I loved my brother. I was proud of him for loving his son and taking care of his wife.

I wondered what went through his mind when he read my letter. Did he understand? Inviting me to his home showed me he still cared. And that meant the world to me.

34

Insecurity

AT SIXTEEN, MY body and mind were changing, and my emotions tried to keep up. It was hard to be a teenager, and even harder because of the trauma of my past. The many wounds skewed my thinking and made daily navigation of life difficult and confusing.

I became self-conscious of my appearance, and of what others thought, especially my peers. I depended on their approval because I disapproved of myself.

I didn't know what healthy romantic love looked like, but I craved it and assumed I was ready for it. The love of a boy, I thought, would somehow fill all the holes that were left empty growing up. I sought after the cutest, most popular boys in school—if *they* liked me, I must be likable. My self-worth depended on it.

To my peers, I had it all together—an outgoing personality, a cute face, and pretty hair. I was smart and witty, and the boys liked me. Where I thought my image lacked, I faked it, or outright lied about it.

Although only five-foot-one, I managed to convince my friends I was a model. I had done some modeling for fun, but I exaggerated the stories behind the photographs. A total of *one* of my photographs was actually published, along with a story, but my added details sounded so much better when I told my friends about it.

I also embellished stories about my dad in California. His material things and the glamor of living in sunny California, so close to Hollywood and Los Angeles, made for more good tales. I left out the part about only having met him last year. The struggle with my anger and confusion as I tried to put my relationship with him into perspective. Pa and I spoke on the phone once a month, but I only saw him for a few weeks in the summer, when he flew me to California.

Self-pity still tormented me. First it wrapped its arms around me and agreed with every negative thing I said to myself. When I needed an excuse to stay in a rut or give up, self-pity whispered, "You poor thing. You're too damaged to do anything hard. Forget your schoolwork. Forget being honest. Forget fighting for better." Then my pity became cruel. "He kept my family. Why did I have to be born? My life is ruined."

I sometimes screamed into my pillow. "I don't want this to be my life!" I punched the mattress and threw books across the room—books that used to be my escape. I stared at the open pages and felt the guilt. Then I pulled the blanket underneath my chin and let pain and helplessness flow. *Why me? Why am I being punished?*

But the good thing about pity is that it ultimately angered me. The flashbacks of abuse triggered my emotions, reminding me I had been to hell and back. Somehow, I survived. I spoke to the pity. *I didn't do anything wrong. I want better than this.*

Some days felt like I walked through a battlefield, full of bullet holes, desperate for the bleeding to stop. I was tired of fighting battles, only to find myself in the middle of another one that I couldn't escape. I didn't understand the war. I just knew I wanted to be rescued again.

I gave my notice at the pizza place and took a job at the grocery store across the street for more pay. Balancing school and work became exhausting, but I made my car payment, paid for insurance, and put gas in the tank. I was thankful for that. I didn't enjoy the grocery store nearly as much as the pizza place, but it didn't dawn on me that I had many choices in life, even then. Somewhere in my younger years, I had been taught to accept what was in front of me and not to try to change it. I had already switched my job once, and I felt stuck.

At seventeen, I had a steady boyfriend who acted like a lovesick puppy that couldn't live without me. He was twenty, shy, and had emotional problems of his own. We met through a mutual friend, and for me, he seemed safe and made me feel needed. My appearance and outgoing personality made it easy to keep my inner chaos hidden. To him, I had become the *fixer* of his problems, because I had it all together.

We talked about getting married after I graduated high school, but underneath my words, marriage terrified me. I didn't know who I was, what I wanted, or how I would ever feel good about myself. I didn't love him, but I was afraid to hurt him. So, I sacrificed my true feelings.

Maggie really liked my boyfriend and even told me she would sign the parental consent if we wanted to get married before I turned eighteen. Her offer surprised me and only added pressure. I was afraid my bouts of depression and self-pity would cause me to give in and get married even though it wasn't what I wanted. *Nobody wants a damaged person.*

During the last semester of eleventh grade, the high school hosted an assembly, inviting representatives from various colleges to speak to the students. We gathered in the auditorium and listened as each representative spoke about their college.

Opportunities. Education. *Wow…college…wouldn't that be a dream?* But I didn't have money for college. *Besides, girls like me don't get to go to college. Too unlucky.*

Each speaker enthusiastically reminded us to visit the tables covered with stacks of applications and window stickers as we left the assembly. Tears threatened to expose my hopelessness as I picked up an Oklahoma State University window sticker but passed by the applications.

I still get irritated when I think of that day. How naïve. Had the representatives spoken about grants, work-study programs, and loans? Had I paid attention? All I knew is that you either had to have a lot of money or a scholarship to go to college. And I had neither.

Eleventh grade ended on a Friday, and the drive home was despairing. Yes, I still had my senior year to look forward to, but ever since the college assembly, my depression deepened. The idea of getting an education beyond high school and making something of myself sounded exciting. But that voice in my head squashed any hope. *You aren't good enough to go to college.* I put the Oklahoma State University sticker on my car window anyway. It was fun to pretend.

That summer began with relief that I could sleep in for the next three months. On Saturdays at the grocery store, we set up an "outdoor market" in the parking lot. I loved working in the sunshine, putting sun-kissed fruit and vegetables into small brown bags with paper handles. It made my insides smile and reminded me of Grandma's garden.

One morning, as I worked the outdoor market, my boyfriend paid me a surprise visit. Our conversation began as typical as it had been for nearly a year, but he blindsided me when he announced, "I don't want to get married."

"You don't?" I was struck with relief. And a shade of hurt.

"I'm just not ready."

He didn't have to convince me. It was the strangest and easiest breakup I'd ever experienced. He left, and I turned back to my warm fruit and vegetables, and brown paper bags.

Now what?

35

Pa's Side of the Story

I SAT AT the kitchen table as Maggie washed dishes at the sink. The late July sun shone across the room as we chatted about how my junior year of high school was over and the start of my senior year was only a few weeks away.

"What will I do after I graduate?" Maggie didn't detect my anxiety. "I mean, I know I still have one more year of high school, but what will I do afterward?" For months I drowned out conversations about college among my peers. I was tired of hearing which college they applied to, or which scholarships they had already received. No one asked me where I would be going to college, and I was glad. *Let them think it's OSU, like the sticker says.* I didn't want to talk about it. There was nothing to say.

"I don't know. Do whatever you want." No help. Maggie had dropped out of high school to marry Uncle Jimmy and have kids. She was content with her choices and had probably never given much thought to other options. At least not enough thought to offer suggestions. Theresa had also dropped out, gotten married, and moved to Nashville.

Brrrrrrring. The phone startled me.

"Hello? Hold on." Maggie held out the receiver. "It's your dad."

I took the phone and the conversation started in its usual way. "How are you doing?" Pa always asked.

"Just fine."

He laughed as he mimicked my southern accent. "Just fiiiiiine." I laughed along.

We talked about what I had been up to since summer break began. I told him about the outdoor market at work, and that my boyfriend and I had broken up. He made a sarcastic joke about not needing a boyfriend anyway, and again I laughed. I wasn't used to opening up to him about my worries, so I didn't mention my anxiety or my need for some kind of direction.

I don't remember if he asked me about my plans for the rest of the summer, or if I brought it up. But I heard myself say, "I'm doing absolutely nothing but working, and that's how it will be after I graduate next year—nothing, because college is a million dollars."

"Not here, it's not. In California, college is free." *Free?* I hadn't expected that. I didn't know any college was free. "Except for your books."

And without thinking, I blurted out, "Well maybe I'll just pack up and move to California." *Oh my gosh, did I just say that?* The thought of moving to California was terrifying; I had only been there for short visits in the summer. I waited for his response.

"Well, start packing and get your butt out here."

"Um, what?" Was it really that easy? No discussion? "Well, I have a car that's almost paid off. I have to work."

"I'll send you some money. Load up your car and drive. You can get a job here."

"Oh." My mind froze, and I searched for words. Did my life plan just change in a couple of seconds? "Okay."

"You'll have to stay in a hotel one night. It's a long drive. How about you plan on coming in two weeks?"

"Two weeks? Okay." *Why is this so easy for him?* It had been settled before I even looked up. I recalled what my dad told me a few years earlier when we first met. "Chris, there's nothing wrong with living in a small town, but it's good to move away, travel around to see what's out there. And if you choose to come back and settle down in that small town, at least it won't be by default." *I'm scared. Me and my big mouth.*

When I hung up the phone, I hesitantly filled Maggie in on my recent *decision.* I hadn't even asked her. She smiled and looked a bit taken aback, but responded with, "Well, if that's what you want to do, I support you." If she was hurt or disappointed, she never showed it, and I secretly prayed that she wasn't. The ease in her voice gave me peace. *If it doesn't work out, I'll come back.*

The two weeks before I left were a whirlwind of packing, goodbyes, and trying to manage the myriad of emotions filling my head.

Excitement. Fear. Sadness. Hope.

My fears disappeared once I arrived in California. Day by day, I watched and followed as I slowly learned what life would be like with Pa, Dodie, and Carrie Jo.

The kitchen and game room were the main hangouts for everyone. Dodie loved to sit at the kitchen table to do her nails and pay bills as she talked to whoever was in the room. She puffed on one cigarette after another, holding it carefully between her fingers, as not to mess up the wet polish. Carrie Jo and I played pool, listened to music, and chatted as though we had grown up together.

Pa often stood in the kitchen sipping on Jack Daniels mixed with Coke as he talked to us through the opening between the kitchen and game room. I learned Pa was smart and had a sense of humor, although at times his humor seemed dry and that made him funnier. He enjoyed long deep conversations, his thoughts were layered, and he spoke sincerely about various topics. I occasionally found myself lost in the conversation, so I focused on his warm tone.

He had strong opinions, and I didn't know enough to argue with him most of the time, so I went along with whatever he said. The anger I felt when I first met him had eased. I decided since he was my dad, I wanted to get to know him better. And for him to know me. I wasn't ready to tell him everything Jack did to me. I wasn't sure if I would ever be ready for that.

Somewhere in the beginning months of living there, Pa tapped on my bedroom door.

"I want to talk about when you and Lane were little. I want to tell you my side of the story."

Am I ready for this? Jack told me my dad didn't want us. Mama never corrected him. Lane and I were expected to believe them. Questions weren't permitted. And my dad's side of the story didn't matter.

Now I sat in front of my biological dad, and he was ready to talk. I prepared to listen.

Pa was honest and open, even when his own words caused his voice to crack. I was free to ask questions, and he answered them as well as his memory allowed.

Pa was a year older than Mama when they met at the movie theater where Mama worked behind the ticket counter. They dated and learned they each had a difficult home life. For Pa, it was the combination of being poor and not having a father since he was ten.

His father had been killed in the Korean War, and Pa carried the pressure of helping his family without the guidance or example of a father.

"Your mom's family was also poor. And a bit dysfunctional." I had never thought of our family as dysfunctional. To me they were normal.

"I was moving up the corporate ladder with K-Mart. Making good money." I nodded and listened.

"We thought we could escape our home lives by getting married, so we went to the Justice of the Peace." I wondered what could be so bad at home that Mama wanted to escape.

"But since your mom was only seventeen, she had to have parental consent—unless she was pregnant." *I'm seventeen*. It was hard to imagine Mama being my age.

"So, we lied and said she was pregnant, and after a brief ceremony, we walked out with a signed marriage license. But we never filed the license with the courthouse to make it official."

"What? Why not?"

Pa let out a sigh and looked at his lap.

"Because we really didn't want to get married."

His words sent a wave of sadness into my heart, a small death to the imagined love affair I had always hung on to. I wanted them to love each other. At least in the beginning.

"We showed the license to our parents, packed our things, and moved into our own place. Lane was born shortly after." Pa's next promotion took them to Joliet, IL, where I was born a few months later. Pa said the problems between Mama and him began when he started traveling more heavily with his work and only being home on weekends.

"I was young and naïve. I thought as long as I sent money to your mom, I was being responsible. I didn't know she was lonely and overwhelmed with two small children and no family around." Pa's eyes moistened. "All that traveling with my job is something I truly regret."

Another promotion took them to Colorado, and by then their relationship was diminishing, as Pa's work travel only increased. While living in Colorado, Mama made the decision to leave him. She took Lane and me back to Arkansas, where she enrolled in a nursing program to become a registered nurse. She rented the little house on 14th street, where I still see myself sitting backward on the couch, looking out the window as I waited for the mailman to deliver a box from a father I didn't know.

"I should have been there," Pa said. "No wonder she left. She needed help." There was nothing I could say. I nodded and listened. "I stayed in contact with your mom. I sent checks every month. I sent gifts to you and Lane."

"Barbies and a G.I. Joe." I wanted him to know I remembered the gifts.

"Yes. And I sent cowboy boots to Lane." Pa's eyes filled. His lip quivered. "Every time I came into town, I came by to see you kids." *He came to see us?* "But your mom had a new boyfriend and wouldn't let me see you and Lane."

"Jack?" My gut stirred just speaking his name.

"Yes. She told me Jack would take care of you kids, and I couldn't see you. I kept sending checks, but she started sending them back."

My heart sunk. *My dad tried to see us.*

"One time, I drove past the house on 14th Street, and you, Lane, Pam, and Theresa were playing in the front yard. Pam was wearing the boots I sent Lane." I pictured Lane and me playing outside with our cousins like we did so many times. *And he drove past. He saw us playing.* A glimpse of reality that didn't fit with what Jack had always told us.

"Then I got a letter. From Jack." *What?* "Jack wrote me a letter and said he wanted to marry your mom, adopt you kids, and raise you as his own. He said he loved you, and only needed my written consent."

My brain went crazy. "He never adopted us! He abused us!"

Pa hung his head. "I know." He wiped his eyes. "I'm so sorry."

My body shook with overwhelming anger. I thought I might choke on the pain in my throat. The evil of that man to say such a noble thing—that he loved us two kids and wanted to adopt us, only to turn around and give us a life of abuse and neglect. An evil I struggled to comprehend. Yet I did. Because I lived it.

"So, you read Jack's letter. Then what?"

"Like I said, I believed it. Jack's letter sounded official. I was afraid I would cause too much disruption in your lives. I wrote back."

Did Pa just say he wrote back to Jack? My mind spun. *No one ever told me this.*

"I told Jack if he could take care of my kids, then he had my blessing to adopt them." Pa's words nearly stopped my heart. My eyes widened. My mouth opened.

He gave us to Jack? Who gives their kids to someone else?

"But I didn't know…" Pa buried his face in his hands. He raised his eyes to meet mine. "I'm so sorry." His chest heaved. His chin shivered. His eyes pleaded. "I thought he was going to adopt you. I thought you'd be okay."

For a moment I had no words, no thoughts, just numbness. I saw Pa's brokenness too. I felt his sorrow, his pain. I knew if he could go back, he would change things. How could he have known what Jack was really like? And though I understood Pa did what he thought was best at the time, it hurt terribly that he could let go of us.

Jack never adopted us. I don't know for sure if he and Mama ever married, even though they said they did. All I know is that from that point on, Lane and I went by the last name of Payton because that's what Mama and Jack told us to do.

Eventually, Pa met another woman, moved to California, and shortly after that, Carrie Jo was born. He said he talked to Mama occasionally throughout the years when he called to see how Lane and I were doing. Mama assured him we were fine, all was well, and everyone was happy. What else was she supposed to say? The truth would have been unbelievable.

I drifted into a wish. What if Mama had said the truth instead? What would it sound like? *Actually, my husband is a controlling, abusive man with an addiction to sex. You should see his porn magazine collection. We even do that wife-swapping thing. Jack really likes that. He doesn't allow us to talk about you, and he never got around to adopting the kids. In fact, he's the one who told me to stop talking to you or accepting any more child support. Oh, and guess what? He mistreats the kids too. He's got Lane on a pedestal so he can control him and let me tell you about Chris. Jack just can't seem to keep his hands off her. Of course, he does it all in private, like the bruises on my arms and legs. But hey, they go by his last name, and I've got lots of good stories to cover up the truth, so no one will ever really know. So, yes, all is well.*

Pa had no idea.

36

Disillusion

MY SENIOR YEAR of high school in California could be described as culture shock. I went from a small rural high school, where everybody knew everybody, to a school with more students than the town that I was from. Lifestyles were drastically different. High schoolers there were not shy about having sex, drinking, smoking, doing drugs, partying, or anything else they wanted to do.

I made a few acquaintances, and Carrie Jo was my only real friend. Depression followed me to California, making school, and life, a daily gruel. By Christmas, I wanted to go back home to Oklahoma. I approached Pa and told him how I felt even though I hated saying the words.

"I want to go home."

"You haven't given it enough time." I hadn't expected that response.

"I miss Oklahoma. I miss Maggie and Uncle Jimmy. And my friends." I had kept in touch with people back home, mostly with letters.

"Give it more time. At least finish out your spring classes."

I held back the tears. Pa got up from the table. My heart sank. I was eighteen and could leave, but I still desperately needed my dad's approval. I wouldn't have it if I went.

After graduation from my senior year, I enrolled in community college. My depression lifted again as I began classes. *College.* Something I thought I wouldn't get to do. There was more freedom in college and less peer pressure. I had no idea what kind of degree I wanted, so I started with the basic class requirements.

I began to date more, got to know Pa better, and spent more time at the beach, which became my favorite place. I loved the sound of the waves crashing over themselves and rolling onto the sand. I delighted in the warmth of the wooden piers beneath my feet as I walked to the end, listening to seagulls above my head. I took in deep breaths of salty air as I watched the surfers ride the waves, crash, and paddle out to do it again. *They're not afraid of the water.* At the beach, all my senses came alive, giving me feelings I never knew existed. *Maybe California will work out after all.*

There were plenty of other distractions, making it easy to forget about going back to Oklahoma. Instead of validating my true feelings, I pushed them away. I learned to avoid and deny anything that I didn't know how to handle. *Forget Oklahoma. Forget the past. Move on.* That's what I was supposed to say, right?

A friend of Dodie's offered me a job at a men's upscale clothing store, which introduced me to a wide array of people. Some were rich, thinking nothing of buying ten suits at a time, then spending hours in front of the mirror while the seamstress pinned and tucked, then instructed them to come back in ten days to pick up the altered pieces.

There were men with women half their age hanging on their arms like a decoration. Some of the men spoke with accents and tried to pour on the charm. I was usually unimpressed and didn't hesitate to show it. There were college guys who needed just one good suit to hang in their closet, just in case. There were men who needed a suit for a special occasion and never planned to wear it again. That baffled me. *Why would someone spend that much money and not wear it for the rest of their life?* It was interesting to see how others in this world lived, to meet men who seemed nothing like Jack, but were still unimpressive to me.

Getting asked out on a date wasn't a problem. I often accepted, but rarely looked forward to it. At the time, I didn't realize I looked at men through an impossible lens. None of them were good enough because all of them were pigs, and it was only a matter of time before any one of them would hurt me. If I didn't like them, I simply didn't go out with them again. But if I did like them, I dated them for a while, then dumped them before they hurt me.

I didn't enjoy my job but liked college. I still didn't know what I wanted to do. I was still conditioned to accept what was in front of me as if I didn't have choices.

Occasionally, I was asked to work at the warehouse in Los Angeles, and to a country girl, it was an entirely different planet. Six lanes of traffic each way, bumper to bumper. People from all over the world. The change excited me.

Parts of Los Angeles were decorated with skyscrapers, sparkling buildings, pristine sidewalks, and perfectly groomed dogs on leashes. Other parts of the city were covered with trash, graffiti, and scary people.

And the *cars*. Cars like nothing I'd ever seen, with names I couldn't pronounce. Once, I stood outside of Warner Brothers Studios, admiring the Lamborghinis and Ferraris parked in the giant circle drive in front of the building. A very eccentric man in a suit approached me and informed me that looking at the cars was *frowned upon,* and with his tightly pronounced words, asked me to leave.

I vowed that day that I would never be like that.

When describing Pa and Dodie to others, I usually said something like, "They are awesome. They like to have *the band* over and throw parties. Very laid back and funny." I referred to the pool parties they sometimes hosted, usually on the Fourth of July, that included a lot of drinking, loud music, Pa getting thrown into the pool fully clothed, and the passed-out guests laying on the stair landing or underneath the pool table.

To a teenager, this seemed just good ole fun, and not enough parents knew how to have fun. They even allowed Carrie Jo and me to drink. What could be cooler than that? I dismissed the nightly arguments between Pa and Dodie as, "They aren't afraid to express themselves."

Pa and Dodie were different people in the daytime. Pa always said, "Dodie really does have a good heart, even though she acts like a bitch."

I wondered if he said that to us in case we heard the nightly yelling. I chalked it all up to "This is just how Californians are." They both poured drinks as soon as they got home from work each day, and by the time they went to bed, they had drunk a few more.

On the weekends, Dodie lived next to the pool—tanning and drinking.

Pa showed me how to mix his Jack and Coke, so he could occasionally ask me to do it for him. He loved projects in the yard when he wasn't studying horse race statistics or doing something on his computer. One summer, I helped him install a putting green complete with a sprinkler system in the backyard.

He also showed me how to take care of the pool. I loved anything that was outside near water—any water. I never understood my love for water when I couldn't even swim. *Something's still wrong with me.*

Nothing around me or inside of me kept stable. I continually changed classes, boyfriends, and jobs. Nothing felt right. Nothing made me happy. Although Carrie Jo and I grew closer, Pa and Dodie continued to drink, smoke, curse, and argue. Their nightly fights became screaming matches—louder, harsher, and longer. I began to wonder where I fit in, or why I was there. Carrie Jo and I couldn't help but hear most of it. We often looked at each other when the screaming in the other room was intense, as if to say, "Yes, I hear it."

It became apparent that Dodie was unhappy with Pa, and she didn't hold back, screaming cruel and cutting words. Pa didn't hesitate to respond in his own defense. Sometimes I sat in my room wishing Pa would just stop talking so maybe Dodie would run out of things to say.

"Dodie is such a bitch," Carrie Jo would say, then seemed to ignore their shouting.

"I know. Wish she didn't treat Pa like that." I wanted to believe what Pa said, that Dodie had a good heart. I tried hard to see it.

"She's always been like that."

It was difficult for me to put the fighting between Pa and Dodie into perspective. Pa didn't hit Dodie or kick her out like Jack always did. With Jack and Mama, the fighting created fear in me. Fear of Mama getting hurt. Fear of getting kicked out again. With Pa and Dodie, I was confused and leaned on Carrie's lackadaisical attitude as a way to deal with it. But the fighting in both sets of parents created layers of anxiety that would last years.

I learned from their arguments that Dodie never wanted me to live with them. I had always thought they both wanted me there, but I heard Dodie yell one night, "I'll bet you've spent a thousand dollars on her since you met her! And I'd pay a thousand dollars to send her back home! Just send her back home!"

I fought back tears and closed my eyes. *Somebody else who doesn't want me.* I knew the plane tickets to California were expensive. And there were two outfits Pa bought me last summer when I visited. But I didn't know the money had been a problem with Dodie. Guilt spread over me. Dodie always seemed nice to me during the daytime when she was sober. Then a stab in the heart, as Dodie continued yelling. "I didn't even know you had other kids!"

What? He never told his wife about us? Who gets married and doesn't tell their spouse about their kids?

Flashes of the various stories Pa told me about his life ran through my mind. Sailing on his boat, playing golf, riding his motorcycle, building a new home, raising Carrie Jo, and marrying Dodie.

He really did move on without Lane and me. He really gave us up. I wanted to yank the knife out of my heart. *No. He's a good guy. He's sorry. He loves me now.* I needed those things to be true.

Pa and Dodie's fighting intensified, and so did their drinking. Their mutual disdain was obvious as they stood at the kitchen counter, poured drinks, and snarled words at each other. At one point, they stopped talking to one another, and instead, wrote notes back and forth, sealed them in an envelope, and stuck it to the refrigerator.

This went on for two weeks until Pa announced he bought a used van and planned to live in it in the driveway. He drove the van to work every day, and eventually got pulled over and received a DUI. His consequences included a mandate to attend Alcoholics Anonymous. He moved back into the house, and the arguments died down, and so did Pa's drinking. But not Dodie's.

I was relieved and welcomed the new calm, but I still didn't understand that life. I knew deep inside, I still wanted to go home.

After living with him for a year and a half, I felt ready to leave, even if he didn't want me to. I loved him, and I wanted him in my life, but I didn't want to live there anymore. I had no regrets about going there, getting to know him, talking with him, and hearing his side of many stories.

It had been necessary for me to experience life with my dad, live in his house, and taste the new life he created after he and Mama split. It was necessary for me to establish a relationship with him, and to be able to say I now have a dad, a real dad. Then and now, I am extremely grateful that I got to know my sister Carrie Jo and experience some life with her. I didn't want that to end.

I learned a lot from living there, more than I would ever have simply by hearing stories. I moved to California with secret hopes that somehow getting to know my biological father would heal all the wounds and pain of the past—it healed *some* of them, a few of them, but a lot of damage still layered underneath the surface. I needed to go home again if there would be any chance to heal the next layer.

I don't know if I was running from something, or to something, or both. All I knew was that my dad wasn't perfect, his life wasn't perfect, but I saw his heart, and it was good. I also knew that I needed to go back home.

It hurt my dad deeply when I left. He didn't understand, and I didn't know how to fully explain. I couldn't even make sense of it myself at that time. I acted on a *knowing* deep inside of me—instinct maybe. It hurts me to this day that I hurt my dad by leaving. But it was the right thing to do. I had to keep healing.

37

I Am Not Powerless

AS I DROVE home from California, I imagined returning to the same world I had left only eighteen months earlier. I pictured several exciting "Surprise! I'm back!" reunions complete with hugs and laughter. I thought since I had settled some of my emotional issues about my dad, and experienced so many new things in California, I would come back a stronger, more evolved person and life would be better than ever. I hadn't even told anyone I was coming back. I just showed up.

But the life I had left in Oklahoma was no longer there.

People had gone on with their lives. Friends had gone off to college or gotten married. My old boyfriend had a new girlfriend. Maggie and Uncle Jimmy moved to a small house in town. Julie was eleven now. Pam had moved out, married, and had a baby. And Theresa had gotten married, had a baby, then separated from her husband and moved back in. The new house was tiny, with barely room enough for all of them and certainly no room for me.

Grandma and Grandpa still lived out at the farm, and Grandpa's Parkinson's was worse than ever. Maggie offered me their old trailer if I wanted to fix it up. "Grandma will enjoy the company," she said. The poor condition of the trailer overwhelmed me, but I was determined to make it my home.

I got my old job back at the grocery store but working there was miserable as the only opening was in the meat department, cutting and wrapping raw meat.

I felt alone again. Left behind, even though I had chosen to leave. I wanted familiarity back. *Did I make a mistake? Should I have stayed in California?*

I kept in contact with my dad, but the guilt of leaving him festered. I wondered how long it would take him to forgive me. *I'm such a loser.*

Now nineteen, a college dropout, I worked a job I hated, and lived in a dumpy trailer, with no sense of belonging or direction. *I blew it by leaving, and I blew it by coming back.*

Depression swooped in quickly, and I became utterly lost again.

I did find one friend from high school, Donna, still single and living in the area with her parents. I clung to her. I needed her.

It had been two years since I saw Lane. He had moved further into his new life with his new family, and it felt like he was a million miles away. I didn't know where he lived or how to reach him.

I decided to visit Mama. I didn't want to see Jack, but I knew I would have to, to get to Mama. My search for direction and some sort of comfort had me nearly desperate. Was I thinking straight? The little girl inside of me still bled, still hoped she'd eventually find a warm place back in Mama's heart. *Maybe after all these years, something will be different.* I didn't really believe that, but it was easier to hope than to let her go.

I needed to hope.

And there was Becky, who was four years old when I was removed from our home. Seven years had passed, and I wondered what she was like now. Had Jack abused her too? *Maybe I can get to know her. She is still my sister.*

Mama, Jack, and Becky lived in an apartment in Van Buren, behind the nursing home where Mama worked. After only a few visits with Mama, I realized virtually nothing had changed. There were several framed photos of Mama throughout their bedroom, dressed in nearly nothing, posing explicitly. Stacks of pornographic magazines and pamphlets from the swingers' clubs laid in plain sight.

Jack still controlled everything, and Mama still sported bruises. I hurt for Becky. I asked her safe questions, careful not to suggest anything.

"You doing okay?" "Things here at home okay?" "Are you happy?" Becky answered everything with "Yes." We weren't as close as Lane and I had been. We hadn't had a chance to be. *Would she tell me if he had abused her too?* I prayed she would.

My friend Donna and I spent a lot of time together, usually at her house. When we weren't hanging out in her bedroom, we were at her brother's baseball games or cruising Grand Avenue on Friday nights.

One day after I spent the night at Donna's house, I went to pick up Becky. Jack had given her twenty dollars, and we were going to Walmart. I tolerated the discomfort of being in the same room with him, ready to flee as quickly as I could. I sat at the kitchen table waiting for Becky to be ready to leave. Jack started talking.

"Chris, I want you to know I've been informed you spent the night at a boy's house last night." His eyebrows were raised, and his chin pulled back into his neck. He seemed proud of himself for being so clever.

A wave of disgust squeezed my stomach. I glared at his contemptuous face. Seconds passed as I absorbed his words. *A boy's house? Someone has informed him? He's following me?* My adrenaline pumped. *He's still a liar.* That voice in my head threatened a subtle attack. *You're powerless.*

No, I'm not. Did I just think that?

I'm not powerless. My eyes turned away from Jack. *Where did that come from?*

Since when did I dispute the voice inside of me? Were there two voices? Did I dare think I had power when it came to Jack? A sudden realization sent courage through my veins. *I can walk out of here, and he can't do anything.*

Returning my eyes to Jack, I spoke clearly. "No, that's not true. I was at my friend Donna's house." The confidence in my voice surprised me. My adrenaline surged, but I wasn't numb. *Why am I not numb?* I was talking to Jack, being confronted by him, standing up to him, and I wasn't numb. Still the voice in my head prodded. *You can't win.* I knew he was lying because I knew where I was. Typical Jack.

Jack's lips pressed together. His nose flared as he sat up in his chair, never taking his eyes off me. "The person that told me this wouldn't lie." His eyes filled with anger.

So did mine. Did I dare dispute what Jack said? Courage formed despite my wild nerves. I realized for the first time in my life, I was not even tempted to back down.

I don't have to play his game. There was that other voice again. "Well, if someone did tell you that, they were lying."

I locked my eyes to Jack's. *He must see that I'm not afraid.* Even though I was.

Jack stirred in his seat. "Now Chris Ann."

Oh, Chris Ann. Here. We. Go. I braced myself.

Jack ranted that his *informant* was an *upstanding individual*, and had no reason to lie, and I needed to watch my behavior because I might damage my mother's reputation by spending the night with boys and all. Yes, he said that.

Then Mama chimed in. *Mama's talking? Is she allowed to have an opinion?* Apparently she was, if it was the same as Jack's.

"Chris, this is a small town." Mama's clenched jaw and wandering eyes exposed her self-doubt. But she kept being obedient. "If you spend the night with boys, word will get around, and I could lose my job at the nursing home."

Mama's words were absurd, but they still hurt. Not because I believed them, but because she was standing by a man who was lying. A man who still abused her. A man who had raped her daughter.

"Mama, I didn't spend the night with a boy." The legs of my chair angrily scooted away from the table. I stood, picked up my purse, and cast my eyes at Jack.

His folded arms moved up and down with his heaving chest, and his face looked red enough to explode.

I glanced back at Mama. She wasn't wearing her usual awkward smile. She tilted her head, pressed her lips together, and widened her eyes. *She wants me to back off.*

I'm sorry Mama, I can't. My eyes went back to Jack. Then came the voices in my head.

You're powerless.

No, I'm not.

You're going numb.

No, I'm not.

You're guilty.

No, I'm not.

"Jack." My voice was clear. "You're lying. And I won't be bullied by your lies anymore." *Oh my gosh! Oh my gosh! Oh my gosh!* I couldn't believe I said that. *Stay calm.*

"Becky, we'll go another time." I wished I could take her with me.

I pushed my chair underneath the table, walked to the front door, and left. My feet couldn't get to my car fast enough. Fumbling with my keys to unlock the door, I finally became numb. *Don't look back.*

The engine started, I threw the car into drive and pulled out of the parking lot. I didn't know where I was headed, just that I had to keep going.

Was that really necessary? That voice again. *Did you have to be so dramatic?* Guilt. Had I just stood up to Jack? Had I called him a bully?

They're laughing at you.

He was lying about me.

You're a joke.

No, I'm not. He was lying about me.

Nobody believes you.

I believe me.

I drove to my run-down trailer at the farm. My purse fell to the floor as soon as I opened the door, and I ran to my bed. My face touched the pillow and my eyes burst, sending me into an unexpected sea of emotions. I cried from the pain. I screamed from the anger. I buried my face in agony, engulfed in bitterness and confusion.

When my body exhausted, I rolled over for air. My mind and body were limp. The ceiling fan blew my wet face. I watched the chain swirl in the air as the blades turned. When my breathing calmed, I felt my forehead slowly wrinkle with a weighty thought.

That voice in my head…it lies.

38

Last Visit with Mama

I PAID ONE last visit to Mama at her apartment. Jack was at work and Becky at school. Mama and I sat on the couch as she folded laundry, and I searched for something to say. The noise of the television filled the moments between our glances back and forth.

"When's Becky gonna be here?" Somebody needed to say something. Mama didn't answer. Her eyes were miles away.

"Chrissy, if you ever want to talk about anything, I'm here for you." Mama's words nearly choked me. *Did she really say that? She called me Chrissy. Chrissy* came from a different place in her heart than *Chris. She's here for me?* Mama had never said that before.

Why did she say that? This mom never noticed my dirty hair or bleeding lips. The mom who dragged us back to Jack *every single time* he kicked us out. The mom who stayed by our abusers' side. The mom who fled from Jack many years ago because he threatened to kill her but couldn't muster the courage to flee him after he sexually abused her daughter.

Now she's here for me?

This mom gave me away. I doubted she meant it. But I wanted to hope.

"Anything?" I looked at Mama's face. She almost looked willing.

"Yes, anything." Mama closed her eyes, then opened them. She displayed a smile of satisfaction, as though she had done what all good moms do—offer to be there for their children.

"Well, there *is* something I've been wanting to ask you for a long time."

Mama straightened her back. "Chrissy, you can ask me anything."

"Why did you give me up?"

"What?" Mama's demeanor changed in an instant. *Oh—I guess that's not what she meant.* Mama's smile disappeared, and she looked the other way. "Not *that*. I didn't mean *that*."

"Why not?" I allowed my hurt to be heard in my voice. *I need her to respond.* My eyes pleaded even though Mama wouldn't look at me. *Please talk to me, Mama. Please.* We sat silent for several seconds, then she turned to me and spoke.

"I gave you up because I knew it wouldn't be fair to make you live there."

I pondered her words. *What does that mean?*

"It wouldn't have been fair to make you live there with *him*." Mama's head hung in front of me. Then she looked away.

My mind froze. *Did Mama just tell me she believed me?* Did she just acknowledge Jack had abused me?

My lips were paralyzed as Mama's words stood in front of me. My arms wanted to embrace her and say *thank you for believing me.* My heart wanted to scream, *why didn't you help me?* She was the one person who could have helped me and *should* have. But she didn't.

Silence.

"I knew you'd be okay."

We stared at the television. The tone in Mama's voice seemed hopeful. *She wants me to believe her.*

More questions flooded my thoughts. Had Mama really thought about me after I disappeared? Had she cared? Had her heart really gone there, even if only for a moment? Why couldn't she tell me *then? I wasn't okay!*

The television screen blurred in my vision, and the sound faded. *She doesn't know how much I needed her. Should I scream my questions? Make her answer?*

I had been broken for years, yet Mama's words broke a new part of me. Apparently, she cared a little. But I didn't get to feel it.

The weather channel came on, and we both watched. A familiar pain bled in my heart—that little girl inside of me, tortured and thrown out. Abandoned, alone, and scared for years. The anguishing aftermath was still not over. Then came anger.

My mind repeated Mama's words. *It wouldn't have been fair to make you live here—with him.* Had she always believed me? Did she believe me when the authorities took me away the first time? What about the second time? Did she believe me when I told her that bag of condoms came from Jack?

As quickly as Mama allowed a tiny crack to open up, she shut back down. I had to leave her apartment before I burst.

"I better go."

"Okay."

The numbness didn't wear off until the next day. I had my Mama for a few seconds, the Mama I knew from many years ago. The one who saw me. Was it fear that snatched her back? Shame? Denial?

Grief set in. *That's all I'm gonna get.* Mama was gone and didn't know how to come back. I cried for the little girl inside of me. I cried for me. I cried for the years I'd been in battle. I cried for the sorrow in my soul and wondered why it had to be that way.

Depression held me down while deep loss smothered me.

I'm so tired. I needed new help, but I didn't know where to get it. I wanted to belong someplace. I wanted someone to love me, and something to fill the void. I was stranded in the middle of my personal war zone.

I had to stop going to Mama and Jack's apartment. It was too toxic there. I wondered about Becky again. *If she's getting abused, will Mama protect her?* Should I send someone to check on her? A social worker?

Eventually, Mama sent a message through Maggie for me to stay away. I was too much trouble. I've always wondered if my presence made it hard for Mama to face the truth, or if it was Jack who couldn't deal with it.

Regardless, I had to move on. I had to keep healing.

39

Mama's Dying

IN MY DREAMS, I would meet a guy who was emotionally healthy, mentally strong, stable, and safe. An honest and loyal guy who accepted, respected, and loved me—all of me. I wanted a guy who didn't regard me as damaged goods or unworthy—the way I saw myself. How free I could be, to love and bond with a guy like that.

But guys like that don't want girls like me.

I married my first husband out of fear of being alone. He had been abused as a child, and together we were a disaster. Two unhealed, unstable people, together for the wrong reasons. He joined the Army when we found out I was pregnant, and we stayed with his mother until he finished boot camp. It was an awkward haven.

I have relived the emotions from my pregnancy many times throughout the years. Never had I felt such excitement or such fear of failure. Having a baby was a privilege I didn't think I deserved. I loved her from the moment I knew she existed. But could I be a good mom? Was I worthy?

You don't know how to be a mom.

I will learn.

You don't have anything to offer.

I love my baby.

You're not enough.

I will devote my life to her.

She deserves more than you.

I worried nightly. *What if I'm not a good mother? What if I can't make her feel loved? What if I can't protect her? What if I fail her as Mama failed me?*

I had nightmares about losing my baby in deep dark water. I stood frozen at the edge because I couldn't swim. I couldn't save my baby. The nightmares punched me in the gut and haunted me for years, even after my daughter was born, as did the voice in my head. *She's not safe with you. You'll lose her.*

I'll keep her safe. I love her. I took care of Becky when I was only a kid.

When I wasn't worrying myself sick, I loved my baby more than myself and believed my love could be enough to make her happy and keep her safe. I caught myself laughing and loving the way pregnancy felt. *When did I stop laughing?*

When I saw my daughter for the first time, the love inside of me swelled into something I had never felt before. Bliss and disbelief that she was mine. *There must be a God, to give me such a precious gift.*

As I attempted to be the perfect mother, my confidence faded and I struggled with what "normal" looked like. What did her crying mean? She's unhappy. Why won't she eat? Something's wrong. Why does she keep spitting up? She's sick. Why won't this diaper rash go away? *I'm stupid.* Am I holding her enough or too much? *I'm failing.*

"You're crazy. A basket case. Emotionally unstable." My husband's words were cold.

I hadn't learned much about healthy child-rearing, and as my daughter grew, I didn't know if I was doing it right. In my wounded mind, crying always meant pain or sadness, so I jumped at every sign of discomfort my daughter displayed. *Keep her happy so she'll feel loved.*

I knew abuse and neglect were wrong, and love and protection were right, but I was still blind to many of the gray areas. The areas where security, understanding, values, and trust are developed. The areas where parents do things intentionally to teach, discipline, help, and grow their children into happy balanced humans. I loved my daughter deeply, but it didn't feel like love was enough. Like I was enough.

The Army moved us to Germany, where we rented a one-bedroom apartment three miles from the military base. After only two months of being there, I received a call from Maggie.

"Chris, your mama's in the hospital. She's got cancer." Maggie's words were deafening.

Not Mama.

"The doctors say she's terminal."

The room darkened around my mind. Like—days? Weeks? Months? What does terminal mean? Mama can't die.

"You there?"

"Yes, I'm here."

"Okay, well, I knew you'd want to know."

"Okay. I'm coming."

We arranged to fly back home for thirty days. After paying the rent, we barely had enough to buy two round-trip tickets. Luckily my daughter could sit on my lap. Upon arrival, I wasted no time getting to the hospital. I wanted to see Mama.

Jack's eyes widened when I walked into the room. *Ignore him.* Family members stood around the walls chatting but became quiet when they saw me.

My eyes met Mama's, and my heart was unprepared. Her body was tinier than I had ever seen it. She barely had hair. Her dark yellow skin drooped against her protruding cheekbones. Dried blood stuck to her cracked lips, and her eyes were disappearing.

Jack stepped between me and the hospital bed. *Of course.*

I painted on a smile and whispered "Hi, Mama" from the doorway. Light chatter began to fill the room again.

Mama braved a smile.

Oh, Mama. How did this happen? The last time I saw her, she was plump with a head full of dark brown hair. *Why didn't anyone tell me?*

Amid the chattering, Jack changed the scene. "Honey, are you tired? Do you want to rest?" He leaned awkwardly over Mama and glanced around the room.

His forged expression of concern for Mama curled my insides. Jack clumsily straightened Mama's blanket and adjusted her pillow. *What a performance.*

Jack looked around the room again. "I'm sure she's tired." One by one, visitors left, and it was obvious I wasn't going to get a moment with Mama.

"You're tired, aren't you, honey?" Jack looked at Mama and nodded his head until Mama responded.

Mama looked at me, then back at Jack. "Yes."

Still obedient.

Over the next few days, I called Mama's hospital room, hoping to catch her alone. Jack always answered and spoke in his matter-of-fact *I'm in charge* tone.

"Your mother is resting."

"I want to see her."

"She doesn't want visitors." *Sure she doesn't—like the other day when the room was full, and Mama was smiling?*

One by one, I spoke to various family members who had witnessed disturbing moments since Mama's battle with cancer started. Many of them received phone calls from Mama because Jack had dropped her off somewhere and never came back to get her.

While one relative kept Mama company in her hospital room, the phone rang. Jack worked out of town during the week but called Mama for updates. Although this family member only heard Mama's side of the conversation, the picture was clear.

"Jack, the doctor came in," Mama spoke carefully. "No... No, I'm not going to make anything up, I promise. He said it has spread."

Mama's face grew pale as she listened. A tear fell to her hospital gown. "Jack, I'm not making it up. The doctor said it's everywhere."

She paused, then spoke again. "No... I'm not... Jack, I'm not..." Tears flowed as Mama held the phone with one hand and clutched her blanket with the other. "Jack, I'm not feeding you a bunch of crap, I promise."

Mama stared into the air as Jack's muffled voice dominated.

"Okay... Okay... Okay, I won't do it again." Mama hung up the phone.

Sometimes the facts are hard enough to think about and even harder to utter. Even as she lay dying in the hospital, Jack continued to verbally and emotionally abuse her.

Another family member stopped by Mama and Jack's apartment to check on Mama. Jack opened the door then returned to the couch where he watched television. The family member discovered Mama crawling in the hallway and rushed to her. "What are you doing?"

"I have to go to the bathroom." Mama was barely able to look up.

That relative helped Mama to the bathroom and back to bed. As she left, Jack said to her, "This cancer crap is all in her head."

When she opened the front door, Jack added, "Hey, if you see that Chris Ann, tell her the statute of limitations is up." He slammed the door behind her.

Jack told another relative who visited Mama's hospital room, "If Chris tries to come up here, I'll call security and have her thrown out." This relative wasn't intimidated by him.

"Jack, if Chris wants to see her mother, she should be allowed to see her." After several more minutes of Jack's ranting, my relative put an end to his words. "Jack, if Chris comes up here, and you call security, I will turn you in for smoking in the hospital bathroom."

Jack closed his mouth after that.

People reported seeing Mama crawling up the outside steps to their apartment because she was too weak to walk up.

Another story from a relative who frequently checked on Mama told me of one day she went to the apartment. Jack had been there for the weekend, but returned to his out-of-town job, and Becky was at school. Mama answered the door, then quickly retreated to another room. Her bruises were big and dark and shone right through her clothes.

"What happened? How did you get those bruises?"

Mama looked away, but muttered, "It's something I don't want to talk about."

"Did that happen from one of the procedures at the hospital? Did someone *do* that to you?" It wasn't the only time she had seen bruises on Mama.

Mama hid the ugly truth. But no one was ever fooled.

I WOKE UP in the morning to the sound of my daughter stirring in her crib. The smell of bacon lingered from my mother-in-law's kitchen. The recent heartbreaking accounts of Mama getting abused weaved heaviness and pain with anger. Only seven more days before our flight back to Germany.

I don't wanna be nice anymore. I had to see Mama.

I took my daughter to her playpen in the living room, picked up the phone, and dialed.

"Hello." Jack's voice was unsuspecting. I usually didn't call that early in the morning and regretted calling at all. *Should've just gone up there.*

"Jack, I will be seeing my mother today."

"Oh no, you won't. She'll be sleeping." His tone turned defensive.

"Yes, Jack, I will." *That felt good.* "I will be coming up there to see my mother, and you have nothing to say about it."

"No, you won't!" Jack's voice cracked. "I'll call security."

"I am not intimidated by you anymore." *Oh my gosh! I said that!* "You don't control me anymore." *And that too!* Unfamiliar confidence arose inside of me.

"Jack, I don't buy your act for one second. You may be able to control my mother, but your days of controlling me are over, you S.O.B." *Oh no, where did that come from?* "And I don't care that the statute of limitations is up. You know what you did." I hung up the phone.

The television was the only sound in the room. My husband stared at me. His mother stood holding her empty breakfast plate. My daughter pushed buttons on her musical toy.

"I'm going to see my mama."

My nerves still quivered as I stopped at a pharmacy on the way. *Mama needs ointment for her lips.*

As I approached the door to Mama's room, I gripped the ointment and rehearsed. *I should have at least two minutes before security gets here. Tell Mama I love her, and I've been trying to see her for days. Smile real big and hand her the ointment as security escorts me out. At least she'll know I care.*

Jack couldn't be on both sides of the bed at the same time. *I'll kiss her forehead if I can.*

Alone in the dim room, Mama sat in bed with a pen and notepad in her hands. *This will be easier than I thought.*

"Hey, Mama." My feet hurried toward her. *Finally.* But Mama stunned me with her words.

"Chris, you can't be here."

My face faded. "What do you mean?"

"You can't be here. You need to leave."

I hadn't misunderstood. My throat lumped. "Mama, I came to see you. I've been trying to see you for days."

Her head tilted forward, and her eyes were big. "You have to leave because of the way you spoke to Jack on the phone."

"Mama, I came from Germany to see you." My heart cracked. I took a few steps and held out the lip ointment. "I brought you this." *Am I choking?*

"I could hear you over the phone, and because of the way you spoke to him, you have to leave." Mama didn't move. *Is this my mama? We finally had a chance to visit alone. No, this is Jack. Coward got Mama to do his dirty work.*

I tried one more time. "Mama, I just want to see you."

"You have to leave. Now." She looked away. I looked at the floor. There was nothing else to say.

I walked out. *It's over. Jack won.* Hatred seeped through the crack in my heart. *Mama chose him again.*

The hallway lights darkened, and the walls closed in. I made my way to the nurse's station and stood at the counter until someone saw me.

"Can I help you?"

"I'm Chris. My mother is in room 632. Will you give her this ointment?"

"Her doctor is getting ready to go in there. I can give it to him."

"Thank you."

From behind, I heard a gentle male voice, "Ma'am?"

I turned to see a man in a white coat holding a clipboard.

"Yes?"

The man introduced himself as Mama's doctor. He invited me to go into her room with him, but I explained the conversation we just had. His eyes were empathetic as he listened.

"I didn't even know she had another daughter." The crack in my heart broke wide open. *Of course not.*

"I'll give this to her." He held up the lip ointment. "And I'm sorry."

I wanted to say thank you, but my voice wouldn't work. I stared at the floor until I could muster enough control to ask, "How long does my Mama have to live?" He hesitated a second.

"She has a 50/50 chance of living another year." *A safe answer. So, a year at the most.* Probably not under Jack though.

I thanked the doctor, walked away, and knew I would never see my Mama again. I walked past her room one last time and whispered, "Love you, Mama."

40

Realization

WE RETURNED TO Germany, Mama continued to go in and out of the hospital, Jack continued to run the show, and my marriage continued to deteriorate.

Maggie and Grandma provided updates. When Jack left town, family members took her to the farm to visit her mother and sister. Mama and I exchanged letters, all of which were mailed to and from the farm so Jack couldn't know. Once again, the farm served as a safe haven.

Mama and I never spoke about that day in her hospital room. I knew from Maggie and Grandma that her time grew shorter. I think Mama knew it too. In her letters, she wrote as if our lives were vastly different from reality. Pretending almost.

She talked about the vegetables she would take home from Grandma's garden, and how she wished I was there to take some too. She wrote of how she pictured my life in Germany and visualized me playing on the floor with my daughter.

She wrote things she had never said to me before. "I send my love." "You are my daughter." "I will love you always and forever." "I'm proud of you."

Her words tortured me. I struggled to find the honesty in them. Hadn't Mama given me away? Hadn't she kicked me out of her hospital room? Her words didn't fit. *Is she in denial?*

I never confronted Mama on anything she wrote. I wanted whatever I could get that resembled a relationship with her, even if we pretended. *She's dying. Why stir things up?*

A family member told me while Mama lay in her hospital bed, she asked, "Do you think God is punishing me for giving my little girl away?" It made me cry for both Mama and myself. *She called me her little girl.* Between life with Jack and cancer, I didn't want her to hurt anymore. *She's suffered enough.*

I read her letters, laid them down, read them again, then cried. The pain of the truth ran deep. *If only we'd been free, Mama. Maybe our lives would have been like those letters.*

Almost a year to the day that Mama ordered me out of her hospital room, the phone call came late in the afternoon. Mama died. I was still numb when we arrived in the States. As soon as I could get to the phone, I called Maggie. "Hi, Maggie. We made it."

"Chrissy, I hate to tell you this, but there's gonna be trouble."

"What do you mean?"

"Jack has spread it all over the family. You can't come to the memorial service." The numbness left and reality hit me. *Memorial service. Mama's gone.*

"Why?" My throat closed. But I knew why. *Because Jack said so.*

"Jack said if you show up, he will call the police." *Is he really doing this again?* My chest deflated as my heart sank. *He's doing this.*

"Still evil."

"Yes, I know, Chrissy. I'm sorry."

The air around me became a haze. I felt exhausted in every way. *Mama's gone.* The tears rolled to my chin. I didn't care. They dripped to my lap. *How long is he going to bully me?*

"Chrissy, you there?"

"Yes—I'm so tired, Maggie. Of him." My heart threatened to stop. Would I ever really be free of Jack?

Bye, Mama. You didn't deserve any of this.

WE RETURNED TO Germany, and for days I simply survived, doing what was necessary through the numbness. I took care of my daughter, cooked, cleaned, and bought groceries. The sunshine outside mocked the darkness inside of me. When I thought about her, I felt empty. I waited for feelings to come but they didn't.

I wondered if Lane and Becky felt empty too. And Jack—what does an abuser feel when his victim dies? *You can't hurt her now.*

I blew up balloons, tied knots, and placed them one by one on my daughter's bed while she napped. My camera lay ready for her expression upon waking up. Mama had blown up balloons for my seventh birthday party. Orange, yellow, and white ones. My mind tried to conclude she was no longer on this earth, but my heart wouldn't let it.

I smiled at my daughter as I placed the last balloon on top of her blanket. Her tiny chest moved up and down, and her peaceful face told me it would be a while before she would awake. A half-eaten cookie lay under her hand, and I couldn't help but giggle. *Oh, how I love you.* I looked at her closed eyes and soft hair. *You will never lose me.*

I started feeling again.

As I passed the bedroom window, my eyes caught the landlord and her young daughter pulling laundry from the clothesline. They shrieked as the wind blew towels across their faces and laughed as they yanked them from the line and tossed them into their basket.

JACK'S WORDS IN the hospital haunted my thoughts. "Karen, are you tired?" Code for *I'm not going to let you talk to her,* and a demonstration of his control. A glimpse of Mama's face as she ordered me out of her room stirred the pain, "…because of the way you treated Jack."

The rejection from Mama's memorial service began to sting. *I can't believe Mama's gone. Did anyone notice I wasn't there?*

My chest tightened as my inner conflict grew. *She's free, but what do I do with the pain? He can't hurt her anymore, but her life was tortured.* Then it dawned on me. *I didn't get to say goodbye.*

Older memories took turns scrolling through my mind. I saw Mama standing in the doorway at the house on 14th street, holding a can of biscuits, "Chrissy! Here you go, playdough."

I saw Mama later walking out of her bedroom with bruises on both arms. I saw her carrying Becky, with Lane and I at her side, walking to the payphone after Jack kicked us out.

I can't hold on anymore. I rushed to the living room couch and let my heart burst. I didn't want to hold it together anymore. I couldn't.

In those moments, my entire being broke for Mama for all the years she remained in Jack's emotional prison. For the pain that lived on her face. I drowned in sorrow. My mama was gone.

"It's Jack's fault your Mama died," Maggie often said. "All those sex partners. She had that HPV virus. And Jack never let her go to the doctor."

Maggie's words didn't register until three years later, at my doctor's office. My gynecologist suggested I obtain Mama's medical records for him to review. The records would answer questions about any inherited risks I might have. After listening to several minutes of medical verbiage, I asked my doctor to simplify what he was saying.

"Christine, your mother's cancer was caused by a sexually transmitted virus called HPV. The cancer grew very slowly. She had a tumor the size of a grapefruit that had been growing for at least ten years undetected."

"Undetected?"

"It started as cervical cancer. A routine exam by her gynecologist could have found it and treated it before it spread." *Before it killed her?*

"My mother didn't have to die?" Disbelief lingered. Had I understood correctly?

"Appears that way."

Summer ended slowly and fall blended the warm sunny days with cooler air and gray skies. Accepting Mama's death meant letting go of hope for things that would never happen. Hope of her someday breaking free of Jack. Hope that one day I would see peace on her face instead of fear. Hope that we would sip coffee together and talk about Grandma's garden. Hope for a reunion with the mama I lost years ago.

Anger and hatred for Jack grew in hope's place. I realized for the first time that I was also angry at Mama. I could say it now. I already lost her. I spoke to her in my thoughts.

I hate him, Mama. I hate what he did to you. And to me. And I'm mad at you. I'm mad at you for not protecting me. Do you know how much I needed you? In fact, I hate MEN. Men are pigs.

Disgusting images of Jack's abuse flashed through my mind. Then came guilt. *Mama was a victim. Beaten down physically and mentally.* She had been gone years before she died.

Then anger again. *How could you give me away?*

Then tears. *I'm sorry, Mama. I know you loved me.*

What Jack did to me damaged my mind. What Mama did damaged my heart. I loved her. I cherished her and longed for her to cherish me back. But she didn't. Her absence has sometimes been harder to deal with than the abuse itself.

41

Another Marriage

AFTER FIVE AND a half years, my marriage ended. We returned to the States to divorce.

I worked as a preschool teacher and attended classes at the community college. I had picked up a few more hours at an online college while living in Germany. *That's it. I'll get my college degree. Then I'll be somebody, and the shame of my past will go away.*

After the divorce, guilt and stress added to my wounded thinking. I parented my daughter with little to no help from her father. I worked hard to give her the things she wanted, and I stressed incessantly over making her happy. *Am I good enough? Does she know how much I love her?*

At the time, I didn't understand the depth of my childhood wounds or the fear it put in me as a mother. I desperately longed to make the daughter I loved so much feel valued and protected, heard, seen, and loved. All the ways I had wanted to feel with Mama. But my crippled thinking created more difficulties than what my heart intended.

As my daughter grew, I ran to her every discomfort to show her I was there for her. If she stumbled, whimpered, or fussed, I felt the need to prove that I heard her, and she wasn't alone. The ache of neglect I experienced in childhood was never going to be felt by my own child. I would make sure of it.

I struggled to tell my daughter "No" when needed. I remembered the sting of Jack's ridicule when I couldn't do anything right—ever. I was afraid to correct her. I wanted her to feel accepted, something I never felt as a child.

It took years of my own healing, learning, and growing to realize the many mistakes I made as a parent. I wish I had known sooner how unhealed I was. I pray that my love for her was stronger than my mistakes.

Life was hard and lonely. The stress of divorce, single parenting, working, and going to college became overwhelming. Never enough money, time, or energy. Anxiety grew. Fear grew. Worry grew. *Does my child miss her dad? Is she hurting? What does she need?* I was lost.

I applied for therapy at a local counseling center. The same place where I met Sally as a teenager. *Maybe Sally is still there. She'll tell me what to do.*

"No, I'm sorry, Sally Goforth no longer works here, but we can set you up with a different therapist."

I began weekly counseling, hoping it would clear up my misery. Every week I spilled my heartache, then waited for my new therapist, Stephen, to respond. He was kind and listened patiently. *He reminds me of Sally.*

Stephen's words sounded good but were difficult for me to believe. They contradicted the shame and worthlessness inside of me.

"You're just as valuable as anyone else."

"I don't feel valuable." That voice in my head convinced me long ago that valuable people don't get abused—then given away.

"You are lovable and deserve to be treated kindly."

"I have to work hard to be loved."

"You don't have to give yourself away to be loved."

Shame pulled my eyes to the floor. *I can't go there.*

"I just want my daughter to be okay. People tell me I'm a good mom, but I struggle to believe it."

"If you're okay, she'll be okay. Let's work on you."

"I don't know how to be okay. My ex-husband told me I was crazy, and I'm starting to believe him."

"Chris, you're not crazy. You're suffering from depression and anxiety." Words I had heard before.

"Didn't I bring all this on myself? I've made some bad choices."

"You aren't perfect. You made some choices that have produced difficult consequences. But you are a good person. You are a good mother. You love your daughter, or you wouldn't be here."

Tears fell. *Wish I could believe that.*

"Why am I so broken? Why do I worry so much? Why do I always feel like I'm failing? Why do I hate men? Why…" The questions never ended.

"You are coming from a place of trauma."

Trauma?

"Look how strong you are."

"I don't feel strong."

"You were neglected, abused, and abandoned. You've lost a lot. None of it was your fault. But it shaped your thinking. Your thinking shaped your behavior."

Stephen's words—*none of it was your fault*—choked me. *Really?*

"Shouldn't I be over it by now? People tell me I should be over it. They say, 'it's in the past.' Why can't I get over the past?" *Because something's wrong with me.* I waited for Stephen's answer. I really wanted to know.

"Just because it's over doesn't mean it's over. You must heal." *Sally had said that too.*

"Healing is an individual process. You're still surviving. You've been surviving for years."

The weight of the truth in his words brought tears. *He gets it.*

"I don't know how to heal." I couldn't comprehend how to get from where I was, in a dark lost world, to where Stephen said I could be, healed and free.

"You still have choices."

I didn't see how that was true. I felt trapped. For months, Stephen never gave up. He repeated the same things in different ways, hoping I would eventually see it. At the end of one particular session, after pouring my guts out, I waited for him to say something that would take the edge off, even if only for a moment.

"Chris, have you ever thought about letting God help you with your problems?"

Those were not the words I wanted to hear. We never talked about God in our sessions, and I wasn't sure if he was allowed to ask me about God, as this wasn't a religious counseling center. Although I didn't sense judgment from him, Stephen's question made me uncomfortable and insulted.

Does he think I'm a lost cause after all? I felt shame. *God doesn't have time for me. I've done too much. Too much was done to me.* I didn't go there to talk about God. I faked a laugh to hide my discomfort.

"Oh, I believe in God and all, but I need *real* answers." I couldn't imagine how God could help me. I didn't have time for that. Besides, I wasn't good enough for God either.

I've heard people say, "You attract the kind of person you believe you deserve." I told myself I deserved the love and kindness my therapist spoke about, but I struggled to believe it. Beliefs that began in early childhood were not easily replaced with new and foreign ideas, no matter how wonderful they sounded.

With my still-healing wounds and broken thinking, I began dating a divorced musician who was twelve years older than me and said all the right things. And once again I ignored the red flags that screamed, "There are problems here!" I desperately wanted to be loved.

When I transferred to the University of Arkansas in Fayetteville, my boyfriend followed. I quit my job to attend college full-time. Still striving for that education so I could feel like somebody.

I applied for government assistance and food stamps. *Just 'til I graduate.* And although I had been divorced from my ex-husband for three years, he initiated a custody battle, sending me into a new frenzy of fear. *Why now? What have I done? I can't lose my daughter!*

Although my suspicions were never confirmed, I believed my ex-husband's actions were motivated by guilt and the need to prove something. He had remarried. A family man again, with a stepson. His younger brother had also recently married and expected a baby.

I was unmarried, on government assistance, and in therapy. The picture painted of me even made *me* doubt myself. And although losing my daughter was the most horrifying loss I could imagine, I determined to fight hard. And I did. As the legal battle progressed, so did my fight, and so did my fears. The cheapest attorney I could find was still a financial stretch.

Thoughts about Mama surfaced. *How could Mama let me go— willingly?* I still didn't understand.

"Okay, I'll marry you." My own words made my heart sink. My boyfriend was on his way home from a music tour in Florida. The tour hadn't led to bigger things as he hoped, and he proposed over the phone. I knew I was Plan B.

What I really wanted to say is "Get lost! I deserve better!" The custody court date came near, and I was afraid of looking bad. *If I get married, I can get off government assistance and food stamps.* My boyfriend had a good job, which added to the appearance of a stable environment.

So once again, I entered a marriage out of fear. With my first husband, it was fear of being alone. With my second, it was fear of losing my daughter.

Two years into my second marriage, the custody battle ended. I did not lose my daughter. But as one nightmare ended, another began.

The red flags I ignored two years earlier became realities. My marriage wasn't good. A pattern of abuse developed, increasing in severity each time. The cycle went something like this: I did something that made my husband angry. Tension grew. He verbally lashed out, then physically, sometimes moving out afterward. Busted lips and lumps on the head were easily covered with makeup and creative hairstyles. But the internal harm hurt the most.

After each episode of abuse, I declared, "I won't be treated this way!" My husband calmed down and promised never to do it again. I believed him because I wanted to, he came back home, and all was well until the next disagreement. The cycle started all over again.

The abuse added more shame. I never thought I would be a victim again. But there I was—more confused, lost, ashamed, and depressed than I had ever been.

As a child, I never understood why Mama would let Jack physically abuse her. It seemed simple to me. "Just leave him, Mama." I never heard Jack's *I'm so sorry* speeches. I never saw that part of the cycle. All I knew was Jack knew how to stay in Mama's life, even after he had hurt her or kicked her out.

It became the norm for my family doctor to bring up depression by asking me the standard questions. Regardless of my reason for being there, the visit always ended the same.

"Do you struggle to concentrate or focus?"

"Yes."

"Do you have trouble sleeping?"

"Yes."

"Do you often have feelings of sadness, hopelessness, or being trapped in your thoughts?"

"Yes."

"Do you feel bad about yourself?"

"Yes."

"Do you ever have thoughts of suicide?"

"No!" My answer was always the same for the last question. "The thought has crossed my mind, but I want to live." *I just didn't know how.*

42

A New Path

MY EYES OPENED to warm sunshine gleaming through the sheer curtains. Birds chirped outside the window. The clock gently ticked. *It's Saturday. I don't have to work.* I lay listening. My mind drifted to my daughter. It was her weekend with her dad. *Wonder if she's awake.* She was only two blocks away, but it felt like a thousand. For a few moments, I soaked in the stillness. *Wish I could feel this all the time.*

My husband had rented his own apartment three weeks ago. We had argued about why I painted my toenails. He seemed sure it was for another man. The argument turned to abuse again and ended when he cut the phone line and left. The silence in the house turned from peacefulness to sadness. *With him, or without him, I'm alone.*

I knew he would eventually show up with sad eyes and arms full of promises that wouldn't be kept. Just like Jack. The pit in my stomach churned. I wanted to ignore it.

What can I do to be happy today? I can paint the bathroom. The paint's cheap.

I swung my legs over the bed and felt a sudden panic inside me. My feet hadn't even touched the floor, and I yanked them back and shoved them under my comforter.

What was that? That feeling… The air became heavy. Something was different. I laid my head down and returned to my thoughts. *I'll clean up the house and wash my car. Then drive through Taco Bell. That'll make me happy.*

I threw back the comforter and tossed my feet over the edge, again gripped with a *don't do it* feeling. My feet stopped just above the floor, and I jerked them back to the bed.

What is wrong with me?

"Don't let your feet touch the floor."

Where did that come from?

I hadn't heard an audible voice, but one from within. Not the lying voice that told me how worthless and unlovable I was. Not the voice that argued with the lying voice. This was a voice unlike the others. I heard this one in my heart. The others were in my mind. I wasn't sure how it got there or what it wanted. *Am I going crazy?*

"Don't let your feet touch the floor, the way things are."

The way things are? What does that mean? My body curled up and my heart grew heavy as if it knew something was coming. *Is this gonna be painful?*

I pulled my pillow close, wondering when I would be able to get up. Thoughts of my life floated in front of me. Flashbacks of abuse. Pits of depression. Screaming matches with my first husband, and with my second. The anguish of my entire life.

What's going on? Am I just too damaged—too messed up—to be happy? I'll stay in bed then.

I heard Jack's words from years ago. "Your daddy didn't want you, and I don't want you either." I heard Mama's words the day she ordered me out of her hospital room. "Chris, you can't be here, because of the way you spoke to Jack." I heard the words of the social workers every time they picked me up to take me someplace else. And the words that spewed from my husband's mouth three weeks ago. "I'm done with you!" *Will anyone ever want me?*

I closed my eyes and breathed in slowly as the years of my life scrolled through my thoughts. In some ways, it felt as though my childhood abuse never stopped. I couldn't shed the shame or the horrible things I thought about myself. I couldn't break free from the depression or patterns of thinking that always led to disaster. I didn't know how to *"just get over it"* like so many people flippantly suggested.

Did others think I enjoyed my prison? Did they think I could simply push a button and all the emotional damage and mental programming would suddenly correct itself? Remarks like *just get over it* and *stop living in the past* sounded wonderful, but those words didn't tell me what to do with the wreckage. I grew to believe I must be weak, a loser, an idiot, for not knowing how to *just let it all go*, so I could be happy. *It's never gonna be better than this. I'll never have what other people have.*

What was I doing wrong? I had been rescued from the abuse as a child. I met my real dad. I went to college. I held down a job, took care of my daughter, and tried to be a good person. But still lost, my life continued in shambles.

I'm gonna paint that bathroom. My feet aimed for the edge of the bed once more, dropped toward the floor but halted in mid-air as the voice in my heart overpowered me.

"If you take another step down the path you're on, your life will never change."

My feet and my thoughts hung frozen over the side of my bed. *Have I heard that voice before?* It reminded me of the voice that said to me "Get out now" after Jack exposed his plan to take pornographic pictures of me. The same voice that told me my protection wasn't going to come from Mama after I told her Jack had given me a bag of condoms.

This voice created a *knowing*, an *awareness* that stemmed from the deepest part of me. One that needed no explanation and left no doubt. Truth. I looked at the floor as if touching it meant the point of no return. My feet recoiled.

I can't keep living this way.

The quandary in my heart showed me what life would look if I let my feet touch the floor without a new path. A new direction for life. I would paint the bathroom and clean the house. My husband would eventually come back with poetic words, and I would let him in. At the next argument, I would get hurt, he would leave again, and the cycle would repeat over and over. And in between the events of my life, I would continue to self-loathe and self-judge until I no longer felt hope. Like Mama.

Tears streamed, then flooded. *It wasn't supposed to be like this. I was supposed to get over it.*

Sally's words from years ago entered my thoughts. "Chris, you are lovable. You are valuable. You didn't deserve what happened, and none of it was your fault."

I remembered the kind people throughout my past, and how their gentle spirits gave me strength—the ladies at church, the couple across the street, my teachers, even strangers. They all saw good things in me that I didn't see in myself. More truth?

If they're right, why don't I see it? I buried my face into my pillow. I agonized and questioned. The lying voice inside of me had always ruled but now seemed weakened. Dozing in and out of sleep, I pulled closer to the voice in my heart. I was desperate for it, like a genuine friend who never lied and would never leave me.

"Don't let your feet touch the floor unchanged."

What am I supposed to do? I've tried everything I know. Would my heart tell me what to do?

"I am the way, the truth, and the life."

Not what I expected to hear. *Where have I heard that before?* It sounded like a God thing. *Did I hear that when I was little? At the church across the street?*

I doubted God was the answer, but I let my thoughts go there. *That's what I want, isn't it? To know the way, understand the truth. To have life—real life.* Was God really all that? I never forgot about the words Stephen said at one of our last counseling sessions, "Have you ever thought about letting God help you with your problems?"

Two hours passed as I lay in bed remembering words, seeds planted in my mind by so many different people throughout the years. I relived the moments in the kitchen with James and Helen King and still felt their love for each other. *They had peace in their hearts.* They loved God and believed the Bible.

I remembered a religious lady I worked with who told me I was going to Hell because I divorced my first husband. She went to church three times a week and knew all the rules but treated me with callousness. She masqueraded as a Christian, but I didn't sense the same peace, like James and Helen. Certainly not the same compassion.

Someone else told me, "God says you're enough." Something I didn't believe.

They said, "He forgives and heals. He takes broken pieces and turns them into something beautiful." *How could my broken life be something beautiful? I'm a mess.*

I laid back and stared at a yellow stain on the ceiling. *Must have been a leak.*

"Are you going to choose the truth?"

It wasn't going away. I wanted to cling to the power I was being drawn to, but was it really God? *I'll think about this God path.* I made one last attempt to get out of bed, but the grip in my heart held me back more tightly. It was as if there were two arms around me, holding on to keep me from jumping off a cliff.

"Another step unchanged leads to death. I am the way, the truth, and the life." I became afraid—afraid of my feet touching the floor without a change inside of me. *This is real.*

My thoughts began clearing. I saw my unchanged life ahead of me. Despair. Destruction. Hopelessness. Pain. Shame. Chaos. I saw myself always searching but never finding the answers. Continually running, but never arriving. *If I don't change now, I never will.*

I wiped my tears and spoke to that voice in my heart.

God, is that you?

Silence.

I don't want to be religious, like that lady at my work. She hurt me. Somehow, I knew she was wrong.

I just wanna know who you are.

"I am the way, the truth, and the life."

My chest grew excited. Then I thought of how my life must look to God—my shame, my mistakes, all my secrets. Hope threatened to disappear.

God, I don't know if you'll accept me. I'm very damaged. I closed my eyes and felt the exhaustion. *I'm so tired of it all.*

"I will give you rest."

Rest? I wanted that to be true. The years of searching, running, agonizing, and fighting left me bitter, lonely, and lost—anything but rested. Could God really give me rest?

The idea of an easier path seemed soothing but unimaginable. Could I really live without shame? Heal from the abuse? Forgive for my own mistakes? Feel peace? Have direction? Know the truth?

Why would you do all that, God? My eyes darted around the bedroom. *Is He in here?*

"Because I love you unconditionally."

Words that stunned my soul. Had they come from any person on this earth, I wouldn't have believed them—I couldn't have. But they came from this indubitable *knowing*. A truth that both filled my heart and broke it.

I couldn't describe unconditional love, or even imagine it. I only knew I had never had it. But I believed what my heart said, and I knew it was a love more powerful than the darkness inside of me. And I longed to have that kind of love.

My closed eyes didn't stop the tears. I was overcome by a pulling, an internal yearning to love God. *I have to have him. He's the way I need to go. He's the truth.* I sat up in bed. It was settled in my heart.

Okay, how do I do this? I looked around the room. I knew what I heard in my heart was God. And my new path must be about Him. But what was I supposed to do now? I spoke to my heart.

"God, I want to live for you, follow your ways. You can have my old life. Please give me a new one." Every word solidified my sincerity. The room was silent, but my heart was hopeful. *Did that work?*

An unstoppable smile crept across my face. My heart came to life. Peace poured over me and in me.

Oh my gosh! He heard me!

I knew my life up to that moment wasn't erased, but my future would set me free. I saw a new path in front of me. A path toward things I ached for, but never knew where to find. Freedom from the shame of what happened to me. Courage to confront the lying voice in my thinking, and boldness to declare the truth.

Forgiveness for my mistakes and failures. Excitement for a life of breathing again, smiling, loving, and being loved.

Living for God became a bumpy learning process—a long long one—a process I'm still in but get better at each day. All I knew on that

Saturday morning was I had stepped off the cycle of destruction, and stepped into a life of freedom, healing, joy, hope, and an awe-inspiring feeling of love. *I feel so clean inside! I can see straight! He loves me!* Feelings I wanted to embrace forever.

I sat mesmerized. *"Because I love you unconditionally..."* Could it be that the God of the universe, the author of love itself, actually loved me? Me?

"Yes!" I shouted as loudly as my voice would let me. I threw the comforter aside, put my feet on the floor, and breathed in the new air of my life.

A fresh start. I couldn't be certain of other people's hearts, but I could be sure of mine. My heart had forever changed. My life would begin again with a clean slate, a new direction, a new focus, and an instruction book—the Bible.

I bought a topical Bible so I could see what God said about specific things I needed to know about—divorce, forgiveness, God's love. I couldn't change the past and I didn't know what my future looked like. I knew I had a lot to learn but I now rested in knowing my heart and mind were where they needed to be.

The rest of me changed one tiny piece at a time. Emotional bondage became replaced with freedom. Truth replaced lies. I acknowledged each hurt, each lie, each fear, and each insecurity as they surfaced. *Yes, that hurt. Yes, that was wrong. Yes, that was a lie. Yes, I've been afraid of that.*

It took practice to replace painful thoughts and demoralized thinking. *Now I'm free to heal. Now I see the truth. Now I can forgive. Now I'm forgiven. If I fail now, I can get back up.*

Faith and time strengthened my confidence. *I don't have to be afraid. I'm strong. I'm lovable. I'm valuable. I'm courageous. I'm healing.*

I began speaking directly to that lying voice in my mind. *You are the voice of my past, the voice of my abuser, and the voice I allowed myself to use. No more! You are a liar. The shame was never mine to carry.*

I was astonished at the things I read in the Bible. *The truth will set me free? I'm a masterpiece? I'm worth more than gold?* Each night I laid my head down and whispered to myself, "I am loved. I am free."

But there were still bumps ahead.

43

Breaking the Cycle

THE COLD STREET froze my bare feet. Pieces of gravel sent tears to my eyes. Dark sky made it hard to see. *Keep running.* I slowed only long enough to see if my husband chased me. He had come in the middle of the night, in a rage, and ordered me out of the house. Every headlight sent me into the grass until it passed, and I could be sure it wasn't him.

I can't believe this is happening. I ran to a convenience store four blocks away. *There's a phone there.* The lighted parking lot and other people were a relief, allowing me to catch my breath. *I gotta call someone.* The sight of the payphone against the brick building triggered memories. I heard the little girl inside of me. *Who you gonna call, Mama?*

My feet moved me to the front of the payphone, but my mind took me somewhere else. I saw myself pressed against Mama inside a phone booth years before. The clanking of her coins as they dropped through the phone sent a hollow feeling through me. I heaved for air as Mama's pained voice spoke into the phone.

Honk! "Hey, your foot's bleeding!"

I snapped back into the present. My eyes darted at a man in an old car with loud music spilling from the window. "You need a quarter?"

"Um…"

"You need a quarter? For the phone?" I wondered how long I had been standing there. I glanced at the dirty blood on my heel.

"No, thank you. I have one." Relieved when he drove away, I dug through my purse. The sight of my shaking hand prompted a flood of truth. *He kicked me out. Just like Jack. He sent me walking—with nothing.* Flashbacks of walking down the sidewalk with Mama and her bruises. Fear on her face. Calling for help—again. But it wasn't Mama this time.

I pondered how I got to that payphone, in that condition. It had been seven months since I began my new life. I kept growing, learning, and changing. How could this be happening?

Thoughts of my daughter cracked my heart. Only hours earlier, I dropped her off at her dad's. Thankful she hadn't witnessed the night's abuse, I looked to the sky. *What's my life doing to my little girl?* She had never walked with me to a pay phone after getting kicked out. Anger stirred my thoughts. My chest drew in the heavy air.

And she never will. How far would the abuse send me next time? *To the hospital? Will he lay a hand on my daughter?* Anger grew. The thought of my daughter being abused, or being told he put me in a hospital, was unbearable.

I can't let that happen. I can't be like Mama.

"The cycle of abuse has to be broken," Stephen once said during counseling. "Has it been broken?"

I fought an internal and external battle. It wasn't only a pattern in my childhood; it'd become a pattern in my marriage, in my life, and in my mind. I had to stop it, for myself. I had to stop it for my daughter. And part of me had to stop it for Mama.

The last words I heard as I fled from my husband's abuse rang in my mind. Amid his horrid attack and foul language, he shrieked, "I want a divorce!" How many times had he said that? How many times had he abused me? How many times did he leave? But I always believed his apologies, and I always took him back.

I stared at the pay phone. *Mama would take him back.* I looked to the sky again. *What do I do?* Then I knew.

I returned home the next day with a police officer. Once my abuser was gone, I had the locks changed. And I prayed for my next step.

Stand firm. I prepared myself for the phone call—the apology, the pleading. *It's all part of the cycle.* I rehearsed my reply, "I won't let you abuse me anymore." I said it to Jack, and I could say it again. *I'm strong. I'm worthy. I deserve to be safe. I will protect myself and my daughter.* I prayed more.

Accept help. I sought counseling again to help me stay focused and strong during my weak moments. I needed healthy people to lean on. I kept praying.

He wants a divorce, but I don't have the money. I vaguely remember the person who told me to go to the local law library. I searched divorce decrees until I found one with the same circumstances as mine—no children born to this marriage, nothing to sell, no money to fight over—uncomplicated.

Using the example as a guide, I typed my own decree, filed it at the Circuit Clerk's office, and served my abuser with a copy. He chose not to respond. After a short waiting period, I called the judge's office and requested a hearing. The judge read the decree, asked me if I worked for an attorney, saw that my husband was not there to contest, signed the decree, and bam—I was divorced.

Breaking the cycle of abuse is complex. I couldn't do it alone. Getting away from an abuser was one thing. Staying away and safeguarding my future, and the future of my daughter, required continued healing—and help.

"You have to be willing to trust again—the right person, at the right time." My new counselor understood my fears.

"I got abused when I trusted."

"Yes, you did."

We faced the facts together. "With Jack, you were a child. You were powerless. You did what children are supposed to do, trust their parents. Unfortunately, you had to get out. And you did get out." Her words swept me with thankfulness. "You survived because you are strong and brave."

Me, strong? Brave? A smile peered across my lips as I listened. *Yes, I am...with God's help now.*

"But I trusted my ex-husband, and he abused me too." *What about that?* "And what if I get married again someday? And what if he abuses me too?" My smile faded and my eyes pleaded for reassurance.

"Chris, you're learning your value. You're healing. You're changing. You're identifying your mistakes. Setting firmer, healthier boundaries. Committing to a better path. You have God now."

I wanted to believe everything she said. *Do I take a chance? Do I ever trust again?*

"God says I'm more valuable than rubies. And if I was the only one out of a hundred who was lost, He would come find me." I didn't look to my counselor for reassurance this time. I didn't need it. I knew in my heart her words were true. "I am lovable."

I trust God.

Hope had never been so strong. And although I knew I still had a lot of work to do, I wanted all that this new path had for me. My eyes looked upward. *Teach me more.*

Shame and fear were the most difficult lies for me to shed after being sexually abused. Toxic demons that took up residence in my mind and deceived nearly every thought. They stole my self-esteem and attempted to take my future.

Shame told me I was less than, damaged, unlovable, unworthy. Shame said I was guilty of the bad things that happened, because I was a bad person. Shame convinced me I would never be good enough.

Fear warned me not to trust people—lest I get hurt again. Fear said to shut down, hide my feelings, pretend to be someone else, or people would laugh at me—reject me.

For years, I believed the lies because I couldn't explain why the abuse happened otherwise, or why I made bad decisions, or why my life seemed to confirm everything the lying voice told me. My mind didn't know how to disagree with shame and fear. Until now.

"I'd rather be alone than be with the wrong man." I spoke those words many times for nearly two years as I continued walking down my path of healing, receiving counseling, and seeking God.

I wanted to be married again one day, but in a completely different way. A way that was right, healthy, safe, and good. *I'm sick of destruction.* Two failed marriages did undeniable damage. I couldn't change what was already done, but I was moving forward into a better future.

I continued to become a new person. The person I was meant to be all along. I kept healing and had truth in my grasp. One by one, the lies in my mind were permanently destroyed and replaced with truth. And with every truth came more freedom.

The abuse was Jack's failure, not mine. Jack's failure did not make me less lovable, less valuable, or less desirable. Jack abused his power. I was powerless.

I am no longer powerless. Shame and blame no longer enslave me. My past does not dictate my future.

I am no longer powerless. I am not abnormal. I was victimized and now I'm healing. The pace of my healing journey is between me and God. What others think is irrelevant.

I am no longer powerless. I am strong. I am brave. I am a survivor.

I am no longer powerless.

44

Forgiveness and Freedom

MY LOVE FOR God grew, as did my love for myself. *If God loves me, I love me. I believe everything that book says. Hasn't failed me yet.* And although life wasn't perfect, and I wasn't perfect, I began experiencing a peace I didn't know I could have. Healing was happening and it felt good. The path I was on continued to surprise me. And I met a man. A truly good man.

Terry embodied the things I wanted most and was a thousand miles away from the things I never wanted again. His blonde hair and blue eyes were alluring, but he was so much more. He loved God, and we were on the same path. He saw beauty and value in me. He held me in high esteem. He was thankful for me. An honor I had never experienced. Terry was stable, secure, disciplined, and calm.

As I write this book, we have been married for twenty-four years. Terry took commitment and loyalty seriously, not only on the good days, but also on the bad. He showed me what it looks like to own our mistakes and do what it takes to change, improve, and grow from them.

He also showed me what forgiveness between two people looks like, and that even strong stable Christians are not flawless people. They are humans with strengths and weaknesses, who must never be above asking for forgiveness when they've messed up. His assurance and trustworthiness are among his most precious gifts to me.

Terry says my emotional strength and compassion for others inspires him like no other. We've made each other better people, by receiving God's guidance to us along the way.

Terry jokingly calls me his "Raging Italian" as I am outspoken, direct, unafraid, dramatic, and often loud. A stark contrast to his reserved, conservative way of communicating. He is my "All American Boy Next Door" who I tease for having the perfect childhood, the perfect family, always doing things *by the book,* and being easily shocked.

Neither of us is as extreme as we jest, but we learned early on that differences can either cause head-butting in a marriage, or they can provide beautiful reciprocal growth, if we will learn from one another. We aim for the latter.

For years, I'd known forgiveness was the right thing, but I didn't always understand why. When it came to Jack, I didn't think I could forgive someone who committed such horrible acts against me and others. It didn't seem fair. *He stole so much from me. And he's not even sorry.*

It took one small scary step at a time to let go of the lying voice in my head and replace the lies with truth. That voice was all I had known growing up and a big part of me. But I wasn't walking alone in life anymore, and every truth I accepted gave me strength and a yearning for more. I believed I would be okay eventually. But could I ever forgive Jack?

Sally once said to me, "Forgive as much as you can. Love as much as you can. Both will grow."

Once I moved past the pity I felt during my teenage years, and my spiteful early twenties, I decided I must have entered into forgiveness of Jack at some point. I wasn't angry anymore and I no longer wanted to get even. I wasn't sure when pity and spite disappeared, only that they had been replaced by more peace. *That's our God.*

The need to feel sorry for myself dissolved, and so did my wish for bad things to happen to Jack. I told myself, "I forgive him. I have no desire to have anything to do with him. But I'm done hating him." Hating Jack had become too big of a burden, a venom that threatened to destroy the healing and peace I kept finding.

When I became a Christian, I went to people I had wronged and asked for their forgiveness. I needed to own my mistakes, and it wasn't always easy. In fact, at times it was excruciating. I hoped each person would have mercy, refrain from crucifying me, and I was always relieved when they did. But even when I received ruthlessness in return, I never regretted doing the right thing. Little by little, my heart and my head were being set free.

By my early thirties, I felt I had entered an even deeper state of forgiveness for Jack. Although what he did to me will never be justified, I hoped he would somehow find peace in his life. I imagined it took a miserable person to do such horrific things to others, and I no longer *needed* him to be miserable in order to be happy. God had shown me that with forgiveness comes healing.

Jack occasionally told us stories about when he was a small boy growing up in Mountainburg, Arkansas. The stories were never happy—a little boy who was emotionally abused, ridiculed, and neglected.

He said he often sat on his front porch in the evening because he was locked out of the house while his family ate dinner inside. I never knew if the stories were true or if they were an attempt to gain attention. I grew to believe there was likely *some* truth to Jack's stories, and my heart broke for that little boy. Whatever happened, he had been hurt.

Did his painful childhood excuse his abusive actions? NO.

Did his childhood explain that he may have some deeply hidden demons of his own? Perhaps.

Abuse is never anything other than ugly cruel misuse of power that imposes physical, mental, and emotional pain on an innocent person. I wondered what in Jack's mind caused him to make those decisions. Would he have made the same decisions if he had grown up in a loving, nurturing environment? Maybe—maybe not.

I cried for the little boy he used to be. *How old was he when he first felt real hurt? Was anyone there for him? When did he start choosing wrong behavior? Was it just easier than to do the right thing? Where did things go so wrong, and why?*

I stood at the sink rinsing dishes and gazing through the window. The trees were bare, and the grass was brown. From the living room, the television talked about snow coming.

"It's gonna get cold tonight." Terry loved watching the weather. "We better turn the heat on."

Turn the heat on. The simple flip of a tiny switch—a luxury I've never stopped appreciating. My mind drifted to that cold winter in Oklahoma, when snow blew in through the cracks of the windows and Lane built a fire in the woodstove. I looked at the window in front of me and sighed with comfort. *We've got good windows in this house.*

"*You need to forgive him. You need to forgive Jack.*"

What? Where did that come from? "Is that You, God?"

I hadn't spoken to Jack in over ten years, since Mama's hospital room. I had come a long way from the darkness. *I've grown. I've healed.*

My life is blessed. I remembered the past, even talked about the pain, but I could then put it back where it belonged. The memories didn't control me anymore. *Forgive him? But I already did.*

I rinsed another pan. Memories of Jack surfaced one by one. The night I met him. His intimidating laugh. His red angry face. His demands. His threats. Mama's bruises. I heard his words, "Chris Ann, bring me my cigarettes," and my jaw clenched.

"You need to forgive Jack."

"Definitely snow tonight." Terry's voice pulled my thoughts back to the present.

Anger I hadn't felt in a while stirred. Glimpses of foster homes, memories of despair, the gravity of all that was stolen from me.

I already forgave him.

I finished the dishes and reached for a dry towel. Surely God knew I didn't hate Jack anymore. I was no longer bitter.

"You need to tell him you forgive him."

What? Like, a letter? That has to be wrong. I had no desire to speak to Jack, and plenty of reasons to maintain my distance. He was dangerous and threatening. He hated me for telling on him years ago. *God, I can't tell Jack anything.*

"Go tell him you forgive him."

Go? Are you serious?

Had God forgotten how evil Jack was? *And how he laughed at what he did to me.* No way was I going to go tell him I forgive him. *I forgave him, and that's that.*

I argued with God for a month. *God, he'll think I caved. He'll laugh.*

"Go tell him."

The thought of seeing Jack's face nauseated me. I had forgiven him in my heart, but I never thought I would have to see him again. The little girl still lived inside of me, and I didn't know if she could look at Jack again face-to-face.

I knew it felt right to go, but I was afraid. Fear made my excuses seem logical. I was disappointed in myself for being afraid of him. *After all these years.*

Okay, I'll do it soon.

Weeks passed, and I held onto *I'll do it soon.* But I didn't think I could. My mind continued to fixate on *why?*

More time passed, more arguing with God, and more compromise.

God, can I just write him a letter instead?

God didn't answer. I knew the answer. But I decided to write a letter anyway.

I told Terry my plan, and that I'd like him to read the letter before I sent it. I respected his thoughts and valued his support even if he didn't fully understand. I wasn't ready to tell him how convicted I felt about not going in person and why. I knew he would have lovingly encouraged me to go, and I wanted to find another way.

45

The Letter

AS I WROTE "I forgive you for everything you did to me," I imagined Jack laughing hysterically. How his face would redden and shrivel as he spewed hatred from his mouth.

Doesn't matter. Gotta do this. The more I wrote, the more my heart tugged from another direction.

What if he's secretly sorry, but can't admit it? What if he needs forgiveness, but can't bring himself to ask? I read over my letter and contemplated what to say next. The tug in my heart said to be honest without attacking.

The purpose of the letter was to tell him I had forgiven him in case he needed to hear it from me. Not to remind him he's an abuser. *He knows that. I don't have to punish him to be okay.* I paused at my own thoughts.

That truth filled me with awe. *I'm really becoming okay, despite what Jack did to me. I'm getting my power back. The power to rise above the evil, to reject the shame, blame, and the lies his abuse instilled inside of me. I don't deserve to be punished anymore.*

I read my words again. The memories still hurt, and I cried. *Even if he retaliates, I'm doing the right thing.*

I wanted to be free from hating him, free from fearing him. How could I love myself but hate another? How could I truly be free if I held onto bitterness?

I rolled the pen between my fingers and marveled at the epiphanies that gracefully entered my understanding. More truth. Every bit of Jack's abuse had been wrong, and could not be excused, not even now. But to hate him perpetuated the poison inside of me. It's easy to hate an abuser. *I don't want to be that kind of person. I don't want to hate.*

I gave Jack nuggets of good memories that have stuck in my mind for years—his train villages that I admired, and the beautiful furniture he built. My words were gifts I didn't have to give him, but my heart told me to. And I had been learning to trust my heart, even if my emotions didn't agree. *He doesn't deserve to know that I saw good things in him.*

It seemed empowering to know I was the only one who could give Jack certain words. As his victim, words from *my* mouth had unique impact. I forced my mind to extract tiny bits of good from all the ugly past. There was always a Christmas tree and gifts. Was he really nice to me those days? Or was I distracted by the presents? Regardless, I focused on the good part of the memory, even if the good was tainted.

By the time I finished the letter, I didn't care much about Jack's reaction. I spoke the truth. I made my point. I was honest about what I appreciated, and I honestly forgave him for the abuse. I needed to express both, and I did.

As I dropped the letter into the mailbox outside the post office, a splinter of panic arose. *I can't get it back now.* I walked to my car and drove away. *Probably never hear from him. I'm okay with that.* I had done what my heart told me to do and felt satisfied.

Ten days later came a letter from Jack. I stared. *It's from him.* Tension churned in my gut. *He wrote my name.*

The drive home from the post office was numbing. I imagined what the letter could possibly say. Part of me dreaded what might be inside. How would I handle whatever he said?

I laid Jack's letter on the kitchen counter and put the dishes away. *Maybe I'll read it and maybe I won't,* I lied to myself. *I don't care what it says.*

When there were no more dishes to put away, I picked up the envelope and opened it.

"Dear Chris...." *Who is he to call me Dear?!* My gut tightened. I didn't want to read any more, but I couldn't keep from it.

Jack wrote how happy he was to get my letter because he had been struggling with depression.

No! We're not friends! I shouldn't have written that letter.

He wrote about losing both his legs from years of untreated diabetes, and the rest of his health was rapidly failing. He appreciated my memories of his trains and said he still had many of them. He mentioned his new wife, Vera, who he married a year after Mama died. Jack said Vera worked long hours at a truck stop, leaving him home alone a lot, with no one to talk to.

Am I supposed to be sad for him? My stomach turned queasy. I shouldn't have written.

Jack's letter said he still built things, although he had to get creative about maneuvering around his workshop without legs, climbing on and off the table, in and out of his wheelchair, rolling from side to side, because it was easier to move *himself* around than the project he was working on. He wrote, "I mainly build cedar trunks now."

He didn't mention my forgiving him. He didn't mention Mama. *Coward.* He spoke mostly about his depression and the fact that he was now a Christian. And he invited me to come for a visit. *A visit! Does he not understand? We're not friends!*

I read Jack's letter over and over. My emotions battled my heart. I opened the back door and let the cool air spill over my face. Snow clouds covered the sky. Tears welled and anger grew. I looked into the sky and wondered if Mama was up there.

I read Jack's letter one more time. *How dare you blow off my forgiveness. You didn't deserve it in the first place. How dare you not mention my mama. So, you're depressed now? So what!*

I knew in my heart I must allow the anger—it was real. But I also knew I couldn't let it determine my steps. *I am stronger than everything he did to me. I won't succumb to hatred.*

A dreaded frustration came next. *Great. He's a Christian now. And he's dying. Lonely and depressed. Why should I care?* Did I have a worse enemy?

Then my heart spoke. I pressed my lips, gazed at the clouds, and listened to the voice I knew I must. *"He's in his darkest hour."*

I knew there were holes in his heart that could only be filled by my words. *Should I go?*

He's dying and lonely. No one deserves to die lonely. Do they?

Don't go. You forgave him. You wrote the letter. That's good enough. I felt tempted to laugh at the irony—he was the reason for *my* darkest hour, and now I must go to him during his?

The clouds thickened. *The weatherman said more snow.*

My heart filled with a slow-consuming desire to rise above *good enough.* Above the abuse. Above the loss. Above simply surviving. I wanted to *thrive.* And to do that, I needed my power back. I needed *complete* freedom from Jack, the past, and the broken aftermath. I needed to do something bigger than what Jack did to me.

I am more than what I've been through. I'm better than what broke me. But the world will think I'm crazy if I go see him. I pondered that truth. I felt the judgment. Then I screamed at the world. *It doesn't exonerate him! It sets me free!*

Telling Jack in person that I forgive him would be the most profound thing I could do. It would prove to the little girl inside of me she was no longer bound by fear and shame. It showed Jack his abuse had nothing to do with who *I* was, but who *he* was.

To extend Jack mercy at a time he didn't deserve it but needed it the most. I couldn't think of anything more powerful than that, more freeing, more healing. It seemed a call for connection, not with Jack, but with myself. *This is who I am.* And for another connection with God. *This is who God made me to be.*

I raised my eyes to the sky once more seeking God's confirmation.

Okay, I'll go tell him.

I shared my heart with Terry. He listened intently, then took my hand and prayed with me. We took turns asking God for what we needed—assurance, peace, strength. *God, please go with me. I'm scared.* And by the time we finished praying we knew I must go, and Terry must go with me.

46

Eyeball to Eyeball

I HAD FEW words as we drove to Jack's house. My thoughts zig-zagged between peace and fear, determination and dread. It was one thing to forgive Jack in my heart and never speak to him again. It was another thing to stand eyeball to eyeball with him as I spoke the words. An unprecedented gift for him. A powerful opportunity for me. *Can I really do this?*

Even though the man who wrote those letters seemed different, I still didn't trust him. I had never felt anything good inside when I was around him in person.

The hum of the tires against the highway disappeared as Terry turned onto the dirt road. I read Jack's written directions out loud, turn by turn, holding tightly to the conviction in my heart. Fear crept in. *What if this is a disaster?*

The car stopped at the bottom of the gravel driveway. The ice was too thick to make it all the way up. We would walk the rest. *Should I turn back? No. I'll do it scared.*

Terry sat patiently. "Whenever you're ready."

A dim porch light glowed in the distance. The dark air outside the car barely showed the trees on either side of the driveway.

"I think I'm ready."

"Hold on, I'll get your door."

God, please help me. The little girl inside of me began to panic.

"You want my hand?" Terry's voice spoke gently. A surge of cold air sent chills up my spine.

"No, I'm okay." I drew in a deep breath. *Relax.* The little girl inside of me clung in fear. The adult in me was nervous, but sure. *It's gonna be okay, I promise.*

Sally once said, "It took courage for you kids to survive some of the bullets of your upbringing."

I relied on that courage as I stepped onto Jack's porch and knocked on his door. I listened to the television on the other side. Had they heard me?

Vera opened the door. In the middle of the living room, Jack lay in a hospital bed. Legless. Helpless. It had been over twelve years since I last saw him, standing in Mama's hospital room. Hatred and compassion battled within me. Forgiveness and bitterness. My strength wavered.

God help me.

"Come in." Vera's gritty voice didn't match her kind face. She stepped back, leaving only the doorway and a few feet of carpet between me and the man who destroyed my childhood. For a second my throat closed, and my chest tightened. A flashback of that little girl walking down the hallway of the trailer, toward Jack's bedroom, hit hard. The past weighed heavy. *Do I really want to forgive him?*

Yes. I want to be free.

I stepped into the living room to cross a daunting threshold that changed my life forever.

The first step toward Jack's bed was the heaviest. An unfamiliar strength carried me across the room and replaced fear with sureness. *Something's taking over. Something good.*

I knew why I was here, and I was anxious to follow through. For the first time in my life, I stood in front of Jack unafraid, ready to seal the victory with the words I had come so far in life to say.

Jack held the remote as his bed slowly sat him up. His eyes looked at me and I didn't look away. I didn't need to.

"Hello, Jack." I marveled at my confidence.

"Hi, Chris. Were the roads real bad?"

"Not too bad. We took it easy."

Vera rolled a wheelchair to the side of the bed and Jack used his arms to lift himself into it. "We can sit over here." He pointed to a spot by the window and rolled toward it.

"Ya'll want some tea? It's sweet." Vera walked to the kitchen and stopped at the door to look at us. Terry sat on the sofa a few feet from my chair.

"No, thank you." I was glad for the distraction.

"Jack, you want beer?" *He drinks beer?* Jack's face flushed.

"I have to drink beer to flush my kidneys." *Why is he explaining this to me? Since when did he care what I thought?* "No, Vera, I'll have tea."

Vera carried a glass of tea to Jack, then sat on the sofa with Terry. "That's my doll collection." She pointed to a wall of shelves full of beautifully dressed dolls, all placed on stands for display. "Jack built me those shelves."

As we listened to Jack and Vera talk about the dolls, I found myself getting lost in a feeling I didn't recognize. I couldn't force myself to listen to the doll conversation—I didn't want to. I wanted to relish in this feeling that was gently hugging me.

I'm not numb. Jack's voice always made me numb. But I'm not numb.
That voice of my childhood tugged at my thoughts, trying to sneak a lie or two in, but I resisted. *Won't work. I know the truth.*

"…and so I bought Vera a rotisserie. You know, there's nothing better than a well-seasoned rotisserie chicken."

I watched Jack's lips move as his words rolled past my ears. *I'm not here because we're friends now. I'm here to tell you I forgive you. To break free from the anger. And the shame you put on me. To leave it all here.*

An airiness formed inside my chest in a space where heaviness had always been, where anxiety and fear had always lived, a space that trapped darkness in and blocked out the light. Now that space felt open—just waiting to be filled with something else.

"…so, I parked my wheelchair in the back of the little country church, and I could hear just fine…" Jack seemed to think I was grasping his every word.

Vera was a Christian when she married Jack. She admitted that he *pulled the wool over her eyes,* making her believe he was a respectable Christian man up until after they got married. She confessed that his true colors came out, and he abused her. She said it would have been fine if he had left and divorced her, but because of her personal convictions, she wouldn't leave him.

When Vera's grown sons from her previous marriage heard about the abuse, they paid Jack a visit, and *instilled some redneck fear in him,* enough to make Jack stop abusing their mother. Then sometime after that, Jack made a legitimate decision to live God's way, producing true remorse and the beginning of real change. Change that was only possible with the help of a higher power.

I listened intently to Vera's down-to-earth stories. I analyzed the tone in Jack's voice. I didn't know the man in front of me. Although the past hadn't changed, Jack was different. Even I knew it.

I tried to imagine a life in which Jack wasn't an abuser, a life of building furniture, creating miniature train villages, going to church—being decent. The thought made me sad. *Mama would have liked that.* Oh, how vastly different our lives would have been.

The news blared from the television. Vera went to the kitchen. Jack lifted himself from his wheelchair to the chair near me. I wondered if the weather would come on soon, so I'd know if we were going to get more freezing rain.

"Chris, I need to say something." Jack's tone was unfamiliar. *He didn't say Chris Ann.* "Chris, I owe you an apology."

Did he just say that? The man who did all those horrible things to me? I heard the words, but even so, I didn't believe anything big would follow. Rather, something like, *I'm sorry I was a jerk when you were growing up.* Or would his apology be for something he *thinks* is big to me, but only shows he really didn't get what he did to me?

I prepared to be irritated, and also ready to forgive him no matter what he said. My freedom did not depend on Jack. I waited.

"Chris, when you were a little girl, I took advantage of you."

NOT what I expected to hear. *Is that all he's going to say?*

Jack looked at me as if he was ready for something. *Does he want me to react?* I wasn't going to so much as make a gesture, a facial expression, or remark that would put him at ease. He vaguely admitted for the first time that he had sexually abused me, but it wasn't enough. *He needs to say more.*

"Yes, you did." My face was cool, without an ounce of fear—something I could not have done a few years before.

Jack continued. "I wasn't a good parent. I didn't know how to be."

No, you weren't, I silently agreed. The Jack I knew would never have said those things.

A moment passed. Neither of us spoke as the weatherman gave the report of more snow heading our way.

"I'm sorry."

Did he just say that? I looked into his eyes. They were weak and looking back at me. An appearance almost too foreign to perceive.

"I'm sorry." Jack's voice conveyed emotions far deeper than his words. His shoulders slumped, and he looked at me like an open book. I saw sincerity in his face, not waiting for comfort, and not about to erupt in explanation. I had never seen that face before. My anger swelled despite his sincerity. *I was a child! I was innocent!*

"Terry, I did horrible things to her." Jack's eyes turned desperate. "And she forgave me. She forgave me."

"Yes, I know." Terry responded in confidence and strength, confirming safety and support for me.

"No, Terry, you don't understand. I did horrible things! Can you believe she forgave me?" Jack's mouth held open; his eyes gazed into the air as he barely breathed.

Jack turned to me with what seemed to be his last ounce of strength. His chest moved in and out while he searched for words. He looked at me as if seeing me for the first time. Horrified. Broken. Ashamed. "I…" *What is he trying to say?*

"I'm so sorry." The whisper in his voice said much more—disgrace, defeat. The rest was too painful, too shameful for words. He knew. And I knew.

"Jack, I forgive you." I had said it in my letter, and now in person.

Jack held his lips together as his eyes filled. "I… I don't know what to say."

"Don't say anything." I didn't know if I could bear another word. My heart gasped from the pain of the moment. Anguish from deep within my soul began pushing its way out. The pent-up shame. The fear. The loneliness. All of it surfaced. *I can't breathe.*

Then my heart gave me strength to continue. "Jack, I forgive you. And I love you." I heard the unplanned words come out of my mouth. They were clear, true, and sincere. *I've never said that before.* But I meant them. I loved the person that was desperate to be loved, to be forgiven. My eyes darted away. *God, I didn't know that was in there.*

The years of abuse and damaging aftermath had kept me in a sense of solitary confinement at a maximum-security prison for decades. But now released because I was innocent all along. They had the wrong person.

An unimaginable rush of freedom flooded me from head to toe. Locks in my mind busted apart, prison doors opened, and chains broke, one by one. Barriers that held in the lies, weighing me down for so long, opened. A rush of fresh air ran through me, bringing light with it. It was a freedom I didn't know existed. Unlocked by three words, *I forgive you.*

My heartbeat felt alive. *When did my heart stop beating?* This new river of freedom nearly took my breath away. Into a place I never imagined.

Who gets an admission? An apology! Who looks their abuser in the eye and hears those words? My mind couldn't absorb the shock. Blindsided by Jack's validation of the truth, anger tried to steal my moment, but I refused to give in. The years of telling the truth about the abuse only to be called a liar by Jack, and the years of wading through the aftermath—it all sat on the table between us.

Trauma had taken over my body, mind, and spirit, but truth and forgiveness were changing it back.

There was power in facing the past—speaking the facts no matter how painful. Even admitting my own failures and regrets and grieving for all that was lost. It all took time but was all part of my transformation.

Then came the power and freedom to move on. Freedom to let the destruction die, and the power to take what I have learned, value my new strength, and embrace the present.

Today I look in the mirror and see a woman of grit and grace. With my long brown hair and short stature, I look like Mama.

I see a woman who had a painful beginning, torturous at times. A woman who walked many miles alone and afraid. A woman with sorrows, regrets, scars, and flaws.

But I'm not Mama.

I am a warrior. *With the power to survive, to forgive, to heal, and to thrive. The freedom to love and be loved, to dream and to laugh.* And although my past broke me, it did not destroy me and no longer owns me. The beauty and strength inside of me is more powerful than the past.

Although I've healed a great deal, the process is ongoing. I've accepted there are some things I will never understand. For some questions, I must be willing to accept, "I simply don't know." And that is okay.

I'm thankful for the kind people throughout my life, and for those who believed in me and helped me. No one did everything perfectly, but everyone did something essential, that played a part in my survival and healing.

I cherish family. I know what it's like to live without them.

I appreciate luxuries like air-conditioning, heat, running water, and washers and dryers. I know what it's like to not have those things.

I believe there has always been a God-given plan for my life—a good plan. A plan meant for only me. I believe despite the ugly past, beauty and power have come from it and play a part in that plan. How much more equipped I am to empathize, understand, and help someone else who has suffered in the same ways I did.

How much brighter is my light in a world full of darkness. How much warmer is my hand to someone who has walked alone in the aftermath of abuse for far too long.

I'm thankful for the power of forgiveness, a chance to be free.

Recently, I told Terry the story of how Jack used to grab me and hold my ankles tightly with one hand, while gripping my wrists in the other. I told him how it hurt as I panicked to get away, and how Jack squeezed tighter and laughed harder. It was a memory I had never told him in our twenty-four years of marriage, not for any particular reason, but because like so many memories, they were hidden away, and sometimes forgotten about.

Terry did what someone should have done decades ago. He closed his recliner, walked over to me, and put his arms around me.

"I'm sorry, honey," he said. And he held me and let me cry.

Me, age 14, the summer I met Pa.

Mama's high school photo, when she smiled freely.

Mama holding my daughter in 1987 with me at her side.

Pa in the 60's when Mama knew him.

Pa, 1963'ish when he dated Mama.

Belle Point Elementary, where I attended various times throughout my childhood, and met Laura Crouch.

House on 14th Street, where we lived with Mama, and where I met Jack.

House on North 12th Street, where we lived briefly
during the second grade.

The cinder block apartments, where we lived during my 6th grade,
where the sexual abuse began. Second door on the left.

Liberty Elementary, where I attended various times
and met Sherry Trammell.

The church Lane and I walked to.

Me with childhood friend, Sherry Trammell, as adults.

My senior high school picture.

Me with Carrie Jo, the summer we met.

Me with Carrie Jo, as adults.

My college photo.

Me with Carrie Jo and Pa in 2020.

Aunt Jeanie "Maggie" and Uncle Jimmy.

Me and cousin Pam, as adults.

Cousin Theresa, as an adult.

Cousin Julie, as an adult.

My childhood friend, Laura Crouch, with her siblings.

My childhood friend, Laura Crouch Luckett, as an adult.

Me with Barbara Crouch, Laura's mom, as an adult.

Laura Crouch's childhood home.

Me with my husband, Terry.

To other victims:

YOUR STORY MATTERS. The days you went unheld, unheard, unseen, and unwanted matter. The tears you cried and fears you felt matter. It was not supposed to be that way. And none of it was your fault.

You may feel that you've been on a never-ending cycle for years, rooted in fear and insecurity, poor self-esteem and negativity. You may be stuck where your abuser put you. The good news is that you can stop the cycle, and you don't have to figure it out alone. Though the past cannot be changed, it doesn't have to dictate your future. You are lovable. You are worth being cared for. You are valuable. You deserve healing, freedom, and peace. You not only mattered when the abuse happened, you matter now.

My prayer is that you will seek the help you need. If you haven't told someone about the abuse, start there. Find someone you can trust with the truth. Accept help, seek counseling, acknowledge the facts of what happened, then dig deep for the courage inside of you. It is there, I promise.

Consider God. In Him you will find the truth you yearn for, the strength you need, and the healing you long for. You will learn to trust, hope, and love again. A little at a time.

Every day, forgive as much as you can. Love as much as you can. There will be days you won't want to do either, so try again the next day. Forgiveness and love will grow, even from the smallest seed. New hope will sprout. New dreams will form. Joy and freedom will follow. NEVER GIVE UP.

ACKNOWLEDGMENTS

TO THE NEIGHBORS and other parents…Steve and Melissa, Barbara and Dale Crouch, Phyllis Trammell…thank you for spending time with a lonely little girl.

To the church ladies…Miss Winnie and Helen Coots…thank you for your warmth.

To the strangers who stood up for me…thank you for your validation.

To those who gave us money and brought groceries…thank you for caring about our needs.

To the mama who fed me soup…thank you for seeing me.

To the teachers who gave encouragement and support…thank you for recognizing value in me.

To Mr. Grimm…thank you for getting us out of that phone booth and sheltering us.

To Janey and Mark Hill…thank you for rescuing me.

To James and Helen King…thank you for showing me what love looks like, and for my Bible.

To Laura Crouch Luckett, Sherry Trammell Dieter, Amy Armer, Regina Munger Goodhue, and Jayan George Gregory…thank you for your lifelong friendship.

To Dr. Sally Goforth…thank you for seeing potential in a lost young girl and giving me support throughout my life.

To Penny Childers (my writing coach), Marcy W. (my editor), Joan Bauer Alley (cover design, editing and publishing assistance) as well as Amanda Wingerter and Lisa LeMaster Woolery …thank you all for your help in this writing journey. I couldn't have done it without you.

To my family…Aunt Jeanie and Uncle Jimmy, Grandma, Pam, Theresa and Julie, my brother Lane and my sisters Becky and Carrie Jo…thank you for your love.

To God…thank you for putting it on my heart to write this book.

RESOURCES FOR VICTIMS & SURVIVORS

National Sexual Assault Hotline 1-800-656-4673 (HOPE)
www.rainn.org

National Child Abuse Hotline/Childhelp 1-800-4-A-CHILD (1-800-422-4453) www.childhelp.org

National Runaway Safeline 1-800-RUNAWAY or 1-800-786-2929
www.1800runaway.org

The National Domestic Violence Hotline 1-800-799-7233 (SAFE)
www.ndvh.org

National Suicide Prevention Lifeline 1-800-273-8255 (TALK)
www.suicidepreventionlifeline.org

National Human Trafficking Resource Center/Polaris Project
Call: 1-888-373-7888 | Text: HELP to BeFree (233733)
www.polarisproject.org

National Center for Victims of Crime 1-202-467-8700
www.victimsofcrime.org

National Dating Abuse Helpline 1-866-331-9474
www.loveisrespect.org

TEENS - Love is respect Hotline: 1-866-331-9474
www.loveisrespect.org

Break the Cycle 202-824-0707 www.breakthecycle.org

CHRISTINE ORSBUN

CHRISTINE ORSBUN GREW up in the Midwestern states of Arkansas and Oklahoma, and as an adult has lived in various states, and two countries. Christine considers her relationships with God and family to be the most important parts of her life. She joyously decorates, cooks and organizes get-togethers in her home as she values time spent with loved ones, and the opportunity to pour love into the lives of others. Christine's heart is especially compassionate toward children. By chance, she has found three lost children in her lifetime, and helped them get back to their parents. *What Happened to Chris Ann?* is Christine's own childhood story, and is her first book.

Find Christine Orsbun on Facebook or caorsbun@yahoo.com

Made in the USA
Middletown, DE
18 March 2023

27058932R00187